JAPANESE
TRADE
POLICY
FORMULATION

●

JAPANESE TRADE POLICY FORMULATION

•

Chikara Higashi

Forewords by
Yasuhiro Nakasone
and
Michio Watanabe

PRAEGER

PRAEGER SPECIAL STUDIES • PRAEGER SCIENTIFIC

Library of Congress Cataloging in Publication Data

Higashi, Chikara.
   Japanese trade policy formulation.

   Bibliography; p.
   Includes index.
   1. Japan—Commercial policy. I. Title.
HF1601.H49 1983   382'.3'0952   83-13878
ISBN 0-03-063509-8

Published in 1983 by Praeger Publishers
CBS Educational and Professional Publishing
a Division of CBS Inc.
521 Fifth Avenue, New York, New York 10175 U.S.A.

3456789 052   987654321

Printed in the United States of America
on acid-free paper

FOREWORD

The United States and Japan are the two largest economic powers in the free world today. Consequently, the United States–Japan relationship is of the most importance not only for the two countries but for world peace and economic prosperity. Both countries but for world peace and economic prosperity. Both countries are common in respecting the values of liberty, democracy and free trade. Although both countries desire a relationship of amity and cooperation, it is also inevitable that complex issues and frictions will arise between two such economic giants, as the same is true for two close neighbors. As the magnitude of trade has rapidly increased between the United States and Japan in recent years, we are faced with sizable discrepancies in industrial and trade structures, international competitiveness, and people's sentiments in the two countries. Thus, exploration of effective ways to resolve, reduce or mitigate frictions attributable to such discrepancies has become a pressing and high priority.

I am glad that Dr. Higashi's book is opportunely published to meet such urgent and great needs. This excellent study systematically and accurately depicts the true nature of the Japanese trade policy formulation process, which no one has ever truly done before. Dr. Higashi is unique in that he was a genuine insider of the Japanese policymaking process as a Ministry of Finance career official, and he also intensively studied the American system and policy formulation process through formal education at The George Washington University and research experiences in the Brookings Institution, and through many other prestigious organizations, including the World Bank. Therefore, the substantive information, perspective and analysis he presents is highly original, unique and unprecedented. It shows an excellent and true understanding of both sides of the policy formulation process.

This book will surely contribute to better understanding of the people in both countries, to greater cultural sensitivity, and thus to a considerable reduction of misunderstanding, misperception, miscommunication, and, therefore, occasions of friction. I am also delighted that this book is authored by a Japanese in English. Although the Japanese have been historically good in learning from foreign writers, the appropriate clarification of Japanese systems and practices has been lacking badly in international communities. This book is, accordingly, of high significance in meeting such enormous and long overdue needs. I hope as many foreign readers as possible will read Dr. Higashi's excellent book and, thus, more correctly and deeply understand the Japanese and their way of acting. This book will certainly help both Easterners and Westerners cooperatively achieve our greatest goals—peace and economic prosperity on a global basis.

Yasuhiro Nakasone
Prime Minister
Japan

FOREWORD

Today's world has become increasingly interdependent. Neither countries nor individual people can escape the influence of events in the international community. As the world becomes more interdependent, countries benefit more from each other but also face more complexities in international relations. Since trade serves as a linking factor in that interdependency, exploration of effective approaches to resolve disputes and resulting frictions in international trade has become particularly important.

Most people concerned understand that trade frictions must often be aggravated because of differences in culture, and political and economic systems. This suggests that trade frictions can be reduced by better mutual understanding. I am pleased that Dr. Higashi has focused on the mechanism and true nature of such trade frictions attributed to cultural and system differences. I believe that as a former Minsitry of Finance career official, and as a special adviser to me as the Minister of Finance he has been at an exceptional vantage point to do so.

I am very delighted that Dr. Higashi has made painstaking efforts to come up with a study spotlighting what many people are aware of but no one has ever before carefully analyzed. Accordingly, I want to recommend that as many people as possible read Dr. Higashi's excellent book on the Japanese trade policy formulation process.

This book provides systematic and pragmatic insights for public administrators, politicians, scholars, students, and, particularly, trade and business negotiators. Such improved understanding will certainly lead to a better mutual appreciation and closer relations between Japan and the United States, as well as the rest of the world.

Michio Watanabe
Former Minister of Finance
Japan

CONTENTS

LIST OF
TABLES AND FIGURES

TABLES

FIGURES

LIST OF
ACRONYMS AND ABBREVIATIONS

CPIMG	"Conference to Encourage the Import of Manufactured Goods"
EC	European Community
EEC	European Economic Community
EFTA	European Free Trade Association
EPA	Economic Planning Association
EROA	Economic Rehabilitation in Occupied Areas
F.R.G.	Federal Republic of Germany
GAO	General Accounting Office
GARIOA	Government and Relief in Occupied Areas
GATT	General Agreements on Tariffs and Trade
GNP	Gross National Product
IBRD	International Bank for Reconstruction and Development
IMF	International Monetary Fund
ITC	International Trade Commission
JCJS	Joint Committee on Japanese Studies
JETRO	Japan External Trade Organization
JNR	Japan National Railway
LDP	Liberal Democratic Party
MITI	Ministry of International Trade and Industry
MOAFF	Ministry of Agriculture, Forestry and Fisheries
MOF	Ministry of Finance
MOFA	Ministry of Foreign Affairs
MTN	Multinational Trade Negotiations ("Tokyo Round")
NATO	North Atlantic Treaty Organization
NIC	Newly Industrialized Countries
NTT	Nippon Telephone and Telegraph Company
OECD	Organization for Economic Cooperation and Development
OMB	Office of Management and Budget
OPEC	Organization of Petroleum Exporting Countries
PA	Personnel Agency
STR	Special Trade Representative

TFC   Trade Facilitation Committee
UAW   United Automobile Workers
UN   United Nations
USTR   United States Trade Representative

1

INTRODUCTION

The subject of this book is the formulation of Japanese international trade policy, in particular, toward the United States. The United States is the largest and Japan is the second largest economy of the free world. Therefore, the trade relations of these two countries affect every nation. The Japanese trade policy formulation process is often misunderstood because Japan's trade policies have only recently undergone a substantial change from a restrictive to a liberal orientation. No other country has experienced such a rapid policy reversal in recent times. Because the change was so drastic, swift, and controversial, erroneous views of Japan have emerged at times in the United States and throughout the world.

In the views of many Americans, Japan is assaulting the United States economically the same way it had assaulted the nation militarily in 1941.[1] Subconsciously, they consider the Japanese unpredictable and unfair. Numerous business executives and even economists ascribe Japan's trade surpluses to dumping, low wages, export subsidies, tariff and nontariff import barriers, closed markets, a closed culture, and other unfair competitive methods. They argue that Japan is not fulfilling its international trade responsibilities and that it had undeservedly benefited from the liberalized world trade system, which had been achieved primarily through U.S. efforts during the postwar years.

The Japanese consider such views erroneous and discriminatory. They see themselves as hard workers and disciplined savers who willingly forego consumption and leisure, who invest wisely, and who are successful in producing and exporting. Yet they believe that they are pe-

1

nalized for these virtues by the United States as well as by the rest of the world. Harald Malmgren, who was Deputy Special Trade Representative in the Nixon administration, has admitted that Japan had been pressured because of its economic success.[2] Herman Kahn and Thomas Pepper summarize the conflicting Western and Japanese views as follows:

> There is an increasingly widespread feeling that the Japanese have benefited more than anybody else from the international trading system, yet have done little to help make it work well. This feeling of irritation is shared, though for quite different reasons, by the Japanese themselves, who feel they have been very successful in beating the West at its own game, and now the West is trying to change the rules in the middle of the game. The Japanese believe their success rests on their propensity to work hard, to save and invest huge sums, to apply themselves diligently and creatively, and to be willing to take great risks. They therefore feel entitled to success, but believe that the West is trying by sheer force and unfair tactics, to hold them back.[3]

Moreover, there is a widespread belief among Japanese of all walks of life that they are inherently "scapegoatable." They claim that Japan has been made a scapegoat by Western countries many times before and, consequently, react emotionally to any perceived unfair criticism. It is, of course, possible that the Japanese are too sensitive to racial or cultural differences and attach more importance to Western—in particular, U.S.—attitudes than they should. Be that as it may, the criticism, often based on erroneous views, combined with Japanese sensitivity, more often than not results in additional misunderstandings, the breakdown of communications and, consequently, the intensification of trade conflicts.

The lack of understanding of the Japanese trade policy formulation process in the United States and throughout the rest of the world is particularly important in this respect. One of the major reasons for this is that the literature on Japanese trade policy formulation is very limited. There are several explanations for this. First, the number of policy scholars in Japan is much smaller than in the United States. Second, there is a wide gulf between academicians and practitioners. There are virtually no political appointees in the Japanese government bureaucracy; consequently, there is no movement of people from government to business or academia and vice versa. This precludes in-depth analysis of the policy formulation process by academicians. Third, the Japanese government has never been attuned to public relations; accordingly it has tended to minimize the release of information.[4] Fourth, the behavioral sciences have not been well developed in Japan; thus, their application to other disciplines in the social sciences is yet to be seen. Psychologists, for example, may keep up with the latest U.S. literature, but their interests are limited to clinical or educational psychology and other related problems. Thus, behavioral or multidisciplinary studies of trade policy formulation are almost nonexistent.

Most of the publications available in English have been authored by U.S. economists or political scientists in collaboration with Japanese scholars. The following section presents a brief review of several of these publications.

REVIEW OF SELECTED LITERATURE

Ezra F. Vogel's *Modern Japanese Organization and Decision-Making*[5] was written under the sponsorship of the Joint Committee on Japanese Studies (JCJS) of the American Council of Learned Societies and the Social Science Research Council. The volume includes analyses of Japanese political, economic, cultural, and educational institutions by 14 scholars. The major contribution of the book is the analysis of Japanese organizations and institutions in dynamic terms, that is, from an ever-changing historical perspective. Some of the authors argue that several of the widespread U.S views about Japan are exaggerated or distorted. For example, they criticize the notion of "Japan, Incorporated," as overstating the mutuality of interest between the government and business and as underestimating tensions that frequently occur. Vogel points out that the *Ringi* system is not used in every type of decision-making, but tends to be reserved for only those issues that are relatively complex and require a high level of coordination.

> General questions of strategy are more likely to be discussed in meetings, and documents may be drafted only when specific measures are required.
>   . . . .As such, *ringi sei* is often not qualitatively different from the clearance system in the U.S. government.[6]

He also argues that "permanent employment and the seniority system apply only to a minority of workers in Japan."[7]

On the other hand, several contributors claim that certain characteristics, such as "groupism," long-range goal orientation and bureaucratic elitism are so visible in everyday Japanese life that they are undeniably very influential factors.

In summary, the collected articles provide a useful general overview of Japan, but they do not deal in any depth with the problems of trade policy and, thus, ignore some important considerations concerning the Japanese trade policy formulation process.

Michael Blaker's *Japanese International Negotiating Style*[8] is one of the most intensive studies of Japanese behavior during diplomatic negotiations. As Blaker states, there has been little effort in the study of modern Japanese diplomacy to blend political science and history and to apply some of the new theoretical concepts to historical data so that fresh insights might emerge. Blaker selected 18 cases from the Russo-Japanese diplomatic exchanges (The Portsmouth Treaty) in 1905 to the U.S.–Japanese pre-Pearl Harbor negotiations in 1941. He identifies the handicaps that Japanese diplomats faced in pursuing negotiations: cumbersome policy formulating processes, ambiguous instructions, bureaucratic rivalries, limited discretionary authority, a lack of flexibility, and a reputation for being unattractive and even treacherous bargaining partners. He argues that in spite of such obstacles, the Japanese were, by and large, successful negotiators, and he points out that Japan's negotiating strategy is the result of the interaction of certain attitudes, decision-making strategies, and patterns of communication:

> . . .the Japanese approach to negotiations was dominated by a philosophy of risk-minimization and confrontation-avoidance. They seemed to prefer doing nothing when it was safe to do nothing and acting only when the pressure of events forced them to act.[9]

It is interesting to note that the first U.S. consul to Japan, Townsend Harris, wrote in a similar vein as early as 1857:[10] "The Japanese took a great while to consider every question; that in this respect they differed from the Americans, who decided promptly on all questions,"[11] and "they have yielded nothing except from *fear*, and any future ameliorations of our intercourse will only take place after a demonstration of force on our part."[12]

In continuing his analysis, Blaker states: "Japanese prewar negotiatory behavior was also molded by domestic political factors, particularly decision-making and government/negotiator communication practices."[13] He contends that the major shortcomings of such a negotiation strategy were: that "Japan's leaders and diplomats attempted cautiously and in private to establish a network of personal relationships among the opposition and to probe the thinking of the other side before beginning formal negotiations;"[14] and that "A second feature of Japanese negotiatory style, most evident during the middle bargaining phase, was to push repeatedly and insistently to force through initial positions."[15] The result of this was that:

Compromises came late, after being postponed as long as possible. Concessions came at the late-middle or final stages and followed concessions by the adversary. . . .

Their consistent crisis-stage technique was to push and push again, to hold fast to basic positions, even badly eroded or untenable positions, while seeking to conjure up some combination of methods that could win without major concessions.[16]

According to Blaker, the lack of individual bargaining skills is perhaps the greatest Japanese handicap. Negotiators would rarely submit a compelling formula or an original solution that would lead to a settlement. He had also discovered a list of tactics that served mostly domestic political objectives: recalling or changing negotiators during bargaining; delaying and deferring concessions; purposefully leaking bargaining information to the press; repeating bargaining positions; issuing evasive or ambiguous statements; and relying on private communication channels.[17]

Blaker believes that all of these tactics are the result of Japan's political system, which determines bargaining content and scope. Bearing this in mind, he points to the liabilities of the resulting negotiation style:

. . .the Japanese diplomat acquired a reputation for duplicity and double-dealing even though his purpose was not to deceive. His observable behavior was frequently misread. Why and how such a negative image evolved are proper and significant subjects for further research.[18]

Blaker's greatest contribution is the application of the new analytical-behavioral research method to historical cases. But while his conclusions are applicable even today, his study also has some limitations. Because the cases are of a pre-World War II vintage, he could not analyze the contemporary policy formulation process and thus has neglected the major changes that Japan has experienced since World War II. Furthermore, his study concentrates on international negotiations, thereby rendering the analysis of the domestic policy formulation process inadequate.

Robert A. Scalapino's *The Foreign Policy of Modern Japan*[19] is the outgrowth of a conference of U.S. and Japanese scholars on the Hawaiian island of Kauai in January 1974. Seventeen scholars participated in the discussion of Japanese foreign policy, and 14 contributed to the volume. Four articles are particularly relevant to the subject of this chapter.

Haruhiro Fukui wrote about "Policy-Making in the Japanese Foreign Ministry" based on his interviews with Foreign Ministry officials.

He concentrated "on identifying the dominant patterns of the policy-relevant decision-making process in the Japanese Foreign Ministry and on drawing a collective profile of the bureaucrats who participate in the process,"[20] and thereby discusses participants in terms of age, education, and rank. Fukui's description of the process is insightful, but is nevertheless limited by the fact that "knowledge and understanding is particularly inadequate with regard to decision processes in routine, noncrisis situations, which no doubt account for the majority of real-world cases."[21] Another limitation is his excessive stress on the tension between career and noncareer officials. Fukui argues that:

> The most obvious and probably the most fundamental source of tension lies in the existing personnel system which discriminates against non-careerists as a matter of principle. . . .
> Apart from the inherent inequity of the system, the systematic exclusion of noncareerists from the high ranks has caused a severe shortage of manpower at the strategic levels of decision-making.[22]

Such tension paralyzes the bureaucracy, and, accordingly, causes the "obvious inadequacies and liabilities of the existing system."[23] Fukui's arguments have some validity, in that tension between careerists and noncareerists—or more precisely frustration among noncareerists—may exist; yet, lack of participation of noncareerists in the final stages of policy formulation does not necessarily damage the process.

Michael Blaker's "Probe, Push and Panic" analyzes the Japanese international negotiating style through a number of specific prewar and a few postwar cases. His thesis is essentially the same as in his previously reviewed book. The analysis is scholarly, and he formulates principles from a careful examination of historical records. Blaker characterizes the Japanese negotiating style as "bound by rigid instructions and directed by relatively uncompromising leaders in snail-paced policy-making groups in Tokyo."[24] In summarizing his views, he argues that:

> Domestic Japanese political habits and practices greatly bear on Japanese negotiating behavior. Its fragmented, inner-directed government processes, in which participants tend to put their own interests above all others, have an onerous impact on negotiating performance, and especially on timing, flexibility, and speed.[25]

The analysis raises at least two questions that need to be examined in more detail. One is whether the characteristics of the Japanese negotiating style are really unique to Japan. Most may simply be tactics inherent in effective international negotiations conducted by any nation. Blaker himself refers to this point at the end of his thesis.[26] The second rather serious question is whether the cases cited, most of which are prewar, reflect the changes that Japan has passed through since World War II.

Gerald T. Curtis' "The Tyumen Oil Development Project and Japanese Foreign Policy" tells how Japanese government–business relations work, particularly when the government is concerned with the multiple implications of its strategies.[27] The incentive of the business community is the relatively clear-cut profit motive; however, the ministries often sharply differ in their policy motivation, as illustrated by the Tyumen oil development project. Curtis' analysis thus casts doubts upon the "Japan, Inc." concept.

Chalmers Johnson's "MITI and Japanese International Economic Policy" focuses on international policy making in the Ministry of International Trade and Industry (MITI). While most of the English language literature exaggerates MITI's influence and power, Johnson perceives and analyzes this organization properly. He finds that "one major deficiency of many foreign summaries of Japanese international economic policy is the failure to stress the extent to which that policy is changing."[28] Accordingly, he relates the policy changes in MITI to the rapidly growing and changing Japanese industrial structures. His analysis of MITI's administrative guidance is also in line with historical developments. The ministry's power was primarily based on "license and approval authority" (kyoninkaken) in the early postwar period, and its administrative guidance was strongly rooted in such a principle. This implies that as the Japanese economy is increasingly liberalized, both domestically and internationally, MITI's future role and influence will be adjusted.

Johnson's paper provides a historical basis for the discussion of the contemporary policy formulation process. Another contribution is his analysis of both the causes and effects of "sectionalism," so characteristic of the Japanese bureaucracy. He attributes sectionalism to the lifetime employment system and correctly recognizes that it hampers the interministerial decision-making process.

T.J. Pempel's *Policymaking in Contemporary Japan*[29] is the product of a panel discussion that took place at the Annual Convention of the Association for Asian Studies in April 1974. Six contributors have tried to generate more "facts" about public policy formulation, mostly through case studies. Two of these are noteworthy.

First is H. Fukui's Chapter 2, "Studies in Policy-Making: A Review of the Literature." Fukui provides an overview of the existing literature in English and Japanese and points out a fundamental dichotomy in the assessment of Japanese policy formulation. Many scholars have viewed Japanese policy formulation from an elitist perspective, whereas others have seen it from a pluralistic point of view. Because of the paucity of

scholarly studies, Fukui could only suggest the need for more para-
digmatic analyses, mentioning some of the more fruitful lines along
which such investigations could develop. Pempel makes the same point
in arguing that "many political scientists, both generalists and Japan
specialists, would welcome increased study of Japanese policymaking at
any level. One must immediately recognize the simple need for more
facts and information about Japanese policymaking."[30]

The second helpful contribution is B. M. Richardson's "Policymaking in Japan: An Organizing Perspective." This is a scholarly attempt to
alleviate the paradox inherent in the efforts to establish a bridge between
theory and case studies. Because of the complex realities, many political
scientists concentrate on case studies, but Richardson properly suggests
that "some bridging conceptual scheme is needed if the findings from
case studies are to serve the purposes of theory building, or even simply
adequate description."[31] His analysis of seven cases of Japanese policy
formulation in 1968 have led him to "dispel the impression that there are
simple and permanent coalitions between a few major actors who dominate all of the policymaking in Japan."[32] Richardson's conclusion is that
the outcome of most policy formulation is the result of intimate interactions between major "actors" whose patterns of participation vary
according to the roles they play and the differences among them. While
Richardson's views are insightful, he did not extrapolate his findings to
the trade policy formulation process.

Michael Blaker's *The Politics of Trade: U.S. and Japanese Policymaking for the GATT Negotiations* is the first in a series to be published under
the auspieces of the "Project on Japan and U.S. in Multilateral Diplomacy," sponsored by the East Asian Institute of Columbia University.[33] It
deals with U.S. and Japanese trade policy formulation focusing on the
"Tokyo Round." The volume presents an insightful analysis of the policy
formulation process in both the U.S. and Japan and of the U.S.–Japanese
negotiations.

In his contribution, "The GATT Tokyo Round: The Bureaucratic Politics of Multilateral Diplomacy," Haruhiro Fukui points out that
"decision-making for the Tokyo Round was largely confined to several
ministries,"[34] and accordingly analyzes the organizations, individuals,
and policy formulation process in four ministries and one agency. Despite several controversial observations, Fukui's stress here on bureaucratic politics balances the excessive stress on political factors in his
other studies. His description of administrative behavior in the trade
policy formulating ministries is, by and large, accurate and is based on
extensive interviews with key officials.

I. M. Destler's and Hideo Sato's *Coping with U.S.–Japanese Economic Conflicts* is the most recent publication on the subject of
U.S.–Japan trade relations.[35]

The volume consists of five detailed conflict case studies (steel, automobiles, agricultural products, telecommunications equipment, and macroeconomic policy coordination) contributed by U.S. and Japanese authors. To maintain a balanced point of view, the information was gathered in both Washington and Tokyo and then combined into an analysis of each of the conflicts that took place between 1977 and 1981.

The authors explain why and how the conflicts emerged, how they were handled by each side, and how they were eventually settled through domestic political maneuverings and international negotiations.

While the five case studies provide excellent information on all of these matters (with respect to a better understanding of Japanese trade policy formulation), the book has two limitations. First, trade policy formulation is explored only in the context of the five specific conflicts. Second, the insights provided are process-oriented and are based almost entirely on political and economic explanations. The behavioral characteristics of Japanese policy formulators are only occasionally mentioned.

THE CONTRIBUTIONS OF THIS BOOK

This book makes two contributions to the English language literature on Japanese trade policy formulation. First, it clarifies the institutions and processes involved. The author's status as a former career official of the Ministry of Finance and Special Advisor to the Minister of Finance provided him with an insider's view of these institutions and processes. Second, the author's approach is multidisciplinary. As the previous brief review of the English language literature has shown, most studies of Japanese trade policy formulation have been authored by economists and, to a lesser degree, by political scientists. Accordingly, most of the studies are narrowly focused. In contrast, this book integrates the ideas of economists and political scientists with those of the behavioral scientists. The resulting approach provides a more comprehensive picture of the Japanese trade policy formulation process.

NOTES

1. Robert J. Samuelson has written that "Japanese–American trade relations increasingly resemble a good cavalry fight. Here are the Japanese ambushing every American industry in sight." *See* Robert J. Samuelson, "Japan's Choices: Act or Be Acted Upon," *Washington Post*, 13 December, 1977, p.D7.

2. In private conversations with the author during 1979.

3. Herman Kahn and Thomas Pepper, *The Japanese Challenge* (New York: Harper and Row, 1979), p. 119.

4. Recently, requests for the release of more information have increased and legislation in this regard is now seriously discussed in Japan. The U.S. "Freedom of Information Act" serves as an example for such requests.

5. Ezra F. Vogel (ed.), *Modern Japanese Organization and Decision-Making* (Berkeley: University of California Press, 1975).

6. Ibid., p. xviii.

7. Ibid.

8. Michael Blaker, *Japanese International Negotiating Style* (New York: Columbia University Press, 1977).

9. Ibid., p. 212.

10. Townsend Harris, *The Complete Journal of Townsend Harris*, 2d ed., rev. (Rutland, Vt. and Tokyo, Japan: Charles E. Tuttle, 1959).

11. Ibid., p. 326.

12. Ibid., pp. 357-58.

13. Blaker, *Japanese International Negotiating Style*, p. 214.

14. Ibid., p. 216.

15. Ibid., p. 217.

16. Ibid., pp. 217-18.

17. Ibid., pp. 221-22.

18. Ibid., p. 227.

19. Robert A. Scalapino, *The Foreign Policy of Modern Japan* (Berkeley: University of California Press, 1977).

20. Haruhiro Fukui, "Policy-Making in the Japanese Foreign Ministry," in *The Foreign Policy of Modern Japan*, ed. Robert A. Scalapino (Berkeley: University of California Press, 1977), p. 6.

21. Ibid., p. 35.

22. Ibid., p. 28.

23. Ibid., p. 35.

24. Michael K. Blaker, "Probe, Push and Panic," in *The Foreign Policy of Modern Japan*, ed. Robert A. Scalapino (Berkeley: University of California Press, 1977), p. 69.

25. Ibid., p. 99.

26. Ibid., p. 101.

27. Gerald T. Curtis, "The Tyumen Oil Development Project and Japanese Foreign Policy," in *The Foreign Policy of Modern Japan*, ed. Robert A. Scalapino (Berkeley: University of California Press, 1977), p. 147.

28. Chalmers Johnson, "MITI and Japanese International Economic Policy," in *The Foreign Policy of Modern Japan*, ed. Robert A. Scalapino (Berkeley: University of California Press, 1977), p. 275.

29. T. J. Pempel, (ed.), *Policymaking in Contemporary Japan* (Ithaca, N.Y.: Cornell University Press, 1977).

30. Ibid., p. 14.

31. Bradley M. Richardson, "Policymaking in Japan: An Organizing Perspective," in *Policymaking in Contemporary Japan*, ed. T. J. Pempel (Ithaca, N.Y.: Cornell University Press, 1977), p. 268.

32. Ibid.

33. Michael Blaker, (ed.) *The Politics of Trade: U.S. and Japanese Policymaking for the GATT Negotiations* (New York: Columbia University Press, 1978).

34. Haruhiro Fukui, "The GATT Tokyo Round: The Bureaucratic Politics of Multilateral Diplomacy," in *The Politics of Trade; U.S. and Japanese Policymaking for the GATT Negotiations*, ed. M. Blaker (New York: Columbia University Press, 1978), p. 81.

35. I. M. Destler, and Hideo Sato (ed.), *Coping with U.S.–Japanese Economic Conflicts* (Lexington, Mass.: D.C. Heath, 1982).

2

THE INTERNATIONAL AND DOMESTIC ECONOMIC ENVIRONMENT OF TRADE POLICY FORMULATION

Trade policy formulation is a part of the general domestic and international economic policy formulation process, which consists of the identification of objectives, the collection, analysis, and dissemination of information, and decision-making.

As such, the nature and thrust of a nation's trade policy is, among other factors, strongly influenced by the international and domestic economic environments in which the policy is formulated.

Therefore, the discussion of Japanese trade policy formulation must begin with a discussion of those key international and Japanese domestic economic developments that during the last 30 years shaped this policy. Particularly important in this respect is the evolution of U.S.–Japan trade relations, because the United States is Japan's most important trading partner. In 1981, Japan's exports to the United States totaled $38,609 billion, accounting for 25.4 percent of total Japanese exports of $152,030 billion. In the same year, U.S. exports to Japan totaled $21,823 billion or 15.2 percent of total Japanese imports of $149,290 billion.[1]

In quantitative terms, Japan is the United States' most important trading partner after Canada. However, from an overall U.S. trade policy point of view, Japan is more important to the United States than any other country in the world. This is due not only to the enormous trade imbalances between the two countries ($18 billion in 1981), but also to the specific composition of their trade.

The United States exports mainly agricultural products and industrial raw materials that are vitally needed by Japanese industries, while Japan exports manufactured products as, for example, automobiles, steel, and electronic equipment. In light of these trade structures, former U.S. Ambassador to Japan Alexis Johnson repeatedly stated that the trade pattern between the United States and Japan was like that between a typical industrialized and a developing country, with Japan being the former.[2]

INTERNATIONAL DEVELOPMENTS

Through most of the post-World War II period, as individual economies grew, global trade grew impressively, signaling not only an increase in the importance of international trade to individual economies, but also growing worldwide interdependence.

As trade growth accelerated, the frequency of conflicts in trade relations—and the resultant need for negotiations—also increased. The mushrooming of trade conflicts had multiple reasons; some were inherent in the political-economic development processes of the contending nation-states while others were primarily attributable to policy choices by governments. One of the most significant international political-economic developments was the change in the role of the United States. In particular, the relative decline in its economic and political power in the 1960s and thereafter made it difficult for the United States to maintain its traditionally liberal and paternalistic trade policies toward Europe, Japan, and the developing countries.

There were no serious trade conflicts between the United States and Japan before the textile issue erupted in the late 1960s. Harmony in U.S.–Japan economic relations for the first two decades after World War II was primarily due to U.S. economic superiority and consequent U.S. policies toward Japan. Politically, the United States attempted to play the role of the world's policeman; as such it encouraged as well as expected its Japanese and European allies to become stronger, particularly after the Cold War began in 1947. Economically, the United States assisted the reconstruction and development of Japan through the Government and Relief in Occupied Areas (GARIOA) and the Economic Rehabilitation in Occupied Areas (EROA) programs. It assisted the European countries through the Marshall Plan and other aid projects. The United States was willing to provide not only badly needed U.S. dollars but also agricultural products and manufactured goods to its allies and other friendly nations. It took the initiative in establishing the General Agreement on Tariffs and Trade (GATT), the International Monetary Fund (IMF), and the International Bank for Reconstruction and Development (IBRD). The GATT set international trade rules that prevented the world from falling back on protectionism as it had in the late 1930s, while the IMF established and reinforced the international monetary system—the so-called Bretton Woods system—in which the U.S. dollar played the role of key currency. The IBRD expedited the recovery of Europe and Japan; later, it began to aid the development of Third World countries through low-interest, long-term loans.

Initially, the United States opened its markets to Japanese and European exports, which promoted economic growth in these countries. During this period, the United States did not insist on the principle of reciprocity in trade with Europe and Japan and even allowed Japan's markets to be closed to U.S. exports. This was in a sharp contrast to the U.S. market, which was open to exports from all over the world.

Such benign international trade policies can be explained by the following factors. The United States was the only major country that remained undamaged by the war and, therefore, could afford to be generous. With general euphoria and elation prevailing long after military victory, for humanitarian reasons U.S. leaders were strongly in favor of helping the ravaged world. Such a policy was the first unequivocal expression in U.S. history of a global "noblesse oblige" attitude. Pragmatic policy formulators also regarded the supportive U.S. role as vital to the reduction of frustrations and imbalances among nations. Without such, they believed, another international crisis might take place.

Furthermore, in light of its humane and peace-seeking objectives, the United States considered expanding world trade as a more desirable means to stimulate other economies than its merely offering assistance. Expanded trade also enabled the United States to import inexpensive, light industrial products and export capital goods, technology, and agricultural commodities. Due to the competitive strength of U.S. industries, policy formulators believed that by encouraging imports, free trade would promote exports without endangering domestic markets. Such policies also made it possible for U.S. multinational corporations to substantially expand their roles in world markets during the 1950s and 1960s.

Finally, after the world entered the Cold War period in 1947, it became politically important for the United States to strengthen its allies, particularly the North Atlantic Treaty Organization (NATO) countries and Japan. Accordingly, the United States did not exert great pressure on Europe and Japan in the economic and trade areas. Such restraint was needed primarily for two reasons. First, for the United States to create a community with its European and Japanese allies for the effective containment of communism, it had to promote European and Japanese geopolitical interests. Second, the United States could not afford to undermine pro-U.S. politicians in the allied countries because these politicians were challenged domestically by procommunist parties. To

Third World countries, the United States was obliged to increase economic assistance and extend concessionary trade terms partly because these nations were gradually outnumbering the more developed countries in the United Nations.

Through the late 1960s, the U.S. economy maintained a strong edge over other economies because of the nation's size, natural resources, and sophisticated technology. As a result, the dollar was stable until its overvaluation became apparent during the early 1970s, when the U.S. trade balance fell into a deficit of $2.1 billion for the first time in 78 years.

With the balance of payments in order for most of the post-World War II period, the U.S. economy grew in absolute terms; however, it began to show signs of instability during the 1960s. The postwar economy was boosted mostly by the nation's affluent consumption patterns and by Keynesian fiscal and monetary policies, which tended to put more emphasis on full employment and high growth rather than on containing inflation. Aggregate demand was more often stimulated than restrained, and the United States took advantage of its role as the world's key currency supplier by printing an excessive amount of dollars for consumers and producers to purchase foreign goods, and for multinational corporations to invest overseas. As a result, by the end of the 1960s, the world—or at least the foreign exchange markets in the developed countries—was inundated by dollars. The value of the dollar started eroding—although belatedly—and this trend was accelerated as speculators became bearish about its future. The vulnerability of the U.S. economy was increased by continued heavy reliance on demand expansion, because the lack of "supply-side" policies eventually resulted in stagnant productivity and high inflation. Thus, the combination of high inflation and slower growth—that is, stagflation—became the most serious and complex problem confronting U.S. economic policy formulators in the 1970s.

As far as the United States' international trade position was concerned, the current account surplus declined from $2.584 billion in 1967 to $611 million in 1968, and finally moved into a deficit of $1.419 billion in 1971 and of $5.744 billion in 1972. Meanwhile, the Federal Republic of Germany's (F.R.G.) current account surplus jumped to $2.502 billion in 1967 and remained in surplus thereafter. The Japanese current account swung between surpluses and deficits until 1967, depending primarily upon the tightening or loosening of Japan's domestic economic policies. It was $1.048 billion in surplus in 1968, $5.797 billion in surplus in 1971, and $6.624 billion in surplus in 1972, until sharp increases in the price of raw materials in 1972 and the oil price rises of 1973 and 1974 put it back into a temporary deficit.

Thus, by the late 1960s, the U.S. economy was faced with the serious problem of slow growth and high inflation domestically and a declining dollar internationally. As described above, the nation's economic decline stemmed primarily from stagnant productivity and declining competitiveness that outpaced demand-pulled growth. At the same time, Japanese and European productivity and competitiveness improved. Japan rapidly recovered from devastation, grew much faster than the United States, and surpassed U.S. competitiveness in numerous industrial sectors as shown by the reversal of the trade balance.

The European and Japanese governments took several years to recognize the fundamental changes that had occurred throughout the 1960s. While the U.S. economy started suffering from stagflation and a dollar glut in the late 1960s, Western Europe became more protectionist. The 1957 Treaty of Rome, through which the European Economic Community (EEC) was established, provided for the extension of reciprocal tariff preferences to the former colonies and dependencies of the member countries. The EEC reinforced these special trade relations through the Yaounde Agreement of 1963 and other ensuing agreements, and also tried to expand tariff preferences to the bordering Mediterranean countries and some members of the European Free Trade Association (EFTA) toward the late 1960s. Japan was very reluctant to liberalize its trade policies primarily because its policy formulators underestimated the country's competitive strength.

The erosion of U.S. international economic predominance was exacerbated by the growing reluctance of foreigners to hold dollars and by recurring dollar crises. By 1968, excessive demand for gold had forced the United States to suspend sales except to official parties; as a result, a two-tier system of official and free-market gold prices emerged. The free-market price of gold skyrocketed, at times exceeding $200 for each ounce.

Soon after taking power, the Nixon administration sought to curb inflation and to improve the nation's balance of payments. However, due to the "stagflation" plaguing the U.S. economy, real economic growth came to a halt in 1970, and the deterioration of the dollar continued. In early 1971, when the economy was allowed to pick up again, imports began to rise quickly and, as mentioned earlier, the United States incurred a trade deficit for the first time since 1893. The pressure on the dollar was also reinforced by the substantive decline in U.S. reserve assets in 1971. Faced with such a difficulty, the Nixon administration blamed its European and Japanese allies for a lack of sensitivity and cooperation.

To secure international cooperation, President Nixon announced a new dollar and trade policy (the so-called "Nixon Shock") on August 15, 1971. The policy included a devaluation of the dollar, a decision to go off the gold-exchange standard, and the imposition of a temporary import surcharge.

The "Nixon Shock" represented an epoch-making change from a paternalistic to a defensive trade policy. The U.S. government's trust in liberalization as the key element of trade policy was substantially reduced.

In December 1971, the United States retracted the temporary import surcharge, but only after Japan, the Federal Republic of Germany, and other European countries agreed to revalue their currencies—a move that led to an effective dollar devaluation of 10.34 percent. However, as these actions could not adjust the fundamental imbalances between the declining dollar and the rising German mark and Japanese yen, the United States had to undertake a second, 10 percent, dollar devaluation in February 1973. Finally, in March, the governments of the major advanced industrial countries abandoned any attempt to maintain the fixed exchange rate system and allowed their currencies to float. This move marked the demise of the Bretton Woods system.

The early 1970s were, therefore, characterized by instabilities and disturbances in the international monetary system. Then, just when the collapse of the Bretton Woods system was upsetting monetary authorities all over the world, two more jarring global events took place. One was a sudden increase in the price of raw materials in 1972, and the other was a quadrupling of oil prices due to the agressive policies of the Organization of Petroleum Exporting Countries (OPEC) in 1973 and 1974.

The rise in the price of commodities had an inflationary effect—particularly in the industrialized countries—because increases in food prices raised the cost of living and, consequently, the wages indexed to it. Increases in the price of raw materials also quickly raised the price of manufactured goods, as well as the revenues of exporters of raw materials who in turn expanded their imports, thereby stimulating an increase in prices as well as in the volume of international trade. Although the oil crises had both a deflationary (due to drainage of dollars outside of OPEC) and a pervasively inflationary impact (due to price increases in oil), policy formulators in the major industrialized countries adopted tight monetary policies to curb double-digit inflation leading to a worldwide recession that was the most severe blow to the indutrialized Western world since the Great Depression of 1929–1930.

The quadrupling of oil prices led to a dollar accumulation by OPEC on such a massive scale that global trade was almost paralyzed. The recycling of dollars, therefore, became essential if the world economy was to survive and continue to function properly. Consequently, policy formulators in all countries recognized that the international monetary and trade systems are two sides of the same coin and that neither system can function without the other. In other words, the international developments of the 1970s called for a comprehensive and systematic review and reform of the international economic system, including national trade and monetary policies.

Recovery from the worldwide recession was quite slow primarily because of the paucity of domestic economic policy tools to deal with the high rates of imported inflation, the substantial declines in production, and the reduction in the volume of world trade. Facing balance-of-payments difficulties and the need for domestic antiinflationary policies, many countries attempted to rely on exports to recover from the recession. However, only Japan succeeded in doing so.

Meanwhile, the U.S. recession bottomed out as early as the first quarter of 1975, and, in the second quarter of 1976, the U.S. economy surpassed its previous highest production level, achieved during the second half of 1973. Compared with the 1976–1978 performance of the other major economies, such growth was impressive. However, the resulting consumption-pulled recovery growth also gave rise to an increase in U.S. imports and a balance-of-payments deterioration. The sharp contrast between the U.S. and Japanese recovery patterns (consumption vs. exporting) portended the forthcoming trade disputes between the two countries. The increasing bilateral trade imbalances are shown in Table 2-1, which presents the balance of trade between the United States and its major trading partners during the 1971–1981 time period.

Table 2-1.   U.S. Trade Balances with Japan, Federal Republic of Germany, United Kingdom, and France 1971–1981 (in millions of dollars)

	U.S. Trade Balance with			
	Japan	F.R.G.	U. K.	France
1971	− 3,647	− 1,043	− 203	218
1972	4,636	− 1,693	− 506	159
1973	− 1,934	− 1,904	− 309	429
1974	− 2,646	− 1,895	274	481
1975	− 2,778	− 561	477	746
1976	− 6,778	− 242	248	768
1977	− 9,671	− 1,712	481	243
1978	− 13,586	− 3,978	191	− 201
1979	− 10,576	− 3,142	2,123	454
1980	− 9,924	− 733	2,852	2,220
1981	− 15,789	− 1,102	− 396	1,490

Sources: For 1971–1979, International Monetary Fund, *Direction of Trade Yearbooks* 1981 and 1982 (Washington, D.C.: International Monetary Fund, 1981 and 1982). For 1980–1981, Japan Economic Institute of America, *Yearbook of U.S.-Japan Economic Relations in 1981* (Washington, D.C.: Japan Economic Institute, 1982).

As can be seen in Table 2-1, the initially modest U.S. bilateral trade deficits (through 1975) increased dramatically beginning in 1976. Except for 1979, each successive year shows a worsening U.S. trade balance through 1981. This was largely due to the pronounced increases in Japanese exports to the United States while U.S. exports to Japan during the same time period grew only by modest amounts.

While the United States and Japan were experiencing contrastive trends in their trade balances, more than 80 countries organized to work for freer international trade through the Multilateral Trade Negotiations (MTN)—the so-called "Tokyo Round"—which were to be completed by December 1978. The negotiators were confronted with the problem of reconciling mounting protectionism with the notion of free trade, because while most governments could readily agree upon the general, long-term principles, they faced sharp conflicts of interests with respect to specific, short-term domestic economic policy goals. The Carter administration, committed to free trade, understandably tried to solve its international economic problems (trade imbalances and the instability of the dollar) by urging surplus countries to stimulate their own economies rather than by disciplining the U.S. economy. It particularly blamed Japan and the Federal Republic of Germany for the trade imbalances. Thus, representatives of the government of the seven major industrialized countries gathered in Bonn for the Fourth Economic Summit Meeting in July 1978, at which Japan and the Federal Republic of Germany were urged to stimulate their economies more vigorously.

In the meantime, Japan's Gross National Product (GNP) grew to become the second largest in the free world, with exports amounting to $103.0 billion in 1979. This was more than the export volume of any other country, except the United States and the Federal Republic of Germany. Yet Japan's dependence on international trade was less than half that of the major European nations. At the same time, both the United States and Japan were the most important major trading countries because of the absolute size of their GNP and trade volumes.

The high Japanese GNP growth rates and even higher increases in the volume of international trade—particularly of exports—had a strong effect on the world economy. The U.S. market was especially strongly affected by the ever-expanding Japanese exports, because approximately a quarter of Japan's total exports went to the United States.

DOMESTIC DEVELOPMENTS

All through the 1970s and early 1980s, the trade balance between the United States and Japan remained in favor of Japan. Until the mid-1950s, Japanese exports consisted chiefly of textiles, apparel, toys, china, and

other light industrial products, but as Japan's industrial structure became upgraded, exports shifted to more value-added items. In the 1960s,
Japanese textile and other light industrial products began to lose their
international competitiveness, because domestic wage levels increased
and because numerous developing countries became more industrialized, establishing light and labor-intensive industries just as Japan had in
the late nineteenth century.

The events of this period were accompanied by two additional developments: the increase of the 1978–1981 U.S.–Japan bilateral trade imbalance to far above the already hard-to-tolerate level of 1977;[3] and the
gradual conclusion of multilateral trade negotiations (in 1979), which
provided the United States with an opportunity to examine Japanese tariff and nontariff barriers in a comprehensive manner.

Beginning in 1978, U.S. policy formulators started to argue that
structural adjustments were needed to remedy the bilateral trade imbalance between the two countries. The concept was only vaguely defined
and implied a change only in the overall industrial structures. Nevertheless, Japanese policy formulators feared that the concept might imply a
rigid scheme to allocate industrial production quotas, as did the Washington Conference for the Limitation of Armaments in 1921-1922 and
the London Naval Conference in 1930. At that time, Japan had no choice
but to succumb to the demands of the Western powers; thus, understandably, most Japanese policy formulators were reluctant in 1978 to enter-
tain the U.S. idea of "structural adjustments." In any event, the proposal
was in essence an acknowledgment of the correlation between trade imbalances and industrial structures.

Despite surprisingly strong resistance by Japanese policy formulators, the country was already on the move toward adjustments in the
trade structure, at least in certain areas. To increase the import ratio of
manufactured goods, the government promoted in July 1979 the establishment of the "Conference to Encourage the Import of Manufactured
Goods" (CPIMG) [Seihin Yunyuu Taisaku Kaigi], made up of importers
and trade-related ministries.[4] The primary objective of the conference is
to expand international trade, while avoiding trade frictions. In its first
meeting, a resolution was adopted to double the per capita manufactured imports from nearly $200 in mid-1979 to about $400 by 1982 (approximately the same per capita level as in the United States).

As can be seen in Table 2-2, Japan's ratio of manufactured imports in
1981 was less than half that of the United States and the Federal Republic of Germany and France, reflecting the nation's industrial and trade
structures of the late 1970s and early 1980s.

The low Japanese import ratio can be attributed to several factors.
First, Japan does not have industrialized neighbors with whom it can
share the benefits of the division of labor. Second, Japan is not well en-

Table 2-2.   The Share of Imports of Manufactured Goods in the Total Imports of Major Industrialized Countries, 1981 (in billions of dollars)

Country	Import Total (A) Amount ($)	Imports of Manufactured Goods (B)[a] Amount ($)	Share Percent (B)/(A)
U.S.	271.2	139.4	51.4
Japan	140.8	24.1	17.1
F.R.G.	162.6	76.9	47.2
Canada	64.9	44.5	68.6
France	120.2	56.3	46.8

[a]Manufactured goods consist of the following categories: manufactured goods classified chiefly by material, machinery and transport equipment, miscellaneous manufactured goods.

Source: Organization for Economic Cooperation and Development (OECD), microfische tables (Washington, D.C.: 1982).

dowed with natural resources. In essence, this signifies a high ratio of raw material and a low ratio of manufactured imports. Third, because Japan's large domestic market was historically closed, opportunities existed for many kinds of domestic industries to emerge, reducing the demand for manufactured imports. In any event, the United States did not accept these explanations and accused Japan of not importing enough manufactured goods from other industrialized countries while fiercely promoting exports.

The U.S. view was primarily based on the Japanese tradition of importing raw materials, adding value to them through processing, and then exporting the resulting end products. The U.S. challenge to such a trade pattern was important because it pointed out to the newly industrialized countries the dangers that they face in establishing their position in the world market.

Japanese productivity developments during the 1960s and 1970s were another factor in the generally strong trade performance of the nation. On the average, Japanese productivity increased annually by approximately 8 to 10 percent in the 1970s. (See Table 2-3) Productivity rates in many U.S. industries started from a relatively high level and remain high in numerous economic sectors. On the other hand, increase in Japanese productivity surpassed that of the United States, particularly in strategically important industries such as steel, automobiles, color televisions, ballbearings, tool-machines, and optical equipment.

Concerning the differences in productivity between the United States and Japan, the *1980 Joint Economic Report* referred to a recent study by Dale W. Jorgenson of Harvard University and Mieko Mishimizu of Princeton University, who wrote:

Table 2-3. Industrial Productivity in Major Industrialized Countries, 1970–1981

Year	Japan Index	Japan Percentage Change	U.S. Index	U.S. Percentage Change	F.R.G. Index	F.R.G. Percentage Change	U.K. Index	U.K. Percentage Change	France Index	France Percentage Change
1970	100.0	...	100.0	...	100.0	...	100.0	...	100.0	...
1971	103.4	3.4	105.4	5.4	106.3	6.3	105.2	5.2	105.2	5.2
1972	113.8	10.1	110.9	5.2	112.8	6.1	112.0	6.5	113.8	8.2
1973	131.2	15.3	114.1	2.9	122.5	8.6	118.4	5.7	120.9	6.2
1974	133.1	1.4	117.3	2.8	123.7	1.0	119.2	0.7	125.1	3.5
1975	128.4	-3.5	117.1	-0.2	127.4	3.0	118.7	-0.4	122.1	-2.4
1976	140.9	9.7	125.8	7.4	133.8	5.0	124.1	4.5	133.8	9.6
1977	147.3	4.5	127.7	1.5	137.0	2.4	124.0	-0.1	135.4	1.2
1978	159.2	8.1	129.3	1.3	139.3	1.7	126.2	1.8	140.7	3.9
1979	172.1	8.1	133.0	2.9	144.8	3.9	128.3	1.7	148.3	5.4
1980	183.3	6.5	133.8	0.6	144.9	0.1	126.9	-1.1	150.3	-1.3
1981	188.8	3.0	136.7	2.2	...	...	135.8	7.0	...	...

Note: Percentage changes over previous year are computed from index figures for each year.
Source: 1970–1971, Japan, Central Bank, International Comparative Statistics, 1980, pp. 19–20; 1972–1981, Japan, Central Bank, International Comparative Statistics, 1982, pp. 19–20.

. . .by 1972 Japanese industries had eliminated the technological gap with their U.S. counterparts in 13 out of 28 industries compared. Japanese industry has been ahead of the United States in primary iron and steel and in primary nonferrous metals since 1967 and in chemicals since 1963 and has been steadily increasing their advantages in those industries. According to the study, which covers the period 1955 to 1972, Japan has been catching up with the United States in other heavy manufacturing industries and is ahead of the United States technologically in a number of light manufacturing and service industries including construction, paper and allied products, printing and publishing, and transportation and communication.[5]

Toward the end of the 1970s, declining U.S. productivity played a major role in increasing inflation. This caused U.S. products to be less competitive, thereby aggravating the external imbalances and the decline of the dollar. On the other hand, among the major industrialized countries, Japan maintained the highest level of productivity growth during the 1970s, except for temporary interruptions in 1974 and 1975 due to the first energy crisis. Many Japanese economists and policy formulators attributed Japan's low inflation after 1975 to—among other factors—productivity growth achieved mainly through the invention of energy-saving and other related technologies.

Japanese industrial structure policies during the last 30 years were another important domestic economic factor influencing the nation's trade policies. Industrial structures involve two critical elements: productivity and the relative size and production share of industrial sectors. Productivity determines international competitiveness, while production share is an important determinant of export volume.

Japanese industrial stategy was quite successful. Through MITI's persistent efforts, industrial policies were based on both domestic and international economic considerations. In the late 1950s, priority was placed on four industries—coal, power, steel, and shipbuilding—because these were regarded as essential for recovery from the devastation of World War II. From the late 1950s to the 1960s, the textile industry was strengthened, followed by the electronics, machine, precision tool manufacturing, and automobile industries. Most recently, the high-technology industries, such as data processing, telecommunications, and other systems industries have been marked for rapid development.

The Japanese industrial development plan, however, was not compulsory, although more than 100 government funds, corporations, and companies supported efforts to upgrade private industry. With government guidance and support, the Japanese private sector was encouraged to develop those industries that showed the most promise of long-run success.

The Japanese government aided private industry using two methods: namely, tax privileges and concessionary financing. Tax privileges involved accelerated depreciation and tax credits for industries so designated by MITI and the Ministry of Finance (MOF) as strategically important.

Concessionary financing meant lower-than-market interest rates, which varied according to the investment projects for which the loans were made. Such financing facilitated industrial upgrading because the loan terms were more favorable than those offered by private financial institutions. In addition, such financing induced private institutions to cofinance the projects because qualification for public loans implied that the investment served the national interest and was economically and financially sound. Of the more than 100 public corporations, 13 engaged exclusively in financing. These included the Japan Development Bank, the Export–Import Bank of Japan, and the Financial Corporation for Small and Medium-sized Business (Chuushoo Kigyoo Kinyuu Kooko).

Together with the use of such financial tools, the Japanese government also used administrative guidance (Gyoosei Shidoo) to help implement industrial policies. Administrative guidance implied government influence over private business exerted through regulations, recommendations, encouragement, discouragement, or prohibition irrespective of statutory jurisdictional authority.[6]

Until about 1970, another tool available to the government was the allocation of foreign exchange. Because dollars were scarce, MITI allocated dollars to individual enterprises in close consultation with the MOF. Through this process, the Japanese government could effectively encourage the import of sophisticated, innovative technologies indispensable to industrial upgrading and discourage purchases of consumer goods from abroad.

Such systematic cooperation between the Japanese government and business was sarcastically characterized as "Japan, Inc." by Eugene Kaplan,[7] a former Department of Commerce official, and by other U.S. businesses involved in trade with Japan. Although the characterization represents a gross oversimplification of a complex relationship, Japanese government-business relations are undoubtedly unique and have played a major role in the industrial upgrading process.

During recent years, in particular 1979 and again in 1981-1982, an increasing number of U.S. policy formulators recognized the importance of industrial structures as they pertain to trade performance. Many believe that there cannot be an effective U.S. trade policy without an effective industrial policy because trade liberalization through the elimination of tariff or nontariff barriers, or improved marketing or export-promotion methods, cannot be effective without competitive products to sell.

U.S. and Japanese industrial structures show both differences and similarities. The differences consist of the following: (1) U.S. agriculture is the most productive and competitive in the world, whereas Japanese agriculture is far less competitive and continues to be protected by quotas for citrus, beef, and some other products; (2) the United States produces lumber, coal, and other natural resources competitively, whereas the same Japanese industries are not internationally competitive; and (3) U.S. traditional industries, such as steel, automobiles, and electronics, are relatively old; therefore, machines and equipment in these industries are frequently dated. On the other hand, the same Japanese industries have shorter histories and are better equipped with modern and highly productive machinery.

The similarities are as follows: (1) the capital- and technology-intensive industries enjoy relative advantages and are internationally competitive; and (2) the labor-intensive industries face competition from producers in newly industrialized countries.

The recent U.S.-Japan trade conflicts occurred partially because of such differences and similarities. The two nations' high-technology and capital-intensive industries engaged in strong competition, with Japanese industries ultimately outperforming the U.S. counterparts. This was attributable to many factors; some relevant to industrial structures were the promotion of innovative technologies, better quality control, and more effective global marketing by the Japanese.

Typically, trade imbalances resulting from competition by similar industries generate stronger trade conflicts than do imbalances resulting through competition by different or complementary industries. It is particularly noteworthy that the Japanese overtook the United States in the textile and optical industries in the 1960s, in the color television, machine tool, and steel industries in the early 1970s, and in the automobile and electronics industries in the late 1970s. It is also important to point out that even when the Japanese economy slowed down during the early 1980s, in particular, during 1981-1982, this slowdown was not accompanied by a corresponding increase in unemployment. Table 2-4 compares Japan's unemployment rates during the 1975-1981 period against the unemployment rates of its major trading partners.

The low Japanese unemployment rates are partly the result of the lifetime employment system. Japanese employees are retained even if their firm operates below capacity, whereas in the United States employees are laid off or recalled in almost direct proportion to operating capacity. In other words, Japanese firms internalize employees while U.S. firms externalize them by putting them on the unemployment rolls. As a consequence, Japanese management is under great pressure to operate at full capacity and to continually expand operations. This, in turn, results in a strong export drive, particularly when domestic demand sags.

Growth in exports usually generates increased employment in the exporting country. On the other hand, the first major effect of growth in imports is usually a reduction in employment in the importing country, although imports may ultimately lead to mutually expanded trade and,

Table 2-4.   Unemployment Rates in Major Industrialized Countries, 1975–1981

Country	1975 (%)	1976 (%)	1977 (%)	1978 (%)	1979 (%)	1980 (%)	1981 (%)
U.S.	8.6	7.7	7.0	6.0	6.0	7.1	7.6
U.K.	4.1	5.7	6.2	6.1	5.6	6.8	11.3
France	4.3	4.7	5.0	5.4	n.a.	6.6	7.4
F.R.G.	4.7	4.6	4.5	4.3	3.3	3.4	5.5
Japan	1.9	2.0	2.0	2.2	1.9	2.0	2.2

Sources: For France, 1975–1979, CIA, Handbook of Economic Statistics 1979 (Washington, D.C.: Government Printing Office, 1980); for remainder, 1975–1979, International Labour Organization, Yearbook of Labor Statistics 1979 (Geneva: ILO, 1980). For all countries, 1980, CIA, Handbook of Economic Statistics 1981 (Washington, D.C.: Government Printing Office, 1982). For France, 1981, OECD Economic Outlook July 1982 (Paris, OECD, 1982). For U.S., 1981, Economic Report of the President February 1982, (Washington, D.C.: Government Printing Office, 1982). For remainder, 1981, OECD Bulletin of Labour Statistics 1982–2 (Paris, OECD, 1982).

consequently, increased employment in both the exporting and importing countries. Understandably, for about 25 years after World War II, most countries tried to attain rapid growth and employment by promoting exports and curtailing imports.

As could be expected, Japanese export drives created economic-political problems in the importing countries, particularly in the United States whose bilateral trade imbalance with Japan was around $10 billion in 1977 and around $18 billion in 1981.[8] The United States claimed that its major industries, such as the steel, color television, semiconductor, and automobile industries had been injured by imports from Japan and—to a lesser extent—from Europe. The unemployed workers and labor unions representing the injured industries wasted no time in demanding protection. They first went to politicians representing their districts, then—directly or through these politicians—to the executive branch. The mass media carried the issue, not only all over the country but also all over the world. In this manner, particularly if the injured industry has strong political influence, a relatively minor increase in imports can trigger strong protectionist responses. This is true as much in Japan as in the United States or Western Europe.

The quality of life in Japan has long been used by U.S. and European policy formulators to, at least, partially explain the supposedly unfair trade advantages from which Japan benefits.

In most major industrialized countries, the quality of life—although its operational definition remains vague—has established itself as the ultimate economic, political, and social goal. Even in communist and developing countries, it is regarded as the ultimate long-run objective, although in the short-run, the governments in these countries are probably more interested in economic growth or military build-up. Thus, it is not an exaggeration to argue that high growth, high productivity, low inflation, low unemployment, and other policy goals are important to the extent that they affect the quality of life.

Improving the quality of life, however, is a costly undertaking. It involves more consumption, higher wages, and more imports to provide consumers with domestically unavailable goods and/or lower prices. In this sense, for example, while free trade had for years contributed to the United States' high quality of life, it also brought with it a deterioration of its trade balance. In other words, an improvement of the quality of life can actually contribute to the intensification of trade frictions.

The impact of the quality of life on the supply side is no less significant than on the demand side. Improvements imply higher wages, more environmental protection, better safety and health standards, and other regulations—all of which increase production costs—thereby reducing international competitiveness. The comparative advantages of developing countries in the labor-intensive industries is attributed mostly to lower wages. However, attention should also be paid to the manner in which industrialized countries increase their production costs through rules and regulations aimed at improving the quality of life. Many of the regulations considered essential in the major industrialized economies are often lacking in the developing countries. As a result, neither the United States nor Japan can compete with developing countries in certain light, labor-intensive industries such as the textile, apparel, or toy industries.

To understand the trade policy implications of the quality of life, attention must be paid to the historical development of this elusive concept. Until recently, even in the United States, smoldering plant chimneys were considered a symbol of industrial prosperity. Through the early 1960s, emphasis remained on economic growth, and the negative aspects of industrial development were ignored. The antiestablishment sentiments that emerged during the 1960s forced policy formulators to pay attention to the quality of life rather than merely to production increases. The quality of life suddenly became a fashionable notion even at the highest policy formulating levels—including the administration, Congress, and the judiciary. The notion of steady economic growth came to be questioned, and a new net measure of GNP—a more relevant indicator of economic performance—was advocated. Such a measure would take into account the negative effects of growth on the environment and/or on health.

Meanwhile, particularly after the late 1960s, the U.S. trade balance suffered. Although, as pointed out previously, the causes were multiple, the measures introduced to improve the quality of life added to the imbalance.

Japan's recovery from World War II began during the late 1940s and early 1950s. Economic growth was rapid and the international competitiveness of its industries continually improved. Believing that the large bilateral trade imbalances were caused by structural factors, U.S. policy formulators argued that the difference in the quality of life between the two countries should be equalized.

The environmental protection, safety, and health standards of Japan were quickly brought up to U.S. levels as early as the mid-1960s. By the late 1970s, the smoggy air and polluted water of Tokyo that characterized the city during the mid-1960s was only a memory. Indeed, some regulations, including automobile emission standards, are now even more strict in Japan than in the United States. However, measured in terms of the length and frequency of vacations, size of dwelling space, wages, social welfare, cultural facilities, parks, and other amenities, the quality of life is still lower in Japan than in the United States. Accordingly, many U.S. and European policy formulators charge that the Japanese save and invest excessively, spend too little, and work too hard and too long for low wages.

Some of these arguments were already studied and acted upon by the Japanese government during the early 1970s. However, the implementation of appropriate policies was interrupted by the oil crises of the mid- and late 1970s as well as by the reduced economic growth of the 1981–1982 period. Nevertheless, both domestic and international concerns continue to make future improvements in the quality of life a major policy goal for Japan.

THE EVENTS OF THE EARLY 1980s

Beginning in 1980–1981, the United States, the Federal Republic of Germany, Japan, and most other industrialized countries of the world were in the midst of an economic downturn, which, by the end of 1982, appeared to be deeper and longer lasting than expected. The United States and Western Europe experienced severe growth and productivity problems, and even Japan—whose economy still performed better—faced problems that were heretofore unknown to its people.

The domestic economic problems of the major industrialized countries were compounded by the increasing competition from the newly industrialized countries with modern technology and low-cost labor.

Neoprotectionist trade barriers—designed to shield traditional industries plagued by structural problems—mushroomed. Not surprisingly, world trade—which had been the engine of the spectacular postwar growth—declined for the first time since 1945.

In addition, the heavy indebtedness of the developing countries (more than $500 billion by 1982) and the need for large-scale debt rescheduling have put a heavy strain on the international financial mechanism.

These problems were even more troublesome because they were tightly interrelated. Attempting to solve just one of them made little sense; there was no way, for example, to reduce the strain on the world's financial system without reviving trade which, in turn, was impossible without accelerating economic growth, particularly in the highly industrialized countries.

The severe worldwide economic problems of the early 1980s were the result of the events of the 1970s, that is, inflation, unbridled international bank lending practices, rapid and largely uncontrolled growth in the developing countries, sudden oil price increases, and the occasional wild gyrations of the floating exchange-rate system.

Conditions were worsened by the determined attempts of the Reagan administration in the United States and other conservative governments in Europe to correct the economic problems generated by the 1970s through tight monetary policies. While inflation in the United States and the United Kingdom as well as in a number of other countries was reduced, prohibitively high interest rates stunted recovery attempts. Layoffs, plant closings, and bankruptcies multiplied around the world, and unemployment in the highly industrialized countries reached more than 30 million, up from only around 20 million in 1980. The United States, the weathervane of the world economy, experienced its most severe and longest postwar recession, which some observers began to call a depression. With more than 10 percent unemployment, sagging demand, underutilized industrial plants, and a strong dollar, protectionist sentiments were increasing not only in Congress but also among the top officials of the administration and even traditionally free-trade-minded Democratic politicians such as Senator Kennedy and former Vice-President Mondale. Because the United States is Japan's most important export market, not surprisingly their anger was directed mostly at Japan.

Although experiencing lower inflation, unemployment, and a higher rate of growth, Japan was also strongly affected by the worldwide economic developments. Domestic demand was slackening, exports sagged, and the increasing wave of protectionism in both the United States and Western Europe put a great strain on the nation's international trade relations.

CONCLUDING REMARKS

For the first two decades after World War II, economic relations between Japan, the United States, and Europe were characterized by cooperation and complementarity. The United States displayed a noblesse oblige attitude that aided the reconstruction and development of the war-ravaged economies of Japan and Europe and encouraged the United States' new allies to become stronger, especially after the onset of the Cold War in 1947.

The vast, open U.S. market absorbed increasing Japanese and European exports, thereby helping to promote economic growth abroad—even though Europe, after the formation of the EEC in 1957, became more protectionist, and Japan remained reluctant to liberalize its trade policies. The liberal U.S. trade policies, generated by humanitarian, economic, and political considerations, strengthened Japan and Europe. In time, however, they also weakened the U.S. economy.

Due to its rich natural resources, relatively abundant capital, sophisticated technology, and high productivity, the United States continued to be very competitive until the late 1960s. By the early 1970s, however, the United States became less competitive, and in 1971 the United States experienced a trade balance deficit of $2.1 billion—its first in 78 years. At the same time, nonetheless, the U.S. economy prospered because of liberal Keynesian fiscal and monetary policies.

As inflation became a more serious problem, however, the relatively steady growth could not be sustained long without adequate growth in productivity. Worse, the restrictive economic measures of the early 1970s reduced economic growth to recessionary levels without lowering the rate of inflation. The result was an increase in domestic inflation and a diminution in international competitiveness, accompanied by a deterioration of the trade balance and a faltering dollar. Meanwhile, Japan and Europe outperformed the United States in economic growth, productivity, and price stability.

Worldwide economic disturbances highlighted the United States' economic problems and made it necessary for the United States to curb inflation and to strengthen the dollar. Thus, the restoration of the U.S. trade balance became necessary for the stability of the international monetary system and the growth of global trade. The accomplishment of this, however, implied further trade conflicts between the United States, Japan, and Europe, because the United States had lost the competitive edge that had made its paternalistic trade policies of the past possible.

Increases in the price of raw materials and oil in the early 1970s amplified tensions in the world trading system. This was primarily due to the accumulation of dollars by a few OPEC countries, as well as by the large trade deficits of most of the oil-importing nations.

The United States and Japan recovered from the 1974–1975 worldwide recession earlier than most other countries. Their trade performances, however, proved to be quite different. Japan's trade surpluses increased, whereas the United States incurred increasingly higher deficits. The bilateral trade imbalances between the two countries also continued to build up, creating serious bilateral trade conflicts beginning in 1977.

The postwar international economic changes were the aggregate of the domestic economic changes experienced by individual countries. During the 1960s and 1970s, in GNP growth rates and productivity, Japan outperformed the United States, and it was also more effective in upgrading its industrial and trade structures. Thus, Japan's rapid economic growth led to increased exports in order to finance imports of raw materials and high-technology products and to meet increased international competition. In addition, through various restrictive trade measures during the 1960s, the Japanese government promoted exports and discouraged imports.

A difference in the nature of economic and trade structures, productivity growth, upgrading of trade and industry, and policies to improve the quality of life caused an increase in exports in Japan and an increase in imports in the United States during the 1970s. This difference also tended to discourage U.S. exports and to restrict Japanese imports, although Japan's import barriers continued to be reduced in the 1970s, especially through the MTN negotiations. As the bilateral trade imbalance between the two countries reached nearly $10 billion in the late 1970s, policy formulators, business circles, labor, and the mass media in both countries lent increased attention to the emerging problem.

The increased attention forced Japan to reduce trade barriers and to promote imports, steps that represented a 180-degree turn-around from previous trade policies. The same events forced U.S. policy formulators, business, and labor to begin to recognize that among others, an important reason for the United States' weakening international trade position was the gradual erosion of the domestic industrial base. Prior to this realization, the United States' weakening trade balances vis-à-vis the Japanese had been almost exclusively ascribed to Japanese subsidies, dumping, high tariffs, administrative barriers, low wages, unique cultural traditions, inefficient or closed distributions systems, and the differing quality of life.[9]

With the onset of the 1980s, the world economy was caught in the most serious and most prolonged recession since the 1930s. Although among the major industrialized countries Japan's economy still performed reasonably well, it was also affected by the worldwide economic slowdown. Economic growth was reduced to a postwar low, unemployment edged up and, most of all, exports were hindered by the emergence of protectionist measures throughout the world, particularly in Western Europe and the United States, its most important trading partners. Of course, the same was true of Japan, where agricultural interest groups successfully pressured politicians—whose survival depends on the satisfaction of agricultural interests—to continue to protect the agricultural sector against, in particular, U.S. exports.

NOTES

1. See, *Yearbook of U.S.-Japan Economic Relations in 1981*, (Washington, D.C.: Japan Economic Institute of America, Inc., 1982), p. 111, Table 37; p. 99, Table 25.

2. Ambassador Johnson made this comment in an interview with the writer in April 1980, as well as in an article in *The Japan Economic Journal*, 17 June, 1980, and in various seminars at the George Washington University and other institutions.

3. See Table 2-1, p. 17.

4. The Conference is chaired by the Chairman of Mitsui Bussan Co., Yoshizo Ikeda, who is also a member of the Trade Council. It has 18 members from the private sector, including major international trading houses, distributors, retailers, and various import associations, and eight members from the public sector, which involves the Economic Planning Agency (EPA), the Ministry of Foreign Affairs (MOFA), the Ministry of Finance (MOF), the Ministry of Welfare, Ministry of Agriculture, Forestry and Fisheries (MOAFF), the Ministry of Transportation, and MITI.

5. U.S. Congress, Joint Economic Committee, *The 1980 Joint Economic Report*, Senate Report No. 96–618, 96th Congress, 2d sess. (Washington, D.C.: Government Printing Office, 1980), p. 32.

6. Ezra F. Vogel, (ed.), *Modern Japanese Organization and Decision-Making*, (Berkeley: University of California Press, 1975), p. xv.

7. See Eugene J. Kaplan, *Japan: The Government-Business Relationship, A Guide for the American Businessman* (Washington, D.C.: Department of Commerce, February, 1972), p. 10. Mr. Kaplan, who worked in the U.S.–Japan Trade Council (renamed in January 1981 as the Japan Economic Institute) after retiring from the Commerce Department, claimed that this phrase was both overused and taken out of context. (Japanese government-business relations are discussed in detail in the next chapter.)

8. See Table 2-1, p. 17.

9. In 1981–1982, many of these arguments were revived. The "manipulated yen" charge was added to the list in 1982.

3

THE INSTITUTIONAL ASPECTS OF TRADE POLICY FORMULATION

As defined previously, the Japanese trade policy formulation process is part of the country's general domestic and international governmental economic-policy formulation process that consists of the identification of trade policy objectives, the collection, analysis, and dissemination of information, decision-making, and negotiations.

Trade policy is formulated by specifically designated entities. These can be divided into primary entities, whose major jurisdiction is the formulation of trade policy across sectors, and sectoral entities, whose trade policy formulation activities cover only the sectors that are under their jurisdiction.

Trade policy formulation is based on information concerning the critical factors in the international and domestic economic environments, the negotiation process—including trade-partner requests—the expectations of domestic special-interest groups, and the attitudes of the mass media and the general public.

In the analysis of the policy formulation process, particular attention must be given to the intraorganizational administrative phenomena. The philosophy and the behavior of individual policy formulators play a critical role in the determination of policies because their perception and interpretation of information provide the basis for decision-making. The identification, loyalty, and competence of these individuals—as well as the quality of their information sources—are additional influencing factors.

The relationship between authority and power is especially important because the combination of these two factors, together with the behavior of individuals, affect and reflect the speed, style, nature—and even the predictability—of the decision-making process.

Authority is statutory and legitimate, while power connotes influence whether legitimate or not. In most cases they coincide, but not necessarily so. The extent of the gap between authority and power varies depending upon the political system, organizational and administrative characteristics, and related behavioral factors.

The trade policy formulation process is continually affected by the organizational and administrative characteristics that may cause dysfunctions. The belated identification of problems, the lack of understanding future implications, bureaucratic sectionalism, bureaucratic hierarchy, poor integration of diversified roles, and bureaucratic "red tape" are the major examples of such impediments. Figure 3-1 illustrates the trade policy formulation relationships in a graphical form.

ORGANIZATIONAL CHARACTERISTICS

The organizational characteristics of present-day democratic governments consist of the structural and statutory aspects and include specifically: the nature of the political system; the structure of the policy formulating entities (in terms of hierarchy-differentiation, jurisdiction, and authority); regulations and procedures; and the integration of trade policy formulating activities.

The Political System

The major differences between U.S. and Japanese policy formulation are due to dissimilarities in the presidential and parliamentary forms of government with regard to status, allocation of power, functions, and impact. Under the U.S. presidential system, the division of power is balanced among the legislative, executive, and judicial branches. In contrast, under the Japanese parliamentary system, the power of the Diet is more limited than that of the executive branch, partly because the cabinet is formed and dominated by the majority party's senior politicians, and partly because historically the central government bureaucracy has de facto always occupied a more powerful position.[1]

Japan began to modernize in 1868, when the power was transferred from the Shogun to the Meiji Emperor. However, this drastic change from the Shogun's feudal reign to the Emperor's modern imperial regime was not a real revolution because it was not accompanied by major social changes.

Figure 3-1. The Trade Policy Formulation Process

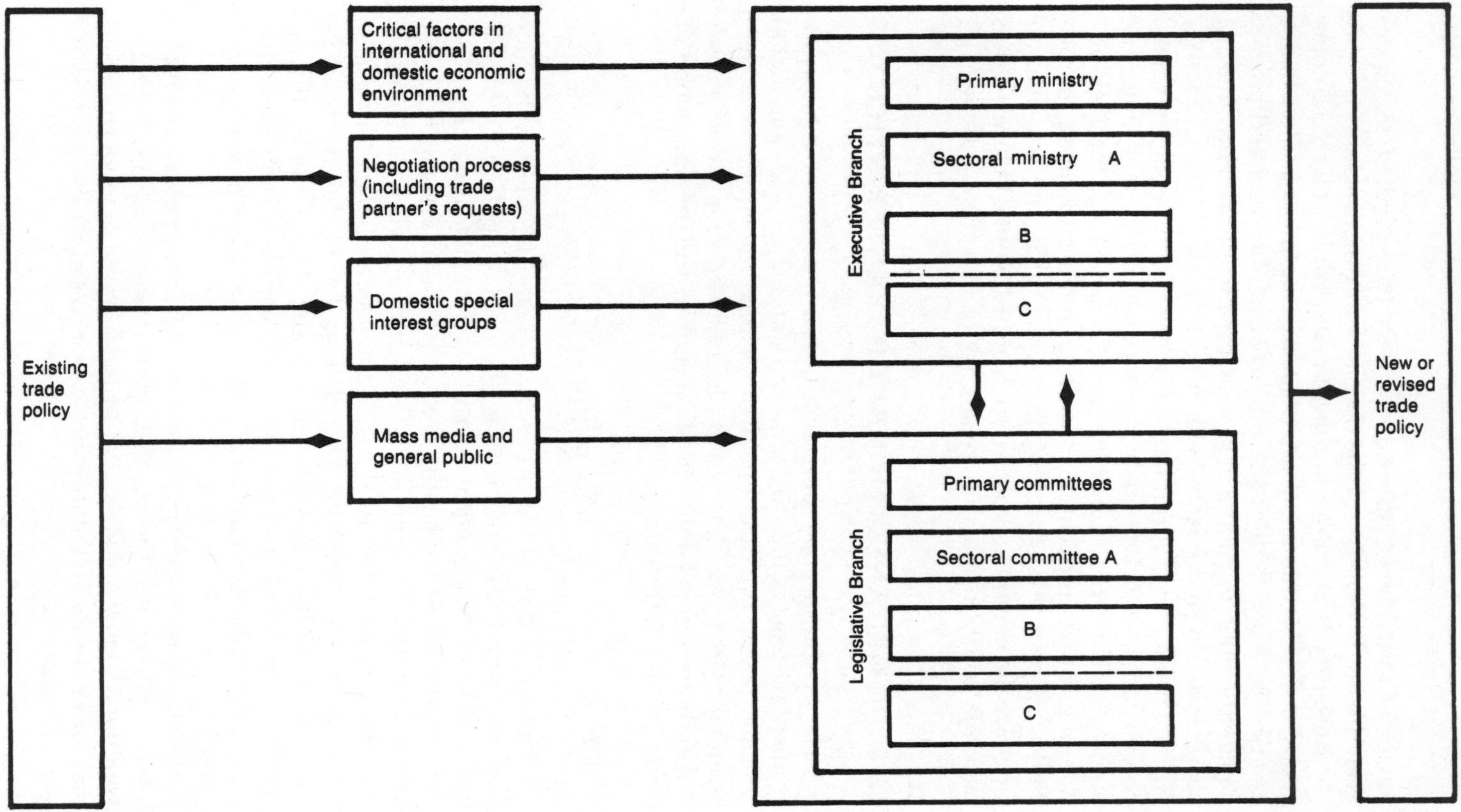

For more than two and a half centuries during the Shogun era, the samurai were the absolute rulers. With their aid, the Shoguns successfully centralized power and through this the Tokugawa Shoguns established a sophisticated nationwide central bureaucracy as early as the beginnning of the seventeenth century. At that time, Europe was still embroiled in divisive wars, and the United States did not even exist.

Many students of current events do not appreciate the importance of this development, which prevented Japan from becoming a colony of the Western powers as other Asian countries did. Furthermore, without an efficient centralized administrative system already in place, the Meiji efforts at modernization would probably not have permeated society as rapidly as they did.

The restoration of power to the Meiji Emperor was implemented through certain factions of the samurai class, most notably those from Satsuma (the southern Kyushu) and Choshu (the most western parts of Honshu).[2] While restoration meant literally a transfer of nominal or statutory ruling power from the Shogun to the Meiji Emperor, functionally it involved a shift of actual administrative power from the feudal forces—primarily the kin of the Shogun family—to the relatively low-class samurai.

Two major characteristics of the early Japanese bureaucracy can be identified from such a historical perspective. The first is its essentially elitist nature. The highly selective Imperial University of Tokyo (today's University of Tokyo) was established by the Meiji government primarily to educate prospective bureaucrats. The second characteristic is its total dedication to the Emperor, who held absolute power.[3] The concept of the bureaucrat as a civil servant was not known until it was introduced by the U.S. occupation forces immediately after World War II.[4] Nevertheless, today's bureaucracy retains its traditional elitism, and this characteristic continues to influence its behavior and public image.

In the Japanese parliamentary system, unless a coalition of several parties becomes necessary (which has not been the case for the last three decades), the majority party forms the cabinet and controls the bureaucracy.[5] The Diet has been controlled by the Liberal Democratic Party (LDP) majority since 1955, particularly by the senior LDP members, who hold most cabinet positions and other leadership posts. The senior cabinet members, in principle, also lead the party, although their effectiveness may vary according to the quality of the prime minister's leadership, the size of his faction, the majority margin of the party, and other political, economic, and social factors. If serious policy differences exist among the factions, settlement is usually reached before a legislative session. Whether this is done through persuasion, "jawboning," compromise, or consensus depends on the issue. There is always the possibility that the party factions will differ so radically as to effect a behind-the-scenes fight, which, however, is eventually settled.

During the Diet session, opposition party members typically criticize and oppose whatever the government proposes, and the majority party members typically deliver supportive statements or remain silent until voting takes place. In the end, however, the majority party is usually assured of the needed votes.

Within the framework of such legislative relations, numerous unique political practices have developed. For example, opposition party members can resort to any measure to delay the proposal and discussion of bills. Government witnesses (either cabinet ministers, parliamentary vice-ministers, or high-level bureaucrats) may assume a low-key posture to avoid extensive discussions by only briefly responding to questions. Of course, while the government does not respond, opposition parties can promote their own policies and ideologies. This results in a weakening of the government's image, while opposition parties appear to be on the offensive.

Finally, legislative hearings are uncommon in Japan. If they are held at all, they are usually limited to exceptional cases, such as criminal investigations. Naturally, such hearings do not provide foreign observers with information that could weaken the country's international negotiating position.

The Structure of the Trade Policy Formulating Entities

The Japanese entities playing a key role in the formulation of trade policy include the Ministry of International Trade and Industry (MITI), the Ministry of Foreign Affairs (MOFA), the Ministry of Finance (MOF), and the Ministry of Agriculture, Forestry, and Fisheries (MOAFF) in the executive branch, and the MITI, MOFA, MOF, and MOAFF Committees in both the Lower and Upper Houses of the Diet. Interinstitutional coordination is not formalized in Japan; thus, no official coordinating committee exists.

The Ministry of International Trade and Industry

The Ministry of International Trade and Industry (hereafter referred to as MITI), as it is known today, was established under the auspices of the U.S. occupation forces in 1949. MITI's primary objective is to encourage Japanese participation in the world economy by promoting the development of export industries.

Of all the Japanese government agencies, MITI has the primary responsibility for trade policy formulation. Accordingly, its decisions are most important, except when they involve budgetary matters. In such cases, the Ministry of Finance plays the dominant role.

The organization of MITI is shown in Figure 3-2. The Ministry contains several semi-independent agencies, including the Agency of Natural Resources and Energy, the Patent Office, and the Small and Medium Enterprise Agency. However, only MITI's Tokyo headquarters is involved in international trade policy formulation.

MITI is made up of a matrix-type organization that mixes functional with sectoral and subsectoral divisions. Officials call the functional breakdown *Yokowari* ("horizontal breakdown"), and the sectoral breakdown *Tatewari* ("Vertical breakdown"). The "horizontal breakdown" involves the bureaus of International Trade Policy, International Trade Administration, Industrial Policy, and Industrial Location and Environmental Protection—which are in charge of planning commercial and industrial policies. The "vertical breakdown" includes the bureaus for Basic Industries, Machinery and Information Industries, and Consumer Goods Industries. These bureaus control, regulate, coordinate, promote, and guide these sectors either individually or collectively. For MITI policies to be effective, a harmonious integration of the bureaus is, of course, vitally important.

The International Trade Policy Bureau, which has primary responsibility for trade policy formulation and international negotiations, is divided into four regional divisions. Particularly relevant to U.S.–Japan trade are the regional division of America–Oceania and the functional division of International Economic Affairs and Tariffs, both of which are in the same International Trade Policy Bureau. The America–Oceania Division is important because its raison d'être is to maintain good trade relations with the United States through effective communications, negotiations, cooperation, and coordination. The International Economic Affairs and Tariffs division is in charge of multilateral agreements (including tariffs) and other policy and administrative affairs related to international organizations such as the United Nations (UN), Organization for Economic Cooperation and Development (OECD), and IMF.

Other units playing a key role are the Information Office and the International Trade Research Division, both of which are also in the International Trade Policy Bureau. The former was established around 1970 after Japanese policy formulators were shocked by U.S. restrictions on Japanese textile imports and realized that a lack of effective communications aggravated the resulting trade conflicts. The major function of the Information Office is to issue public-relations pamphlets overseas and to brief foreign diplomats and journalists assigned to Tokyo. The office's research division collects statistics on international trade and publishes

Figure 3-2. Ministry of International Trade and Industry*

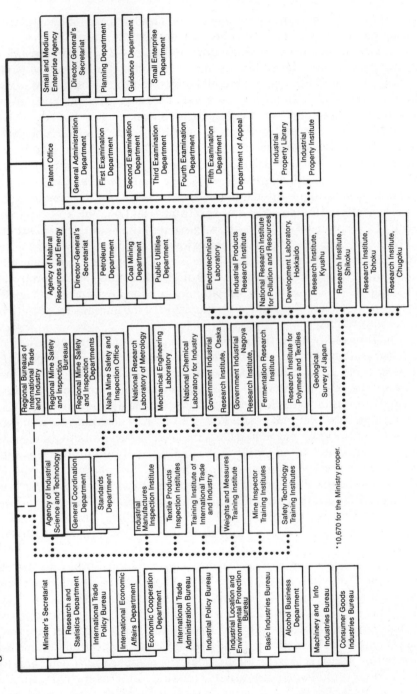

*10,670 for the Ministry proper.

Source: Japan, Administrative Management Agency, Prime Minister's Office, Organization of the Government of Japan, (Tokyo: Abe Printing Co., Ltd., 1980), pp. 20–21.

the annual MITI "White Paper," which is now widely accepted as the official report on Japan's industrial performance.

MITI uses several key committees. Of these the *Hoorei Shinsa Iinkai* (Law and Ordinance Review Committee) (hereafter referred to as HSI) is the most substantive. It includes representatives of all MITI bureaus and, as such, reviews all proposed policies or policy changes before these can be adopted by MITI. Thus, HSI provides officials an opportunity to be informed on a range of matters, including those outside their current responsibilities. The intensive HSI discussions usually generate policies that are free of misunderstandings and errors attributable to parochialism. They also promote organizational identification through the development of a common set of values and a sense of fraternity.

While the formal committees are the major institutionalized decision-making bodies, the frequent informal, ad hoc policy meetings may be of more significance because, through such arrangements, career officials of all organizational levels can interact. They include intra- and interdivisional as well as intra- and interbureau meetings that are attended by junior officials as well as by the administrative vice-ministers. To be effective, MITI needs challenging and innovative ideas and constant policy adjustments; accordingly, even its most inexperienced young career officials are encouraged to participate in informal policy discussions.

MITI maintains 33 *Shingikai* (councils) staffed by experts and including almost all the industrial sectors and subsectors under its jurisdiction. The best known is *Sangyo Kozo Shingikai* (the Council of Industrial Structure), which develops long-term industrial-structure policies. As institutionalized occasions for the exchange of information and views on MITI policies by business, academic, and other interest groups, the *Shingikai* perform a special role.

A key MITI policy tool, the so-called "administrative guidance," or *Gyoosei Shidoo*, is particularly well developed and effective for the following reasons: (1) As MITI deals with diversified and rapidly changing industries, its administrative guidance is more flexible, timely, and effective than legislation that cannot be quickly completed or changed. (2) As the Japanese economy was heavily regulated before, during, and after World War II, MITI has many instruments with which to guide besides laws and ordinances. This makes its "carrot-and-stick" approach— which during the post-World War II years included licensing, allocation of quotas, and control over foreign exchange—very effective. (3) As Japanese industries have always suffered from excessive competition, moderation and coordination by a reliable and authoritative third party has been necessary to promote growth and profit potential. (4) MITI's historical role as a caretaker, coordinator, and leader has helped establish the close government-business relations that are reinforced by MITI's formal network of *Shingikai* (councils), informal contacts, and exchange of personnel.[6] Finally, (5) MITI recruits and trains competent and reliable personnel. This has facilitated the effectiveness—as well as the acceptance by industry—of its guidance, coordination, and arbitration.

The Ministry of Foreign Affairs

The responsibilities of Ministry of Foreign Affairs (hereafter referred to as MOFA) include: (1) planning and implementation of foreign policy; (2) protection and promotion of commercial and navigational interests; (3) the formulation of treaties and other international commitments; (4) participation in international organizations, conferences, and the promotion of international cooperation; and (5) the general coordination of international relations.

Since Japan was isolated under the Shogun regime, diplomatic activities began only with the Meiji restoration in 1868. Facing the threat of imperialist aggression by the Western powers and Russia—and realizing that diplomacy without industrial and military strength could not be effective—the national goal of "a rich country and strong military" (*Fukoku Kyohei*) was adopted to help Japan emulate the West. Thus, while Japan acted imperialistically toward its Asian neighbors, it resorted to diplomatic means to become a member of the group of industrialized nations.

In the post-World War II period, constitutional limitations on military forces made it necessary to put more emphasis on economic than on politico-military relations. Thus, the historically imperialistic Asian diplomacy of Japan was replaced by a low-keyed economic approach centering on trade, capital investment, and economic assistance.

While Japanese postwar diplomacy placed high priority on economic ties with all countries, relations with the United States were by far the most important, because, in accordance with the U.S.–Japan Security Treaty, the country's security was—and still is—guaranteed by the United States' military might.

As shown in Figure 3-3, MOFA has both regional and functional bureaus. In this respect, MOFA is not so different from the U.S. Department of State, although the latter is more of a matrix-type organization than MOFA, which has a relatively rigid overall structure. Fortunately, the informal associations typically formed in Japanese bureaucracies—particularly among career officials—surmount to some extent the dysfunctions inherent in such rigidity.

The major responsibility for economic relations with the United States rests with the Second North American Division in the North American Affairs Bureau. In general, due to the significance of U.S.-

Figure 3-3. Ministry of Foreign Affairs

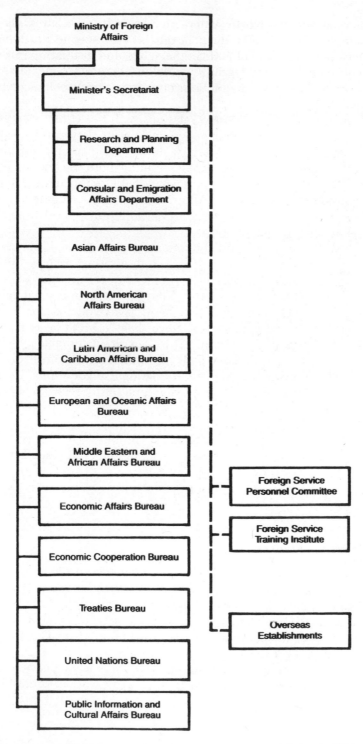

Source: Japan, Administrative Management Agency, Prime Minister's Office, *Organization of the Government of Japan*, (Tokyo: Abe Printing Co., Ltd., 1980), p. 14.

Japanese relations, the North American Affairs Bureau is regarded as the most important unit of MOFA. The duties of the Second North American Division consists of collecting, analyzing, and evaluating information specifically concerning U.S. trade and economic matters. The division also makes recommendations concerning trade policies toward the United States.

However, while Japan's trade relations with the United States are handled by a regional division in a regional bureau, they are also subject to adjustments by the Economic Affairs Bureau. For example, during the multilateral negotiations of the "Tokyo Round," both the Second North American Division and the First International Organizations Division were required by the Economic Affairs Bureau to coordinate and integrate their efforts since the multilateral negotiations were an aggregation of many bilateral negotiations.

All of MITI's trade responsibilities are more or less duplicated by MOFA. The distinction between the two ministries' responsibilities, however, is clear. MITI is in charge of trade policy formulation which, in turn, not only affects but is also affected by domestic industrial policies and conditions. MOFA, on the other hand, is responsible for international negotiations and agreements. Nevertheless, MITI takes the position that the collection of information through direct contacts with trade partners is essential for effective policy formulation; therefore, the ministry should be allowed to engage in international negotiations. To retain control over international relations, MOFA naturally seeks to bar MITI from such direct contacts. Thus, the two ministries are frequently involved in jurisdictional conflicts.

One important limitation of MOFA's jurisdiction is its lack of control over any industrial or economic sector and, therefore, its inability to influence industrial or economic policies. Such policies are developed and carried out by MITI and/or the other sectoral ministries, such as MOAFF.

The Ministry of Finance

The Ministry of Finance (MOF) was established in 1869, the second year of the Meiji restoration. In addition to financial matters, the ministry's original functions included the procurement of civil engineering and other construction services and the promotion of the textile industry, functions that today are under the jurisdiction of the Construction Ministry and MITI respectively.[7]

The law governing the present day MOF was legislated under the influence of U.S. occupation forces in 1949. However, as domestic and international politico-economic environments changed, more than 100 major and minor amendments had been added to the law by the late 1970s. The ministry's major mission, in any event, remained unchanged.

MOF is mainly involved with the development and management of fiscal and monetary policies, including budgeting, taxation (inclusive of tariffs), and the management and control of cash flows and state properties. Furthermore, MOF supervises financial institutions and manages and analyzes international financial and economic matters. Accordingly, MOF is by and large equivalent to the U.S. Treasury Department, the Office of Management and Budget (OMB), and the Securities and Exchange Commission combined, but because of its statutory and actual budgeting authority, it is probably even more powerful than such an aggregation would be in the United States.

MOF's budgeting authority represents the ultimate step in the policy formulation process. While the U.S. OMB's budget proposal is probably revised by Congress, MOF's assessment of budget requests is usually not changed by the Diet because the majority party forms the cabinet which, in turn, controls the bureaucracy. In other words, while the U.S. OMB externalizes the budget process, MOF internalizes it, in that it incorporates requests from the majority party prior to their receiving legislative approval. Herein lies the significance of MOF's budgeting authority, and, accordingly, its power.

MOF's acceptance of policy proposals is an assurance that such proposals will be adopted for the next fiscal year. Conversely, a rejection by MOF signifies that the proposals will be jettisoned, despite the time and energy spent on them by the requesting ministries. Therefore, because no distinction is made between budget authorization and appropriation, MOF's decisions de facto determine policies for the following year. It must, however, be pointed out that over the years the Liberal Democratic Party, through channels institutionalized between itself and MOF, has considerably increased its influence over the budgeting process.

The organization of MOF is shown in Figure 3-4. In contrast to MITI and MOFA, MOF does not have a matrix-type structure. It is often described as having many bureaus and no organizational identity because the responsibilities of individual bureaus are diversified in either a complementary or conflicting manner. The budget and tax bureaus, for example, may be complementary, but they are also quite different from the banking and securities bureaus.

MOF's most internationally oriented divisions are the Customs and Tariff Bureau, the International Finance Bureau, and the Office of *Zaimukan* (Vice-Finance Minister for International Affairs). The Customs and Tariff Bureau is in charge of the analysis and formulation of

Figure 3-4. Ministry of France*

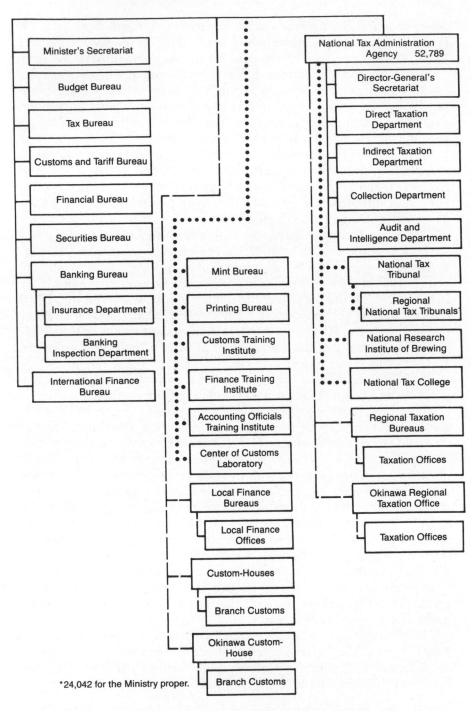

Minister's Secretariat

Budget Bureau

Tax Bureau

Customs and Tariff Bureau

Financial Bureau

Securities Bureau

Banking Bureau

Insurance Department

Banking Inspection Department

International Finance Bureau

Mint Bureau

Printing Bureau

Customs Training Institute

Finance Training Institute

Accounting Officials Training Institute

Center of Customs Laboratory

Local Finance Bureaus

Local Finance Offices

Custom-Houses

Branch Customs

Okinawa Custom-House

Branch Customs

National Tax Administration Agency   52,789

Director-General's Secretariat

Direct Taxation Department

Indirect Taxation Department

Collection Department

Audit and Intelligence Department

National Tax Tribunal

Regional National Tax Tribunals

National Research Institute of Brewing

National Tax College

Regional Taxation Bureaus

Taxation Offices

Okinawa Regional Taxation Office

Taxation Offices

*24,042 for the Ministry proper.

Source: Japan, Administrative Management Agency, Prime Minister's Office, *Organization of the Government of Japan*, (Tokyo: Abe Printing Co., Ltd., 1980), p. 15.

trade policies, while the International Finance Bureau is chiefly concerned with international monetary matters, capital transactions, and economic assistance programs. The Office of the *Zaimukan* assists the Vice-Finance Minister for International Affairs.

The Minister of Finance is MOF's highest-ranking official, but it is the administrative vice-ministers who manage the day-to-day operations in close consultation with the minister. MOF has two administrative vice-ministers, the *Jimu-jikan* (Vice-Minister) and the *Zaimukan* (also Vice-Minister). The *Jimu-jikan* is in charge of all areas under MOF's jurisdiction—including international affairs—whereas the *Zaimukan* manages the operational aspects of international affairs, the coordination of the bureaus, and the representation of MOF in international negotiations or conferences, particularly if and when MOF plays a leading role.

As mentioned before, the major responsibility for trade policy is held by the director-general of the Customs and Tariff Bureau, who is assisted by two deputies. The bureau's entities devoted to trade policy and negotiations are the First and Second International Affairs Divisions. The First International Division is in charge of research, planning, and policy formulation concerning multilateral tariff agreements. The Second International Affairs Division is in charge of managing similar trade and tariff matters but on a bilateral basis. Since trade negotiations often involve bilateral discussions in a multilateral frame, cooperation between the two divisions is always critical.

Another important organizational unit is the Export Affairs Division, which produces the official statistics on exports and imports by country and commodity on a customs-clearance basis. Finally, the activities of all of these units are integrated by the *Soomu-ka*, or Coordination Division, which not only coordinates the trade and tariff policies, but also administers all customs rules.

In the Japanese bureaucracy, the coordinating division is uniquely powerful, because it performs a key role in the consensual decision-making process. The director of the MOF Coordination Division is senior to all other divisional directors and has the power to decide who is recruited, assigned, released, promoted, or demoted—although he does so in close consultation with the bureau chiefs and their deputies.

MOF's decision-making process is typical of the Japanese consensual, participatory decision-making system. Although the ministry is known as a conservative and passive organization where rigid seniority prevails, this does not bar extensive participation by even very junior career officials on informal occasions. In formal settings, however, their involvement is either limited or nonexistent.

The Ministry of Agriculture, Forestry and Fisheries

The Ministry of Agriculture, Forestry and Fisheries (MOAFF)[8] is responsible for promoting Japanese agriculture and insuring the nation's food self-sufficiency in the production of food.

Figure 3-5 illustrates the organization of MOAFF. The Secretariat of the Ministry is charged with policy formulation, but there are several additional bureaus of importance, as shown in Figure 3-5. Of these, the Economic Affairs Bureau is in charge of agricultural imports and international negotiations, such as the "Tokyo Round" in the 1970s. This bureau also supervises the Central Bank for Agricultural Cooperatives. Other bureaus worth noting here are the Animal Industry Bureau, which handles the distribution of quotas for beef imports, and the Agricultural Production Bureau, which handles orange-import quotas.

As can be expected, the MOAFF, through its contacts with farm cooperatives, is closely tied to farm interests. Traditionally, it has always been more concerned with protecting and improving the farmer's lot than with external affairs or the nation's overall trade balance.

As is typical with most Japanese ministries, the MOAFF is rather independent of other government institutions and jealously guards its independence. While the MOAFF consults with agencies such as the MOF and MITI, it is, in fact, rather well insulated from other agencies. Indeed, it has a long history of doing as it pleases.

MITI, MOFA, MOAFF, and MOF Committees in the Lower and Upper Houses

The MITI, MOFA, MOAFF, and MOF Committees in both houses play an important but uniquely Japanese role in the formulation of trade policy.

According to the postwar Japanese constitution adopted under the auspices of the U.S. occupation forces, the Diet has supreme power over the bureaucracy of the executive branch. However, because Japan has a parliamentary form of government, the Diet functions differently from the U.S. Congress. The head of the majority party is also in charge of the policy formulation of the executive branches. The Diet's legislative process is, therefore, quite predictable, because bills introduced by the executive branch usually pass without any major encumbrances. The most opposition parties can do is to embarrass the government through delaying tactics. Accordingly, the critical stages of the legislative process are not the committee reviews, but rather the discussions and agreements held in advance between the executive branch and the majority party's ranking politicians in charge of policy formulation and committee operations. Once these individuals are satisfied, the accep-

Figure 3-5. Ministry of Agriculture, Forestry and Fisheries

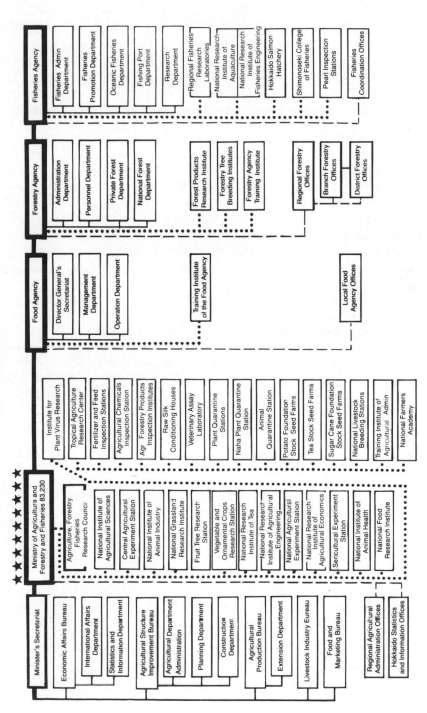

Source: Japan, Administrative Management Agency, Prime Minister's Office, Organization of the Government of Japan, (Tokyo: Abe Printing Co., Ltd., 1980), pp. 18–19.

tance of a bill or policy is virtually guaranteed because party discipline makes voting defections very rare.

As can be expected, a great deal of energy and time is spent on the discussions held prior to committee review. For a bill to pass or for a policy to be accepted, the groundwork must be laid in the majority party's (LDP) Policy Deliberation Commission. If agreeable, the commission passes the bill on to the executive council. If this council also agrees, what follows is an almost routine approval by the appropriate Diet committees and, finally, by the entire parliament.

In the "Tokyo Round" negotiations, the MOFA and MOF committees played an important role. The MOFA committees were involved with the ratification of the Multinational Trade Negotiations (MTN) agreement, while the MOF committees dealt with the domestic implications of the agreement. The MITI committees played a secondary role, because MITI lacked juridictional authority over the resulting laws, while the MOAFF committees dealt only with the citrus- and beef-import quota issues.

The Diet committees are not as well supported as their congressional counterparts. Members of parliament have only two officially assigned aides, and there are no independent committee staffs as in the United States. Furthermore, the General Accounting Office only audits government agencies and does not engage in independent research in response to Diet requests. The National Library of the Diet, with a staff of about 200, is in theory the counterpart of the Library of Congress. In practice, however, it is not nearly so well equipped, nor so fully staffed, nor so extensively used by Diet members.[9]

Regulations and Procedures

Japan does not have any regulatory trade disincentives. Its antitrust policy, for example, is quite anemic compared with that of the United States, because the government of Japan places a high priority on the upgrading of industrial structures and on the enhancement of productivity. Large-scale mergers are promoted, and the cartelization of economically weak industries is normally permitted.

On the other hand, for some time Japan imposed complicated import regulations and procedures. The situation changed, however, when the restrictive Foreign Investment and Foreign Exchange Law of 1950 was repealed and a new, more liberal Foreign Exchange and Foreign Trade Control Law went into effect December 1, 1980.

During 1978–1979, the import regulations and procedures consisted mostly of product standards, inspections, and approval methods that were developed for internal health, safety, and environmental reasons.

However, these regulations emerged over time and reflected Japan's geographical and cultural distance from the Western world.

Despite recent procedural simplifications, some problems cited by foreign businesses and governments remain to be solved. Yet, Japanese import regulations and procedures, like those in other countries, are the result of historical forces. They have become a tradition and are supported by vested domestic interests that do not want them changed.

The Integration of Activities in the Formulation of Trade Policy

Japanese interinstitutional relations and coordination are notably different from those in the United States. There is no established inter-ministerial coordinating committee; therefore, coordination among ministries is more on an ad hoc basis. It is also strongly affected by Japan's strong bureaucratic sectionalism attributable to the lifetime employment system.

There is very little exchange of personnel between MITI, MOFA, and MOF. Each ministry is a far more closed organization than its U.S. counterpart; therefore, the sharing of information among the ministries is also limited. The policy of rotating career officials as widely as possible within but not outside a given ministry prevents the formation of an informal interministerial trade fraternity.

As a consequence, Japanese interinstitutional relations tend to be competitive—even conflictive—rather than cooperative. Due to the increasing importance of international trade relations during 1978–1979, Prime Ministers Fukuda and Ohira appointed Ambassadors Ushiba and Yasukawa respectively to the position of Minister for External Economic Affairs. While the newly created position was the equivalent of the position of Robert Strauss in the U.S. government, the supporting staff seconded to it from MOFA, MITI, MOF, and other ministries were assigned only on a temporary basis. Thus, such staff continued to represent largely their own ministries, making it very difficult for the incumbents to coordinate trade policies or to prevent jurisdictional conflicts.

The best known conflicts, those between MOFA and MITI, were frequently reported in the Japanese—and even in the U.S.—press. U.S. officials, naturally well aware of such infighting, have observed that Japan's bargaining power is sometimes reduced by the resulting premature release of information. Of course, at times, the release of uncoordinated and conflicting information may strengthen negotiating positions.

The aggregate loss due to bureaucratic sectionalism, however, outweighs any possible gains. The MITI–MOFA conflict over international relations illustrates this point well. MITI officials believe that trade policy should be consistent with domestic industrial policy, which they manage in cooperation with the business sector; therefore, MITI—and not MOFA—should have the mandate to formulate international trade policies.

In contrast, MOFA officials stress that, by law, only they can represent the nation internationally and that only they possess the diplomatic skills needed to reconcile economic with political considerations. From MOFA's point of view, MITI's arguments are dangerous because if accepted they could severely limit MOFA's role in international economic relations, thus leaving it with mostly protocol functions and little substantive authority.

Struggles between MOFA and MITI waste administrative resources and promote bureaucratic sectionalism. It is reported, for example, that MITI officials assigned to the United States frequently call or cable MITI headquarters in Tokyo from their Washington residences or offices to transmit sensitive and critical information without passing it through the embassy channels supervised by MOFA. They do this in spite of their status, which requires that they report only through the embassy.

To strengthen its international role, MITI always sought more embassy positions; however, MOFA—in control of such assignments—for a long time did not accede to MITI's demands.[10] MITI, nonetheless, quickly found a way to circumvent MOFA's authority: it seconded its officials to organizations under its jurisdiction—such as the Japan External Trade Organization (JETRO)—and then had the officials assigned to the United States.

Not surprisingly, interministerial conflicts are sometimes carried to political levels, that is, to cabinet members or to parliamentary vice-ministers. In such cases, high-level officials from the various ministries may clash quite openly. According to one of MITI's parliamentary vice-ministers, the high-level conflicts between MITI and MOFA are usually dysfunctional and sometimes even "childish." The same vice-minister has recently, in cooperation with his counterpart at MOFA, developed a policy according to which MITI and MOFA officials must meet regularly to discuss trade issues.

The conflicts between MITI and MOFA are conspicuous and persistent, and they can have serious negative consequences. Yet, the role of MOF in trade policy formulation is also frequently questioned. The officials of other ministries believe that they can do little without MOF's consent, because MOF has either sole or joint jurisdiction over tariff policy, the Export-Import Bank, the Overseas Economic Cooperation Fund, contributions to international organizations, and other similar matters. Any policy with budgetary implications also needs MOF's approval during the budget assessment process. Thus, although many observers see MOF as too domestically oriented—and, therefore, insensitive to international matters—its power and influence over trade policies is substantial.

MOF officials, particularly those in the so-called "international group" (the International Finance Bureau, the Customs and Tariff Bureau, and the Office of the Vice-Finance Minister for International Affairs), believe that they have no less international sensitivity, expertise, and experience than their counterparts in the other ministries.

ADMINISTRATIVE CHARACTERISTICS

The administrative characteristics refer to the processes and practices through which trade policy is formulated. More specifically, they include the location of power, the nature of leadership, and decision-making styles.

The Location of Power and the Nature of Leadership

There is a clear distinction in the Japanese bureaucracy between career, quasi-career, and noncareer officials. To be a career official requires a university degree, a successful upper-civil-service examination, and recruitment by a cabinet-level ministry. Quasi-career officials usually meet the first two of these requirements but are typically recruited by a lower-level agency supervised by a ministry.

Almost without exception, policy formulating officials are career officials. In a cabinet-level ministry, noncareer officials are unlikely to go beyond the divisional deputy-director level, but this does not mean that all policy formulating officials are above this level. On the contrary, most policy papers are generated at the deputy-director level, and young career officials are often invited to informal policy formulating meetings held on different occasions.[11] For example, a division chief (Kachoo) often invites lower-level career officials to talk about policy matters—most probably after 5:00 P.M. when the daily duties are completed and noncareer officials and secretaries have left for the day. Since Japanese divisional directors normally do not have their own private offices (although their desks are larger than those of subordinates and their chairs have white cotton covers), those who are invited to participate in the discussions are likely to flock together around the director's desk. If such an informal exchange is sponsored by a high-ranking official, the only difference is the availability of a private office and the presence of additional high-level participants.

Thus, in Japan it is the career officials who hold the power, and from this it follows that Japanese career officials have more functional similarities with U.S. political appointees than with U.S. career officials. This similarity is unmistakable at high levels; however, even at middle or lower levels, Japanese career officials are more similar to U.S. political appointees, who, by and large, occupy high-ranking positions.[12]

More often than not, Japanese career officials stay in the government for shorter periods of time than do U.S. career officials, due to the rigid seniority system under which they may be forced out as their entry group moves up the pyramidic government hierarchy.

In principle, the average 30-year-service span of Japanese career officials should promote institutional memory, but in reality this is not necessarily true. As mentioned earlier, during their rotational periods, career officials are normally assigned to a position for only one to three years. Senior officials in particular may stay only for a year; their positions are then handed over to the junior career officials moving up the ladder. Furthermore, since Japanese career officials are normally encouraged to be generalists, even a bureau chief who is responsible for policy formulation and implementation is not necessarily a specialist in any field although he may be a very able general public administrator. Thus, Japanese institutional memory may be limited and fragile, but close informal relations among career officials and strong organizational identification promote its survival.

In other words, the Japanese bureaucracy maintains policy consistency as a result of the power and influence of its career officials. A minister, of course, is the highest level authority, but his actual power is often tempered by the bureaucracy, whose members possess the necessary information, skill, seniority, and the loyalty of subordinates. Basic policies are formulated by the career officials, while ministers are usually satisfied with the achievement of some personal project benefiting domestic constituents or political supporters. Japanese ministers are often willing to be mere figureheads who accept without hesitation the recommendations of career officials.

The Japanese style of leadership is democratic and open. Because the lifetime employment system guarantees jobs and promotion based on seniority, participation is encouraged. In the bureaucracy, even the most junior career officials have an opportunity to express their views to top officials on informal occasions, and, typically, their ideas are at least reviewed and discussed as alternatives.

Such extensive participation requires leaders who are skillful in delegating and coordinating rather than commanding. Thus, Japanese leaders are not forceful and domineering, as they must be sensitive to the feelings of others. Leadership is expressed through personal warmth and the admiration and confidence it inspires rather than through the forcefulness of views, the vigor of decisions, or the degree of expertise.

The attitude displayed by leaders toward subordinates is expressed by the term *onjo-shugi*, or "parental concern," which assumes an appreciation of the subordinates whose opinions and wishes are carefully considered. In general, the more "fatherly" the leader is, the more effective he is likely to be, and the more well-qualified followers he can attract.

Such a style of leadership, however, places a special burden on the top officials of Japanese organizations. That is, they are fully responsible for all that transpires under their leadership. In the event of major problems, therefore, top leaders may be expected to resign, even though from a U.S. point of view they should not be held responsible for what has happened.

Thus, Japanese leadership is not so given to commanding as is its U.S. counterpart; however, it does require complete responsibility for organizational performance, as well as an ability to coordinate and to prevent conflicts from getting out of hand. Former Secretary of State Henry Kissinger put it this way:

> The West developed a system of government based on a concept of authority: the right to issue orders that are accepted because they reflect legal or constitutional norms. Japan relies on consensus. A leader's eminence does not imply a right to impose his will on his peers, but the opportunity to elicit their agreement—or at least give the appearance of doing so. High office in Japan does not entitle the holder to issue orders; it gives the privilege of taking the lead in persuasion.[13]

Such leadership is effective in Japan, because organizational identification is strong, membership is homogenous, rules and practices are well established, organization boundaries are clearly drawn, and predictability prevails.

Decision-Making Style

Throughout history, Japanese organizations were characterized by *Kafuchoo Sei* ("family head management system") in which the male head of the family, firm, or ministry acted like a father who possessed absolute power and responsibility. Through centuries of feudalism, this traditional system prevailed until well after World War II.

The Meiji constitution accommodated the *Kafuchoo Sei* system and therefore, as Ruth Benedict noted, Japanese organizations became pervasively hierarchical.[14] In analyzing the Japanese decision-making style, it is, nonetheless, important to understand that the rigid hierarchy was always juxtaposed with at least two other characteristics: an egalitarianism based on ethnic homogeneity and closed organizational boundaries. Throughout Japan's feudal history, ethnic homogeneity helped egalitarianism survive under even the most rigid social classification systems. After the Meiji government abolished the social caste system, mixing and reshuffling occurred at almost all social levels, although uneven access to higher education made it much more difficult for certain individuals to enter the government as career officials.

The closed organizational boundaries achieved primarily through the lifetime employment system promoted egalitarianism, fraternity, and a consensual atmosphere. Therefore, it was natural that a family-type atmosphere could not only coexist with rigid hierarchy, but sometimes even transcend the latter without damaging the formal rules and procedures.

Japan's present-day bureaucracy is still marked by such organizational characteristics. As a consequence, high-level Japanese government officials today are amenable to listening to junior career—or, on occasion, even noncareer—officials. Japanese policy formulators are constantly encouraged to *Genba no Koe Wo Kiku* (to listen to the opinions of the "actual workers" before making major decisions).

It is, however, important to understand that such participation takes place only through the informal organizations so characteristic of the Japanese career bureaucracy. In a formal setting, Japanese officials behave very autocratically and do not elicit or welcome suggestions or differing views from junior or even lower-ranking senior officials. Open exchanges and debates are discouraged, and silence is viewed as a positive contribution to the decision-making process. Comments are made freely only by the top decision maker.

The informal arrangement through which extensive participation takes place is known as *Nemawashi*, or "root binding."[15] During *Nemawashi*, egalitarianism and fraternity prevail, and differences are explored and settled so that the formal stages in the decision-making process are not interrupted.

Since the beginning of the Meiji era, the *Ringi* process has been widely used in Japan as a means of decision-making. The word *Ringi* means literally "subordinates asking opinions or permission from superiors with considerable awe." Kiyoaki Tsuji, formerly a professor at the University of Tokyo, defines *Ringi* as a decision-making process in public administration in which lower-level officials draft a paper and then send it to higher-level officials for their approval, until the paper finally reaches the ultimately responsible official.[16]

According to Professor Tsuji, the implications of this definition are threefold: (1) Lower-level officials who do not have authority to make the decision in question, and who are not in a position of leadership, draft the paper. (2) The paper is circulated and, in principle, is checked by the officials of the concerned divisions and bureaus, but is not collectively discussed. (3) Although only the head of the organization (e.g., the minister) has the statutory authority to approve the paper, the entire circulation process is regarded as the *Ringi* system.

The system has several advantages and disadvantages. The advantages include: large-scale participation, an opportunity to veto, the development of a comprehensive record of comments, and the promotion of coordinatorial leadership.[17] The disadvantages are inefficiency caused by potential delays, obscured responsibility, and lack of leadership.

The advantages, except for the promotion of coordinatorial leadership, are self-evident. The *Ringi* system emphasizes coordinatorial leadership by making it possible for officials with good interpersonal relations—but without a technical specialty—to approve "blindly" a highly technical decision with their *Mekura-ban*.[18] The disadvantages of the process, however, are more complex and require more detailed discussion because they are the result of special Japanese behavioral characteristics and practices.

Under the best of circumstances, the circulation of the *Ringi* paper involves a considerable amount of time, and—because approval is given individually—an official's absence or disapproval may cause considerable delay. This is an important point because Japanese officials are eager to avoid face-to-face confrontations and, consequently, are not wont to oppose anything openly. Thus, if a mid-level official wishes to withhold his approval, he merely keeps the *Ringi* paper for a while, or he stamps his seal upside down. Since the paper passes by many officials, it is highly vulnerable to such delaying tactics.

The second disadvantage of the *Ringi* system is obscured responsibility. The Japanese bureaucracy is of German heritage; thus, the ultimate responsibility rests with the minister. Accordingly, all other officials—from the vice-minister to the lowest-ranking—are in a sense merely assistants whose review of the *Ringi* paper is a necessary but not sufficient condition of the final decision.

It is particularly difficult for outsiders to find out with whom the authority and responsibility for a *Ringi* decision rests, because the Japanese bureaucracy does not maintain detailed job descriptions. Only general and somewhat abstract descriptions of positions can be found in the laws, by-laws, and regulations.

The third disadvantage, the lack of leadership, is inherent in the *Ringi* system because the decision process is begun by lower-level officials. Higher-level officials not only have to wait for propositions to come to them, but also have to move their own ideas through the system for their own approval. Those who attempt to sidestep this process usually fail, as their unwillingness to cooperate causes ill feelings and distrust among their colleagues.

These procedural characteristics suggest that the *Ringi* decision-making process is "slow-quick" as compared with the "quick-slow" U.S. decision-making process discussed previously.[19] The Japanese take time to make decisions, or—more correctly—they take time to determine why and when decisions should be made.

The *Ringi* system also performs a special administrative function. As pointed out earlier, the Japanese bureaucracy sharply differentiates between career and noncareer officials. The former monopolize all important organizational decision-making positions and, as such, represent a powerful elite. In the Ministry of Finance, for example, career officials account for 400 out of approximately 60,000 employees. These are frequently rotated and promoted and enjoy very high status. Noncareer officials, on the other hand, remain in their narrowly defined positions much longer, obtain fewer promotions, and have lower status. For routine decision-making purposes, the *Ringi* system effectively connects these two sharply distinct groups of officials.

Thus, the *Ringi* system combines Japan's traditional organizational processes with the modern organizational and technological methods taken from the West. It must, however, be pointed out that the advantages notwithstanding, *Ringi* has helped promote the strong bureaucratic sectionalism that is so prevalent in Japan. The participatory decision-making process, together with the paternalistic atmosphere of the "closed" organization, enable career officials at various levels in a given ministry to share information and ideas. Out of such knowledge come sectional interests, which play an important role in the interministerial conflicts over jurisdiction and responsibility. Consequently, the Japanese, who show remarkable skill in reaching a consensus within their own organization, often fail to cooperate in interorganizational situations.

Finally, it is important to understand that *Ringi* is used throughout the Japanese bureaucracy only for routine decisions. As a consequence of the increase in the number of complex, urgent, and mutable decisions, the Japanese bureaucracy has come to rely increasingly on a different type of decision-making process. For important and urgent decisions, a meeting is convened by the career official most responsible for the problem. This person can be a divisional director, a director general of a bureau, the administrative vice-minister, or even the minister. All higher-level career officials who will be affected by the decision are invited to the meeting. The resulting discussion quickly comes to the point and becomes open and dynamic. The decision is made on a consensual basis, although inevitably the presiding senior official—either directly or indirectly—exerts a strong influence. This official does not, however, express his own views, until the discussion begins to foreshadow a decision. At that point, a mid-level official—usually a divisional deputy-director—elaborates and refines the consensus into an operational document. Following this, a more ritualistic meeting is held to formalize the decision.

Thus, the type of decision-making process described above is both collective and expeditious—but top-down rather than bottom-up. The *Ringi* paper serves chiefly as a record and as a source of information for those officials who were not invited to the meeting, but who are nevertheless affected by the decision reached. The strong organizational identification prevailing in Japanese ministries facilitates the consensual approval of the decision reached even under such conditions.

CONCLUDING REMARKS

In the Japanese parliamentary system, power resides in the bureaucracy, which is supervised by the executive branch. The bureaucracy has the information and the skills necessary to formulate policies consistently. The power of the Diet is much more limited than that of the U.S. Congress, although the majority-party members of the Diet coordinate their activities with the executive branch. Therefore, the views of the legislature on any policy issue do not differ very much from those of the executive branch. The prime minister, elected by the majority party, can count on his party members to unite behind him in the Diet.

The resultant policy formulation process is more consistent than that of the United States, but it is also less flexible. Except for cabinet ministers and parliamentary vice-ministers, all other top policy formulators are career officals who remain in their positions for about 30 years, and whose views on policy and whose personal attitudes are predictable. A change in prime minister rarely entails a change of policy, since the top bureaucrats continue to stay, and since a cabinet shakeup signifies only the replacement of the senior leadership group of the majority party.

Of the key Japanese trade policy formulating entities, MITI plays the most important role, although MOFA through its negotiation authority and MOF through its budgetary control may exert strong influence. MOAFF's trade policy formulating role is limited to agricultural matters; however, since U.S. agricultural exports to Japan occupy a major position in the recurring trade frictions between the two countries, its influence can be important.

Relations between the ministries are very often competitive and conflictive. The more-than-a-decade-old feud between MITI and MOFA is a good case in point. Such jurisdictional conflicts emanating from bureaucratic sectionalism can slow the trade policy formulation process substantially. Furthermore, although the Diet committees are subject to control by the majority party's leadership, the precommittee political negotiations may also take up a great deal of time. Finally, Japan does not have a central coordinating entity to oversee the formulation of trade policy; therefore, coordination must take place through interministerial negotiations, the pace of which is determined by the slowest ministry involved. On the other hand, in contrast to the United States, Japan does not have any regulatory trade disincentives.

Japanese trade policy formulation is also strongly influenced by administrative characteristics such as the location of power, leadership styles, and decision-making processes.

Particularly important in this respect is the bottom-up, "slow-quick" participatory style of decision-making because it can result in considerable delays irritating the nation's major trading partners, in particular, the United States.

NOTES

1. "There is strong criticism of the bureaucracy's power over the legislative process. The Diet members themselves often complain that they do not have enough legislative staff to compete with the government agencies in drafting legislation." Japan Economic Institute, "Japan's National Diet," *JEI Report No. 24*, 26 June, 1981 (Washington, D.C.: Japan Economic Institute, 1981), p. 3.

2. *See* Taketsugu Tsurutani, *Political Change in Japan* (New York: David McKay, 1977), pp. 36–37.

3. "The characteristics of the Japanese parliamentary system derive from the modernization that began in the late nineteenth century, when all power was vested in the imperial monarch. When the Meiji Constitution was proclaimed in 1889, it defined the Imperial Parliament as a consulting body to the Emperor. Only after 1945 did the Diet acquire the legislative functions it has today. However, the power of the bureaucracy, emphasized since the Meiji Period, has not diminished and most legislation continues to be drafted, introduced and negotiated by the bureaucracy." Japan Economic Institute, "Japan's National Diet," p. 1.

4. Robert W. Ward states that "the conception of a bureaucrat as a 'public servant' was almost totally absent from both Japanese political theory and practice until it was inserted in Article 15 of the new Constitution by Americans in 1946. Before 1946, a Japanese bureaucrat was officially viewed as a chosen servant of the emperor, a politically and socially superior being who derived status and privileges from his imperial connection. The old

Tokugawa adage, *kanson mimpi* ('officials honored, the people despised') well describes the prewar bureaucrat's attitude toward the public." Robert E. Ward, *Japan's Political System*, 2d ed. (Englewood Cliffs, N.J.: Prentice Hall, 1978), p. 163.

5. "In Japan the political unit that counts is the faction, . . . all conditioning their support of the premier on the number of Cabinet and top party posts they receive. . . . Japanese Cabinets have been formed or reshuffled 27 times in the last 20 years, or an average of once every nine months." Ken Ishii, "Japan Shuffles Along to the Familiar Tune," *The International Herald Tribune*, 7 December, 1981, p. 6.

6. The exchange of personnel between MITI and private enterprises is not necessarily a one-way process, like *Amakudari* (retirement of officials to industry), despite the lack of lateral entry. MITI accepts future business executives in temporary postions at the entry, section-chief, and deputy-director levels. Such exchanges are rewarded by immediate and long-term personal contacts which contribute to the promotion of government-business relations.

7. It is interesting to note that Kazuo Yasuhara attributes the current belief that MOF officials are the "elite of the elites" to the fact that the ministry's original jurisdiction included financial as well as industrial policy. Kazuo Yasuhara, *Ohkura Sho* (Gyossei Kikoo) [The Ministry of Finance: Administrative Series No. 3], (Tokyo: Kyooikusha, 1976), p. 25.

8. *See* U.S. Congress, Senate, Committee on Finance, *MTN Studies 2: Tokyo-Geneva Round: Its Relation to U.S. Agriculture* (Washington, D.C.: Government Printing Office, 1979), pp. 18–21.

9. Japan Economic Institute, "Japan's National Diet," p. 2.

10. One additional position in the Washington embassy was finally appropriated to MITI in the FY 1982 budget on the condition that MITI not interfere with MOFA's jurisdiction.

11. This is true in the MOF, MITI, and other ministries, but not necessarily in MOFA. A high MOFA official, who was once seconded to the MOF as a divisional director, told that it was surprising to him that a typical director at MOF rarely needs to write any paper himself, because his deputies write all papers, whereas in the MOFA, a bureau chief or a director general (*Kyokuchoo*), or an ambassador abroad, has to write his own papers. This is so because the information he gets from high-level foreign officials is usually not shared with subordinates, who are not allowed to be present at many of the meetings for protocol reasons.

12. Of course, career officials reach high positions in some U.S. departments—notably the State Department—as well. In contrast, in the Japanese ministries recent developments indicate an erosion of the power of political appointees, whereas the power of career officials remains intact.

13. Henry Kissinger, *Years of Upheaval* (Boston: Little, Brown, 1982), p. 735.

14. Benedict observed that "Japan's confidence in hierarchy is basic in her whole notion of man's relation to his fellow man and of man's relation to the state. . . ." Ruth Benedict, *The Chrysanthemum and the Sword: Patterns of Japanese Culture* (New York: The New American Library, 1946, reprinted, 1974), p. 43.

15. *Nemawashi* is an informal, private, and usually face-to-face exchange of views. It involves persuasion to obtain understanding, agreement, and support. According to Ezra Vogel:
> The term originally comes from gardening, where it designates the careful untangling and binding of each of the roots of a tree before it is moved. The Japanese bureaucracy . . . are in close touch with all relevant groups to make sure they understand the evolving decisions, that their roots are bound.

See Ezra F. Vogel, *Japan as Number One: Lessons for America* (Cambridge, Mass.: Harvard University Press, 1979), p. 94.

16. Kiyoaki Tsuji, *Shinpan Nippon Kanryoo-Sei no Kenkyuu* (Study of Japanese Bureaucracy), new edition (Tokyo: Tokyo Daigaku Shuppan Kai, 1976), p. 155.

17. M.Y. Yoshino, "Emerging Japanese Multinational Enterprises," in *Modern Japanese Organization and Decision-making*, ed. Ezra F. Vogel (Berkeley: University of California Press, 1975), p. 159.

18. *Mekura* means "blind" and *ban* means "sealing."

19. "Slow-quick" refers to slow decision-making but quick implementation.

4

ADDITIONAL CONSIDERATIONS

In addition to the historically conditioned institutional arrangements, Japanese trade policy formulation is strongly influenced also by other social and cultural traditions, including the behavioral practices of government officials. While the number of factors that could be discussed in this context is almost limitless, the following are the most influential.

THE SELECTION OF POLICY FORMULATING OFFICIALS

The Japanese employment system is based on a lifetime commitment by both the institutions and the individuals. Concerning the historical origins of the system, Peter Drucker observed that:

> I cannot, from the sources accessible to me, find out when payment by seniority coupled with lifetime employment became general, but it was unknown for rank-and-file employees before the 1920s. It may have been fairly common for managerial employees before that date, and apparently it had become fairly common for government employees even before that time. Yet there is no precedent for it in pre-Meiji times.[1]

The Japanese government recruits its career and quasi-career officials from universities and noncareer officials upon graduation from high schools.

Potential career officials must pass an examination given by the Personnel Agency (PA), primarily in law, economics, and public administration. From the 40,000–50,000 applicants, usually about 1,000 succeed, and these are listed by the PA as qualified for career positions if they also pass a personal interview. The interviews are not demanding; thus, most of the candidates who have passed the written examinations are put on a "final" list. Once on this list, they must be recruited by a ministry or agency within a year or retake the examination.

As can be expected, the ministries and agencies compete for the individuals with the highest scores. Those individuals not selected by the ministry of their choice may forego a public career and accept a position in private industry.

The ministries in greatest demand—MOF, MITI, and Interior— usually get the best qualified applicants. MOFA does not recruit from the PA list; rather, its officials must pass the special Upper Diplomatic Civil Service Examination, which emphasizes language skills and international relations.

An important characteristic of the Japanese employment process is that it draws applicants not from graduate but from undergraduate programs. In Japan, graduate students are candidates for academic careers rather than for careers in government or business. Thus, as the applicants eventually selected do not initially possess professional qualifications, personality, integrity, basic intelligence, group orientation, and flexibility are more important at the entry level than are specialized skills.

In other words, the Japanese government recruits for potential, which is realized through lifetime training and employment. Accordingly, the recruitment process plays a vitally important role because it determines the long-range future of the institutions involved.

The recruits selected by the ministries have invariably attended the best universities. The 15,000 students of Tokyo University are acknowledged to be among the best of the 2 million Japanese university students. Of the 20-odd graduates entering a key ministry as career officials each year, perhaps 15 to 19 come from Tokyo University while the others are among the top graduates of other national universities, such as Hitotsubashi and Kyoto, or of prestigious private institutions such as Keio and Waseda.

Distinguished educational backgrounds, together with a careful selection procedure, ensure that Japanese career officials are not only very able but are also surrounded by an aura of respect similar to that enjoyed by the elite bureaucrats of France.

While MITI, like MOF, is one of the most difficult ministries to enter, it tends to recruit a more diversified group of individuals than MOF. Given the fact that the environment in which its officials formulate industrial and trade policies is subject to continuous change, MITI attempts to address such changes. Accordingly, even students with a "B" average and a relatively low-ranking in the Upper Civil Service Examination are eligible for recruitment if they possess some special talent, or if they are perceived as having the potential for becoming creative, dynamic, and balanced officials. MITI is known as an active and aggressive ministry, and it is generally believed in Japan—as well as by U.S. officials who come in contact with Japanese government officials—that its officials are more aggressive, active, and flexible than those from other ministries.

Once recruited, Japanese career officials are not expected to carry out professional activities immediately. Rather, especial attention is paid to the new officials' future potential and psychological ability to act as group members rather than to their current knowledge and special skills. Newly recruited officials are given long and intensive in-house, on-the-job training.

By the time career officials reach their thirties, they will have experienced several different assignments and probably will have been appointed as deputy-directors of one of the bureaus. By this time, they can already identify the individuals who are most likely to reach top positions some two decades later. Such predictions are possible because of the stability of Japanese government organizations.

By the time they reach their late forties, the top members of the same entry group become chiefs of key divisions, while some of the others gradually begin to transfer to top positions in local agencies or retire (Amakudari) to take important jobs in business. Most retirees obtain top managerial positions in either private or public companies because their access to the ministries and their proven abilities make them valuable managers. Some retiring career officials, however, may shun such employment and seek "election to public office after they retire from the civil service at an early age."[2]

An important characterisitic of the Japanese government employment system is the lifelong commitment by both the institution and the individual. There are relatively few opportunities for lateral entry or transfer because once a person joins a government ministry or agency he stays there for life. A change of jobs usually occurs only when there is no other choice, that is, probably for negative reasons such as extreme incompetence. The credibility and skill acquired in one job cannot be carried over to another organization where promotions are given on the basis of seniority rather than past performance elsewhere. Consequently, the Japanese are loyal to their organizations, for failure to live up to this tradition would result in loss of seniority and an interrupted career.

As stated earlier, the Japanese bureaucracy offers no possibilities for lateral entry. For example, no one can move laterally into MOF except the finance minister and the two parliamentary vice-ministers. This contributes to the high prestige of career officials whose positions are so secure that they can serve the country with a long-term perspective in mind. Of course, they can leave government employment any time, but once they do, they cannot return.

The Japanese hold strongly to the traditional belief that officials should be nonpartisan and serve all interests equally well. Although the LDP's influence over the bureaucracy cannot be disputed (the party has been in power since 1955), Japanese officials are statutorily required to be free of partisan influences, let alone of partisan activities. Most career officials are proud of their neutrality and political independence, and believe that it is they—and not the politicians—who are running the country. In fact, the majority of bills submitted to the Diet are drafted by career officials, because politicians are generally too preoccupied with campaign matters to investigate and develop legislative proposals. Undoubtedly, there is another reason for this.

Members of the Japanese Diet have only two staff aides on the government payroll, and these are recruited by the members themselves primarily through personal contacts. One of the two aides is usually a female receptionist, the other a male administrative assistant who is seldom qualified to do research or to design policy. Most of the aides' duties are limited to administrative matters such as the arrangement of constituent visits to the Diet or the handling of routine requests.

In other words, Japanese Diet aides are not well qualified to do legislative-support work. This limitation is aggravated by the Japanese lifetime employment system, which makes it difficult for the aides to move between the executive and legislative branches. Under these conditions, it is understandable that Diet members are not well prepared to draft bills or to initiate policy formulating action and that their interests center on campaign and constituent matters. As a result, until some of them obtain cabinet- or subcabinet-level positions through which active participation in the work of the executive branch becomes possible, they have little influence over policy formulation.

Thus, given the sheer volume and complexity of governmental tasks, it is the bureaucracy that is called upon to perform most of them. As pointed out earlier, aside from the posts of political ministers and the generally uninfluential parliamentary vice-ministers, the top positions in the ministries are held by career officials, as are the staff advisory and coordinating positions that aid the prime minister and other cabinet members during the formulation of policy. Accordingly, the views of career officials, institutionally nurtured, are critically important determinants of policy. In general, these officials in the closed and rigid Japanese bureaucracy are conservative, and not readily responsive to environmental changes. Thus, as the politicians who lead the bureaucracy are also conservative senior LDP Diet members, Japanese policies change very slowly.

GOVERNMENT-BUSINESS RELATIONS

Outside Japan, Japanese government-business relations are usually viewed as cooperative, if not collusive. It is also often heard that the Japanese government places high priority on economic growth, while the U.S. and European governments emphasize the quality of life. Although such generalizations are by and large true, they still represent oversimplifications.

Japanese government-business relations are the product of special historical events. When in the middle of the nineteenth century Commodore Perry succeeded in opening Japan to the West, he ended the country's centuries-old isolation. The Meiji Restoration in 1868 disclosed an astonishing lack of industrial development, technology, science, and other factors of modernization. Therefore, with nearly all of the surrounding countries already colonized by the Western powers, it was critical for Japan to modernize its socio-political system, industrialize its economy, and strengthen its military.

As external political threats mounted, Japan was compelled to import Western technologies and skills rapidly to achieve its goals. The country lacked natural resources; yet, it had a population of over 30 million to feed. Fortunately, under the Shogunate, capital had accumulated in the small-scale private sector for about 260 years, and a large pool of disciplined and potentially productive labor was also available.

Under such conditions, government initiatives were necessary to negotiate both the official and private importation of technology and capital goods. Government support was also needed to develop large-scale industries because individual enterprises lacked the knowledge, experience, and capital to do so.

Japanese industrialization projects were initiated and developed by the government and then often transferred to private interests for a nominal price. Business groups took advantage of the government's willingness to fully finance or subsidize projects in the national interest whenever projected profitability was too low or too uncertain or whenever private capital was not available. In doing so, government bureaucrats experienced the satisfaction of serving the country (but not individual citizens), and business not only willingly accepted the bureaucrats' authority, but also shared their sense of satisfaction. Thus, the foundations on which the uniquely close Japanese government-business relations are based were established by the Meiji regime, although pros-

perous businessmen had already started exerting influence over the ruling samurai through their earlier loans and donations.

In modern imperialistic Japan, the social status of Japanese mer-
chants and industrialists quickly improved, as already during the late
nineteenth century the dominant ideology of mercantilism assigned a
major role to business. In other words, patriotism, mercantilism, and the
national goal of emulating the West helped to establish a high degree of
cooperation between the Japanese government and business, particularly big business. Such close relations remain basically intact today—
and it is these relations that are portrayed as "Japan,Inc." by some
U.S. observers.

Unlike the peoples of Asia who were colonized, the Japanese could
always depend on small-scale enterprises for industrial development,
and the mutuality of interest between government and business assured
individual enterpreneurs of an ideal opportunity to expand. An early example of this was the cooperation of the Meiji government with Mr.
Yataro Iwasaki's Mitsubishi Company. The government protected and
subsidized the company, while ordering it as early as the 1870s to open
sailing routes and to operate under contract the military logistical
system.

Today the Japanese government continues to be engaged in a substantial amount of guiding, projecting, organizing, and restructuring of
the national economy, with the result that it has a strong influence over
business activities. In particular, the government regularly designs, reviews, and implements both long- and short-term national plans, including the annual budget.

The overall national plans consist of growth targets for industry, agriculture, transportation, education, and other key sectors. The targets
developed by the Economic Planning Agency (EPA) are based on the
goals submitted by the respective sectoral ministries. In addition to
growth objectives, EPA also projects the balance of payments, aggregate
demand, and developments in the supply side. Before these estimates
and projections are submitted to the parties, councils, and the public at
large, they are carefully scrutinized by MOF. The rather meticulous
scrutiny is justified by MOF's budgeting responsibility, which includes
both the estimation of revenues and the authority to set priorities.

The government also owns and operates more than 100 businesses,
while numerous additional firms are run by local authorities. Through
such interactions, public enterprises link government and business,
thereby playing a special role in the country's economic life.

While the Japanese government has always maintained close relations with business, these relationships are far more complex than gen-

erally believed and are not free of conflict. Furthermore, in contrast to the United States, the exchange of personnel between the government and business is very limited and restricted to *Amakudari*, the one-way retirement of government officials to industry.

This affects not only the nature of government business relations, but also the behavioral patterns of government officials during the policy formulation process. Japanese officials develop their negotiation tactics at the macrolevel and usually understand little of the needs of individual businesses at the microlevel. This can be seen, for example, in their readiness to accept demands from the United States for voluntary export restraint whenever trade conflicts between the two countries intensify.

BEHAVIORAL PRACTICES

The behavioral practices of Japanese government officials are marked by the fact that today few peoples are as homogeneous as the Japanese, who are 118 million individuals of a single race, culture, and language. In part, this homogeneity is a result of Japan's past isolation from the rest of the world, both for geographic and political reasons. For more than two centuries, from 1638 to 1853, Japan's rulers sealed off the country. Thus, "As an island country closed to the world for several centuries, Japan entered the modern era a highly homogeneous society.[3]

Homogeneity makes the Japanese group-oriented, egalitarian, compassionate, and communicative. Homogeneity helps facilitate the establishment of informal ties among individuals, transcending the rigid hierarchy and vertical structure of society and of organizations. However, it may also isolate the Japanese from other peoples. Thus, what are strengths at home can turn out to be handicaps when dealing with the outside world.

Despite the "assimilation of Western technology and culture, the Japanese have succeeded to a remarkable degree in maintaining their own values and forms of social intercourse."[4] Through these, "they have also maintained a sense of uniqueness and separation."[5]

According to the "Wise Men's Report":

This sense of separateness, which has been reinforced by Western prejudices and discrimination against Japanese, has made it difficult for the Japanese to fully participate in the international community, in spite of the high degree of interdependence linking Japan economically and politically with other countries."[6]

Japanese collectivism is based on the concern for belonging and is expressed by an individual's identification with the collective goals of the group to which he belongs. "Groups of every . . . sort abound throughout Japanese society and usually play a large role and offer more . . . self-identification than do corresponding groups in the United States."[7] As Reischauer points out:

> Between various societies there can be great differences in the relative emphasis placed on the individual and the group. Certainly no difference is more significant between Japanese and Americans, or Westerners in general, than the greater Japanese tendency to emphasize the group, somewhat at the expense of the individual.[8]

The group focus affects Japanese interpersonal relations. Its stress upon harmony and consensus generates pressures for conformity to group norms and discourages individualism. Idiosyncrasies and dissension are avoided or suppressed; a team player is more appreciated "than a solo star and team spirit more than individual ambition."[9]

In the bureaucracy, aggressiveness is discouraged, and the ideal officials are tradition- and routine-oriented, while "the nail that sticks out gets banged down."[10] Cooperation, fairness, and understanding of others are the virtues most admired—not personal drive, forcefulness, and self-assertion. Indeed, the personality type that in the United States seems merely assertive is viewed by the Japanese as neurotic.

Collectivism begets cooperation and solidarity. The sentimental desire for the feeling of *ittaikan* (feeling of oneness) with fellow group members is widely shared by the Japanese. This desire is reflected in the Japanese decision-making process, in which decisions are not the prerogative of any one individual, but are reached through consultation and collective efforts. Consensus, that is, an agreement to which no one objects, is the goal of collective action. Harmony is important for this process, and to preserve it the Japanese try to avoid face-to-face confrontations.

In such a behavioral climate, decisiveness is discouraged to the point that relatively minor mistakes can be fatal to an individual's career. *Genten Shugi* (the system to rate the performance by the score of loss rather than by that of gain), which prevails in the Japanese bureaucracy, affects the behavior of officials who believe in *Koto Nakare Shugi* (no challenge, no mistake). The rotation of career officials among a wide range of positions every couple of years also encourages *Koto Nakare Shugi*, while discouraging leadership roles that might cause fatal damage to long-term career prospects. Risk avoidance prevails because even a small, one-time mistake may ruin an established career, whereas conformity to collective, consensual decision-making does not.

These age-old behavioral characteristics combined with the consensual decentralized trade policy formulation process—which frequently involves interministerial conflicts—leads to considerable delays in policy formulation. Japan's trading partners, in particular the United States, have great difficulties accepting the delays and usually ascribe them to duplicity or insincerity. This is not to say that delays are never created purposefully. Japanese officials, just like Americans or Europeans, occasionally find that delayed decision-making serves their purposes. However, most of Japan's trading partners overlook the fact that the "slow-quick" approach to policy formulation is a long-held tradition that is rooted in the nation's cultural history. In this connection it is worth mentioning that while Americans in particular are often exasperated by the Japanese trade policy formulation process, the Japanese very frequently are also frustrated by the "quick-slow" approach of the Americans who may make decisions very quickly but then take a long time to implement them, if at all. The extent to which U.S. officials may misunderstand Japanese policy formulation is well illustrated by Henry Kissinger who wrote:

> When I first came into office, there was no major country I understood less than Japan. Like most Americans, I admired its extraordinary recovery from the devastation of World War II. But I did not grasp Japan's unique character . . . .
> It took me a long time to grasp how decisions are made, and even after I had understood some of it intellectually I did not always perceive the application to specific circumstances.[11]

Delayed decision-making influences the Japanese negotiation style. It is well known in international trade circles that because of their negotiation style, the Japanese often fail to earn even the credit that they deserve. They are slow in responding and often seem reluctant to compromise, unless forced to do so. The "Wise Men's Report" observed that:

> The problem of misperception between the United States and Japan in negotiating situations is often exacerbated by different bargaining styles. While Americans often employ an adversary style of bargaining, emphasizing the negative aspects of the case of the other side, (as lawyers do in court), Japanese tend to remain reticent.[12]

The style of Japanese negotiations results from the traditional behavioral tendency of avoiding confrontation whenever possible. Deputy USTR Hormats, in a 1980 statement before a subcommittee of the House Foreign Affairs Committee, put it this way:

One reason why Japan, despite major import liberalization, is perceived to be so protective of its market . . . . is its style of negotiating—its seeming inability to act unless faced with major pressures to do so and then, seemingly, only with the greatest reluctance.

. . . . Japanese approach to negotiation is a legacy from an era when Japan was too weak to play a major role in the world economy and was not expected to.[13]

Exactly the same point was made by the first U.S. consul general to Japan, Townsend Harris, more than 120 years ago. He wrote in his diary: "They have yielded nothing except from *fear,* and any future ameliorations of our intercourse will only take place after a demonstration of force on our part."[14]

In other words, since the beginning of bilateral political and economic relations, generations of U.S. policy formulators were disappointed by Japanese procrastination and resorted to pressure as an effective means of obtaining compromises. The postwar occupation undoubtedly enhanced this psychological tendency. But such a strategy is not without its dangers. As Henry Kissinger sees it:

The erosion of distinctions between the official and the unofficial, the oblique manner of presentation, the seeming (and misleading) imperviousness to counterarguments can confer a maddening quality on encounters with Japanese diplomats. It can also lead to grave misunderstandings. . . .

Only amateurs would seek to pressure an individual Japanese minister; even when he yields out of politeness, he cannot carry out his promise. But when the consensus has formed, for whatever reason, it is implemented with speed, determination, and breadth unmatched by any Western country.[15]

Another explanation for the Japanese negotiating style is organizational. As mentioned before, Japan relies on a decentralized process of trade policy formulation because it lacks a USTR type office. Furthermore, orthodoxy has always been more valued than originality or creativity; so in the highly structured, seniority-based, lifetime employment system, overly dynamic officals could become a problem. The ideal Japanese officials are tradition- and routine-oriented.

One of the basic rules for negotiations is to use offensive and defensive tactics alternately. But the nonconfrontational Japanese approach to international negotiations means that the Japanese do not present a structured agenda to the other side. Thus, by not suggesting issues for which they can be on the offensive, Japanese trade negotiators usually limit the proceedings to the discussion of the other side's demands.[16]

This is particularly critical in U.S.–Japanese negotiations where the U.S. representative always offers a clearly structured agenda. If the Japanese properly appreciated the U.S. approach, they would always ask for "reciprocity," a concept they strongly subscribe to but are rarely able to enforce in actual negotiations, because of their passivity.[17] As a consequence, Japan frequently accepts U.S. demands without presenting any counterdemands. Eventually, Japan typically gives in to the U.S. demands, and the inevitable failure to perform according to the U.S. expectations tarnishes the Japanese image and increases U.S. suspicions.

The behavioral characteristics of the Japanese trade policy formulation process are even more pronounced by language barriers. While interpreters can convey factual information fairly accurately, they are less successful with the diverse cultural and political nuances that frequently do not translate from Japanese to another language. In addition, because they communicate only indirectly, negotiating trade officials become less precise than they should be, relying on interpreters to surmise the exact intent of the discourse. Finally, the negotiating sessions are more formal than they would be without intermediaries, so that the parties are unable to develop the mutual trust necessary for the elimination of misunderstandings and suspicions.

Although many Japanese study English, very few Europeans or Americans even attempt to learn Japanese. According to the "Wise Men's Report":

> The difficulty of the Japanese language for non-Japanese to learn undoubtedly also contributes to foreign perceptions of Japan as a closed society. With the Japanese language's unique structural characteristics, its complex writing system (which includes the use of Chinese characters and two separate phonetic syllabaries), its rich vocabulary and subtle forms of expression, not many Westerners have achieved working fluency in Japanese and only a handful can be said to have "mastered" it. Although the Japanese are hardly to be blamed for the complexity of their language or the failure of the foreign businessmen to devote enough time to its study, its difficulty contributes to a general sense of Japanese society as closed and impenetrable.[18]

While many Japanese do study English, few of them acquire a good command of the language. Although recently, more Japanese career officials have been sent to U.S. graduate schools, their English ability remains relatively poor when compared to that of other nationalities. This is due to the linguistic, cultural, and perceptual differences between the rest of the world and, in particular, the United States and Japan.

Several U.S. government officials have expressed the view that Japan needs high-level officials and business executives who can deal with the U.S. mass media in good English in order to correct the widespread misperceptions about Japan.[19] Some pointed out how effective the late Egyptian President Sadat and Israeli Prime Minister Begin were in appealing directly to the U.S. public in English, despite occasional grammatical errors.

Finally, it should be pointed out that during the negotiation stages of trade policy formulation, the Japanese are not very effective in using the so-called "back channels," that is, officials or institutions without former negotiating authority that Americans or Europeans use very extensively and usually with good results. "Back channels" can be quite effective in breaking a stalemate, particularly when reliable and capable negotiators are available on both sides. In the United States, experienced lawyers, consultants, and former government officials are available due to the administrative practice of frequent government-business personnel changes. In contrast, few Japanese qualify for such a task because of the stable lifetime employment system and the one-way (*Amalcudari*) government-business personnel exchange.

By the same token, the Japanese attribute far more importance to heads-of-state meetings (summit channels) than their trading partners. Because the Japanese feel that all possible sources of conflict should be eliminated before meetings with heads-of-state, the officials in charge of the arrangements are usually very tense and, consequently, vulnerable. The other side can usually take advantage of Japan's concerns to eliminate conflicts, especially if the preparatory time is limited.

It is also an old Japanese tradition to carry *Miyage*, or a gift to the country visited. Thus, whenever Japanese prime ministers visit one of the major trading partners, Japanese officials are not only concerned about eliminating any conflicts prior to the summit meetings, but also, about taking the appropriate number of *Miyage*—that is, trade policy concessions—to the country visited. While there are numerous examples of such gestures in U.S.–Japan trade relations (for example, Prime Minister Ohira's visit to Washington during the highly controversial NTT negotiations in May 1979), the visit of Prime Minister Nakasone with President Reagan during January 1983, is the most recent case in point.[20]

Almost as soon as Mr. Naksone took office in November 1982, speculation in Tokyo was rife that he would take with him as a *Miyage* to Washington an easing of import quotas on farm products and a reduction of tariffs on over 40 other items. Such expectations were continually heightened by the steady drumbeat of demands and expectations emanating from Capitol Hill and the various administration offices throughout Washington.[21]

THE ROLE OF PRESSURE GROUPS

While the non-Japanese, in particular, U.S. view of the country's political economic system is one of a monolithic "Japan, Inc.," the reality is quite different. Undoubtedly, as pointed out before, Japanese government-business relations are closer than in the rest of the world. The behavioral practices of policy formulators and of the public in general reinforces the special quality of this relationship.

It is, however, erroneous to assume that Japanese trade policy formulation is free of conflicts between the government and special interest groups. As a matter of fact, government officials frequently do not fully appreciate the special needs of the various interest groups and, consequently, for the sake of stable international trade relations are often willing to ignore the same. The 1980–1981 conflict between trade policy formulators and the automobile industry concerning export restraints to the United States is a case in point. Most Americans and Europeans did not know about the bitter exchanges that took place between the two sides, and many otherwise well-informed people do not know of this conflict even today.

As international economic competition became more intensified during 1981-1982, other industry groups also became active. The Japanese Spinners Association, a group that represents 77 companies that make cotton yarn, for example, is pressuring trade policy formulators for protection against yarn shipments from Korea and Pakistan. With lower labor costs and sometimes with more advanced technology (in steel and shipbuilding, for instance) producers from the "Newly Industrialized Countries" (NICs) have also started threatening the domestic and international markets of many Japanese producers. While the general policy of the government (MITI) is not to protect industries that are gradually replaced by low-cost producers from the NICs, these industries are not giving up without a fight. The Japanese government cannot ignore such domestic political realities for the same reasons that the U.S. and European governments cannot ignore the pleas of their maturing, that is, increasingly noncompetitive industries.

The most active and influential Japanese pressure groups, however, are in agriculture. The approximately 5 million Japanese farmers who make up only about 9 percent of the nation's labor force work and live under difficult conditions. In contrast to large-scale U.S. farming methods, they grow their products on steep hillsides that are rocky and volcanic. This makes the use of labor-saving machines difficult, if not impossible. Long-held traditions combined with the departure of the young people to the large cities in search of better paying and more respected jobs has resulted in a farm labor force that is rapidly aging and is unwilling to give up the small family plots despite official encouragement to do so.

The Japanese agricultural sector has a great deal of political influence. Because the allocation of parliamentary seats favors rural areas, the LDP holds a large percentage of seats, and many politicians from such areas hold important agricultural policy positions in the Diet and the party. Moreover, Japanese farmers are organized in the very effective Zenchu (the national farmers' organization) through which they maintain direct contact with politicians. Because almost all of Japan's 5 million farm households belong to this organization, it is not an exaggeration to claim that more liberal agricultural import policies could threaten Japan's political stability. Without the farmers' support it would be difficult for the LDP to stay in power and, therefore, the Japanese government cannot easily give in to demands for farm import liberalization. Most Japanese agricultural and trade experts believe that it will probably take at least another 10–15 years before the Japanese agricultural market can be completely opened to imports.

The uncompromising position of Japan's farmers and the political dilemma of the LDP is deepened by the conflict between the farm and industrial lobbies. The latter group, representing the country's highly efficient, export-oriented manufacturing sector, is the LDP's major source of funds. Concerned about protectionism in their major export markets in response to the continuation of the agricultural import limitations, industrialists are pressuring the government to do away with the limitations even if it means sacrificing the small family farmer. Of course, the Zenchu leaders reject the notion that they must give up their interests to accommodate the exporters of manufactured goods.

Trade policy formulators, thus, are caught in an intense conflict between the requirements of domestic politics and pressures from abroad, in particular from the United States and Europe. The interests that are most deeply entrenched in the political system—the farmers and industrialists—are precisely those who are most threatened by whatever course of action the policy formulators decide to take.

THE ROLE OF THE MASS MEDIA

The mass media in general and newspapers in particular play a major role in Japan's political and economic life. Of the five major daily newspapers the No. 1, *Yomiuri*—which appears in the morning—has a circulation of well over 8 million, the No. 2, *Asahi*, over 7 million in the morning alone. These circulation numbers exceed the combined circulation of several major U.S. newspapers such as the *New York Times*, the *Washington Post*, and the *Los Angeles Times*.

The influence of the mass media and, in particular, of newspapers is increased by their tendency to follow a common line of argument, particularly with respect to U.S.–Japan trade relations. The United States is usually portrayed as a large, but by now inefficient country that is continually trying to bend a much smaller, but very efficient Japan to its will.

In order to perpetuate this distorted view, Japanese journalists assigned to Washington continually swarm all over Capitol Hill and the government agencies, hoping to find politicians or officials who would provide them with negative views on Japan. While most of them have never carefully analyzed the trade problems between the two countries, they claim that the mounting frustration in the United States could easily lead to the kind of protectionism that would completely ban Japanese automobiles, steel, television sets, and other major industrial products from the U.S. market.

Japanese television and magazines usually follow suit and are spreading fictitious stories about the frustration and anger engulfing Congress and the entire United States. Thus, Japan, a country far away from the Western world, is continually inundated by second-hand information that is promptly discussed by the populace. Journalists thus have a powerful influence over the perceptions of businessmen and the general public, the majority of whom do not have first-hand access to relevant information. Of course, policy formulators receive better quality information, but even they cannot escape the influence of the all-pervasive Japanese press when listening to the representatives of the various interest groups that rely heavily on news reports.

Ironically, very often the Japanese press claims that even those international trade deals with the United States that favor Japan result from U.S. "bullying." This indicates that the press is far more a prisoner of its own prejudices than the government, which it continually chides for not giving up "preconceived notions." Japanese journalists simply cannot believe that agreements with the United States can be reached through equitable negotiations and without Japan giving in to the United States.

However, it is important to point out that the Japanese government never collaborates with the press. The government considers the press a strong critic of its policy and the press, in turn, is proud of this critical stance, because it views itself as a major force in preventing government abuse of otherwise almost unchallengeable power. In short, the Japanese press, while nationalistic in an international context, is antigovernment domestically. It is this quality of the Japanese mass media that makes it a force that cannot be disregarded by government officials during trade policy formulation.

THE SPECIAL ROLE OF "U.S. PRESSURE"

As pointed out in the previous section, the favorite international trade theme of the Japanese press is the ongoing battle between the U.S. "Goliath" and the Japanese "David" who is constantly badgered to give in to the unreasonable demands of the stronger opponent.

This theme and its importance has its origin in two characteristics of the Japanese press: first, its conviction that ever since 1853, when Commodore Matthew G. Perry came to Japan, the country had been under continuous U.S. pressure; and second, its sensitivity to trade conflicts with the United States, which far exceeds that of the U.S. press.

Because the United States is Japan's most important trading partner and because "U.S. pressure" plays such a key role in the country's international trade relations, a discussion of Japanese trade policy formulation would be incomplete without an exploration of the special role of this theme.

Americans, impatient with the consensual decision-making process, often pressure the Japanese to act quickly. Although Americans believe their tactics to be effective, actually, pressure only weakens relations between the two countries, making the United States appear arrogant and Japan stubborn. Also, pressures intensify trade frictions by making the Japanese resentful of "bullying."

The "U.S. pressure" theme is widely shared in Japan. While the "scapegoat" mentality of the Japanese may on occasion exaggerate the extent and importance of U.S. demands, the theme is not without historical merit. Commodore Perry did pressure Japan to open up to the West in 1854, and in 1858, Consul General Townsend Harris did pressure Japan to open several ports to commerce, as well as to sign the treaty of Amity and Commerce with the United States. Also, Japan resorted to war in 1941 as a result of persistent U.S. pressure for withdrawal from China. After having acknowledged U.S. victory and power through unconditional surrender in 1945, Japan accepted a U.S.-type constitution, dissolved the *Zaibatsu* (conglomerates), and implemented a U.S.-inspired tax reform and program for broad economic stabilization and development. Finally, it was under such pressure that Japan established self-defense forces in 1954, liberalized trade policies in the late 1960s and 1970s, improved economic assistance programs, and continues to pay careful attention to U.S. demands during the 1980s.

U.S. pressure is manifested in several different ways, some rather obvious, others quite subtle. It is, however, important to keep in mind that the pronounced cultural differences between the two nations, in particular with respect to interpersonal communications, may to a large extent determine what is obvious or subtle.

Congressional hearings and special studies, as well as the potential rejection by Congress of international agreements reached by the administration, are among the most obvious forms of U.S. pressure on Japan.[22] Others include newspaper reports and editorials that the Japanese frequently consider just as erroneous and misleading as the reports and editorials about the United States in the Japanese press are considered by Americans.[23]

The U.S. proclivity to portray "honest" and "open" talk as the most desirable form of interpersonal communication is perceived by many Japanese as a subtle form of pressure. In heterogeneous U.S. society personal drive, forcefulness, creativity, and individualism are not only encouraged but expected, especially from those in positions of leadership. The Japanese, however, are raised to avoid confrontation; that is, "open" and "honest" talk is not only discouraged, but frowned upon. Thus when U.S. government officials or politicians invite the Japanese to an "honest exchange" of views they are conveying an unintended message.

Of course, very often the Japanese badly misinterpret U.S. actions and see unreasonable pressure where none was intended or possible. The *Wall Street Journal* of December 9, 1982, reported a good example of such misinterpretation. In discussing the role of the Japanese mass media, the article states:

> In October 1981, a relatively junior Democratic Congressman from North Carolina, Stephen Neal, introduced a resolution calling for Japan to pay the United States 2 percent of its gross national product each year as a "security tax" in return for the military protection the United States provides. Like many of the countless congressional resolutions introduced every year, this one on its face had zero chance of approval, and it wouldn't have had a binding effect on the United States, much less Japan, even if it had passed. But it was big news in Japan. Most Americans, a State Department official complains, aren't even aware of some of the "screwy resolutions" the Japanese press plays up.[24]

The Japanese also mistake the highly structured U.S. approach to international negotiations as a form of pressure. As mentioned previously, Japanese negotiators usually do not go to international negotiations with a clearly defined agenda. This lack of structure usually forces them to accept the highly formalized U.S. agenda that the U.S. negotiators develop whenever they negotiate with anybody, not just the Japanese.

Real or imagined U.S. pressure also plays a much less well-understood role in Japanese trade policy formulation. Major ministries, such as MITI and MOFA, frequently use it for their own purposes. They resort to it to rationalize the dysfunctions caused by the consensual decision-making process and bureaucratic sectionalism. For instance, during recent trade debates, when MITI did not want Japanese manufactured exports sacrificed for the sake of domestic agricultural interests, it joined MOFA in emphasizing the dangers of strong U.S. pressures for concessions. It contended that the U.S. position reflected frustration, which could trigger protectionism and exacerbate bilateral trade frictions to such an extent that the U.S. market would be closed to most Japanese manufactured goods. Of course, MITI officials also admit that occasionally they simply pretend to be frightened by U.S. pressure because otherwise, MITI cannot obtain any support from the Japanese public, the press, policy formulators, and particularly the politicians representing agricultural constituencies. MITI believes that a global free-trade system is not only in the best interest of Japan, but represents the only realistic economic goal. In order to establish and maintain such a system, its officials are willing to resort to any strategy needed to deal with domestic political realities.

In opposition to MITI, MOAFF believes that Japan needs a certain degree of self-sufficiency in food. This consideration is an important policy factor because MOAFF cannot only mobilize more followers than any other ministry, but also enjoys the support of most LDP politicians who represent agricultural interests. To counter such powerful forces, MITI and MOFA occasionally use the argument of U.S. pressure. Some high U.S. trade officials acknowledge that their Japanese counterparts occasionally advise them when and how to exert pressure. Because they believe that it is essential for the achievement of common goals, they cooperate.[25]

Although several ministries use the argument of U.S. pressure, MOFA uses it most frequently to demonstrate that owing to its diplomatic expertise and competence, only it can foresee the serious consequences of U.S. demands. However, because it has been used over a long period of time, the effectiveness of the argument has gradually diminished. As Japanese confidence increases and the United States' relative influence declines, the bilateral economic and trade relationships gradually become one of equals.

It must be pointed out, however, that already during the 1970s many Japanese officials, particularly of the younger generation, resented the argument of U.S. pressure, and their response was either a counterproductive toughness or an immature condescension. They told Americans how unwise and ineffective pressure tactics were, for the resulting public uproar made it even more difficult for the Japanese government to be accommodating.

Not surprisingly, some U.S. officials both in Washington and the Tokyo embassy express embarrassment, frustration, and even anger at the abuse of the argument. Of course, most of them know that Japanese officials often solicit U.S. pressure in order to obtain an agreement in the Japanese consensual decision-making process, particularly when strong sectional interests are involved. Thus, responsibility for reliance on the overused argument must be shared by the U.S. side.

The Japanese response to U.S. pressure consisted, most of all, of an increase in the number of career officials in the United States, particularly in Washington and New York. The short-term mission of these officials is to collect and analyze information about the United States' real intentions and, if needed, to provide U.S. policy formulators with information about Japan. In the long run, they are expected to familiarize themselves with the American language, culture, society, and policy formulation processes, and also to become acquainted with as many Americans as possible. Such assignments are, of course, made easier by the lifetime employment system of the Japanese government.

Japanese firms also opened offices to collect political and economic information. Naturally, international trading houses came first. Mitsubishi, which opened its Washington office in 1971, was followed by several other large trading companies, including Mitsui, Marubeni, C. Itoh, Sumitomo, and Nissho Iwai. The automobile industry also sent representatives. Honda, Toyota, and Nissan, the three largest Japanese automakers, opened their Washington offices in May 1978, August 1978, and August 1979, respectively. Soon afterwards, they began systematically to monitor the sentiments of U.S. policy formulators, management, and labor.

Such activities engendered a relatively new phenomenon in the Japanese policy formulation process. When MOFA and MITI were concerned about U.S. pressure and considered voluntary automobile export restraints in 1980 and early 1981, Mr. Toyoda, president of Toyota Motor Manufacturing, Co., defied them by publicly stating that many American policy formulators and economists were strongly opposed to the restraints because of their potential inflationary effects.

CONCLUDING REMARKS

Japanese policy formulators are from quite homogeneous socio-economic and cultural backgrounds. As nonprofessional graduates of the most prestigious universities, they enter the various ministries as career officials only after a thorough selection process and in relatively small groups. Furthermore, they undergo strict in-house training programs that involve frequent rotations. Employed for life and looking forward to an approximately 30-year career, they internalize a set of bureaucratic values. Living by the Japanese value of the supremacy of group over individual goals, they lack individualistic tendencies and behave cautiously. Such qualities, combined with a high degree of organizational loyalty, result in a Japanese policy formulation process that—from a non-Japanese viewpoint—is slow, nonresponsive, and elusive.

While Japanese government-business relations are different from those in other industrialized countries, the characterization of what was historically indeed a close relationship as "Japan, Inc." in the 1980s is not only erroneous, but also very misleading. Current government-business relationships are far more complex and controversial than the simplistic "Japan, Inc." notion implies.

In the homogeneous Japanese society, group interests take precedence over personal ambitions, generating pressure for cooperation and conformity. While such a behavioral climate fosters nonrisktaking attitudes and slow, deliberate decision-making, it also insures that once a decision is reached it is speedily implemented.

However, the slow, consensual decision-making combined with the passive siege mentality of Japanese officials, inadequate delegation of authority, bureaucratic sectionalism, and a generally timid and nonresponsive negotiation strategy, creates a lot of problems for the nation in its international trade relations. Non-Japanese, in particular Americans, often ascribe the results of such behavioral practices to insincerity and duplicity.

The flexibility of Japanese trade policy formulation is additionally limited by the very active agricultural and industrial pressure groups as well as by the highly nationalistic mass media, which reports every trade policy move of the government in minute detail.

Finally, most non-Japanese do not appreciate the extent to which real or imagined "U.S. pressure" influences Japanese trade policy formulation. This theme, developed and perpetuated by the mass media and not without some historical merit, is so important that it is even used by the different ministries to fuel or settle bureaucratic rivalries.

NOTES

1. Peter F. Drucker, "Economic Realities and Enterprise Strategy," in *Modern Japanese Organization and Decision-Making*, ed. Ezra F. Vogel (Berkeley: University of California Press, 1975), p. 241.

2. Dell G. Hitchner, and Carol Levine, *Comparative Government and Politics*, 2d ed. (New York: Harper and Row, 1981), p. 259.

3. *Report of the Japan-United States Economic Relations Group*, Nobuhiko Ushiba and Robert S. Ingersoll, Co-Chairmen, (Washington, D.C., and Tokyo: The Japan-United States

Economic Relations Group, 1981), p. 65. (The report is generally known as the "Wise Men's Report.")

4. Ibid., pp. 65–66.

5. Ibid., p. 66.

6. Ibid., p. 66.

7. Edwin O. Reischauer, *The Japanese* (Cambridge, Mass.: Harvard University Press, 1977), p. 132.

8. Ibid., p. 127.

9. Ibid., p. 135.

10. Ibid.

11. Henry Kissinger, *Years of Upheaval*, (Boston: Little, Brown, 1982) p. 735, 737.

12. *Report of the Japan-United States Economic Relations Group*, p. 102.

13. Robert D. Hormats, Deputy United States Trade Representative, Testimony presented to the U.S. Congress, House, Subcommittee on Asian and Pacific Affairs and Subcommittee on International Economic Policy and Trade of the Committee on Foreign Affairs, 18 September, 1980.

14. Townsend Harris, *The Complete Journal of Townsend Harris*, 2nd ed., rev. (Rutland, Vt. and Tokyo, Japan: Charles E. Tuttle, 1959), pp. 357–58.

15. Kissinger, *Years of Upheaval*, pp. 737, 739.

16. The typical Japanese attitude is that ". . . we will do our best (or make all appropriate efforts) to take the necessary measures aimed at resolving the problems."

17. The Japanese inability to demand reciprocity can best be illustrated by the Alaskan oil case. During the 1978 U.S.–Japan trade negotiations, Japan could have asked the United States to sell it Alaskan oil. This would have helped Japan and could have substantially reduced the trade imbalance between the two countries. When the author suggested the idea to a senior MOFA official, he immediately denied its usefulness by pointing out that such sale was against U.S. federal law. It had never occurred to him that Japan could have asked the Americans to take another look at the law.

18. *Report of the Japan-United States Economic Relations Group*, p. 66.

19. During interviews in Washington in 1980.

20. The visit is discussed in detail in Chapter 6.

21. The role of "U.S. pressure" in Japanese trade policy formulation is a special factor to be discussed on the following pages.

22. The so-called "Jones Reports" released in 1979 are a good illustration of the type of Congressional publication which can have a very strong impact on U.S.–Japan trade relations. See U.S. Congress, Committee on Ways and Means, *Task Force Report on United States-Japan Trade*, Committee Print 95-110, 95th Congress, 2nd sess. (Washington, D.C.: Government Printing Office, 1979).

The argument often heard from U.S. negotiators that "Congress will not accept this" is another form of American pressure.

23. Of the many possible examples, see the 9 August, 1982, editorial of *Business Week* (p. 96) which concludes with the statement that ". . . . Experience with the Japanese shows that they respond only under pressure. Now is not the time to ease up."

24. "Black and White: U.S. News is Big News in Japan, but the Angle Always Seems the Same." *Wall Street Journal*, 9 December, 1982, p. 1.

25. In a recent article describing the use of threatening rhetoric against Japan, it was noted that ". . . many Japanese government and business officials privately welcomed the outside pressure because they believe it will make it easier to bring about what they view as needed changes . . . Indeed, the outside pressure is not altogether resisted by Japan." *See* Steve Lohr, "Japan Sees Use for Trade Threats." *International Herald Tribune*, 14 October, 1981, p. 9.

5

SELECTED INCIDENTS OF
TRADE POLICY FORMULATION

As shown in the previous chapters, Japanese trade policy—except for certain social-cultural traditions—is subject to the same type of influencing factors as the trade policy of other major industrialized countries.

The social-cultural traditions, however, are unique enough to result in a trade policy formulation process that Japan's trading partners have difficulties understanding. Such a lack of understanding, combined with the trade partners' own social-cultural traditions, leads to miscommunications, errors in judgment, and, finally, trade conflicts. Negotiations, designed to reduce such conflicts, often intensify the misunderstandings and, consequently, the conflicts.

The political-economic history of Japan during the last ten years is rich in incidents that illustrate why and how the nation's trade policy was influenced by the previously discussed factors. The following pages present a selection of such incidents in the context of U.S.–Japan trade relations between 1977 and early 1983.[1] The incidents were selected on the basis of how well they illustrate those aspects of Japanese trade policy formulation that non-Japanese observers are most apt to misunderstand or not to appreciate. However, during the discussion reference will be made also to those aspects of U.S. trade policy formulation that the Japanese misunderstand or cannot appreciate. The resulting broader view may help reduce future misunderstandings about Japanese trade policy formulation not only on the other side of the Pacific, but also throughout the rest of the world.

THE MACROECONOMIC POLICY INCIDENT[2]

In 1977 and 1978, U.S.–Japan trade discussions were conducted in the context of an unprecedented imbalance of trade that grew in Japan's favor from $5.4 billion in 1976, to $8.1 billion in 1977, and $11.7 billion in 1978, setting a record in each year.[3]

In light of the trade imbalances, U.S. officials asked the Japanese to change their macroeconomic policies, which they partially blamed for the situation. Specifically, they were concerned with the 1978 rates of growth and yen-dollar exchange, as well as the economic policies necessary to achieve the projected growth.

The Japanese trade surplus of 1977–1978 originated in the inflationary explosion of the early 1970s. Spurred by a combination of expansionist economic policies and the OPEC "oil shock," Japan's 1974 consumer and wholesale price indexes rose 23.2 and 31.4 percent, respectively, over those of the previous year.[4] However, the government's tight monetary and fiscal policies through the end of 1975 restored price stability so that the wholesale price index, for example, rose by only 3.0 percent in 1975 and 5.0 percent in fiscal year (FY) 1976.[5] During the same period, consumer prices rose 11.7 and 9.4 percent, respectively.

As a consequence, Japan's recovery from recession was delayed. But when it did occur, it was led by exports, resulting in a substantial current-account surplus. When Fukuda became prime minister in December 1976, he wanted to correct the imbalance by strengthening domestic demand. While his budget for FY 1977 called for increased public works spending, Japanese economists wondered if investment and consumer spending would grow enough to attain a real GNP growth rate of 6.7 percent and a current-account deficit of $700 million, as expected by Fukuda.[6]

In contrast, the U.S. economy had rapidly recovered from the recession, and the Carter administration determined to accelerate the progress. It promoted the "locomotive" thesis, originally proposed by the Organization for Economic Cooperation and Development (OECD) in the summer of 1976. OECD wanted the three advanced industrial economies, the Federal Republic of Germany (F.R.G.), Japan, and the United States, to grow rapidly to "haul" the other countries out of the recession.

The U.S. motive behind the "locomotive" thesis was questioned by some economic experts. According to Hollerman, "[The U.S.] interest in the locomotive strategy . . . seems primarily inspired by the wish to be rescued from the balance of payments consequences of its own inflationary policies."[7] He noted that if the United States alone stimulated the economy, it would risk a larger trade deficit, declining dollar, and heightened inflation. But through the "locomotive" approach, the United States could stimulate recovery in cooperation with other countries and thus share the economic burden. Hollerman added: "It might also be noted that prior to abandonment of the Bretton Woods system, when the United States was in balance-of-payments surplus, it demanded that deficit countries assume most of the burden of adjustment. When it was in deficit, it demanded that surplus countries assume the burden."[8] Indeed, the United States was now demanding that Japan assume the burden of the U.S. trade deficit.

Vice-President Mondale promoted the "locomotive" thesis during his postinaugural trip to Europe and Japan. At the London economic summit in May 1977, and at the OECD and International Monetary Fund (IMF) meetings that summer and early fall, the United States, as well as the United Kingdom pressed for stronger Japanese (and F.R.G.) growth. However, for domestic reasons, Japan preferred to follow a more modest, noninflationary growth strategy, which, while contributing to stable and noninflationary growth in the world economy, failed to satisfy the United States, which criticized Japan for not helping to offset the surplus of the Organization of Petroleum Exporting Countries (OPEC).[9]

In order to achieve growth, the United States urged Japan to expand domestic demand and thereby increase imports. But domestic demand remained sluggish and exports expanded; thus, contrary to government projections, the trade and current-account surpluses rose. U.S. officials viewed this as a major international problem, that is, a drag on world economic recovery, which, in combination with the trade disputes and the growing U.S. deficit, threatened to encourage protectionism in the United States. Consequently, the United States and Japan held sub-cabinet level discussions to explore the trade imbalance. While state and treasury officials emphasized the burden that Japan's growing current-account surplus was placing on the world economy, the Japanese neither challenged the U.S. position nor proposed remedies. From U.S. point of view, this was a good example of the nonresponsive Japanese attitude toward U.S. international concerns.

Japan's exchange rate policies were also carefully examined by the United States and other nations. They urged the Ministry of Finance (MOF) and the Bank of Japan not to forestall the rise in the value of the yen as they had, U.S. officials believed, in 1976, when the yen's value remained around 270 to the dollar, a result of what they thought to be a conscious "dirty float" policy.

The eventual rise of the yen—which reached a postwar high of 253 to the dollar by mid-October—was generating discontent with Fukuda's economic policies in the Japanese export community. Together with the

Ministry of International Trade and Industry (MITI), exporters called for increased fiscal stimulus. Encouraged by such demands, and indirectly supported by MITI officials who wanted expansive fiscal policies to prevent the yen from continuing to appreciate, the United States increased pressure.[10] In contrast to MITI, MOF officials preferred an exchange rate adjustment. These differences were a good illustration of the frequent interministerial conflicts that influence Japanese trade policy formulation.

To resolve the international and domestic conflict, Prime Minister Fukuda eventually changed his cabinet and convinced his new government that it should accept the 7 percent growth target demanded by the United States together with the necessary record spending deficit.[11] Thus, U.S. pressure was a major consideration in the formulation of Japan's macroeconomic policies for FY 1978. Such pressure was effective because of the deep divisions among the formulators of Japanese economic policy and because of the sluggish domestic demand which necessitated stimulation.

Meanwhile U.S. and Japanese officials were trying to find a way to reduce the massive Japanese trade deficit. After protracted negotiations, during which the U.S. side strongly pressured the Japanese in both private and public, the now well-known Ushiba-Strauss joint communiqué was issued on January 13, 1978.[12]

Although the Ushiba-Strauss joint communiqué imposed obligations on both sides, it did not represent an equitable agreement. While Japan was assigned specific duties, the U.S. obligations remained vague.[13] For example, Japan agreed to a specific growth target of 7 percent, whereas the United States had to grow only at a "substantial" rate. Japan was persuaded to achieve an equilibrium and even to accept a deficit in the current-account, whereas the United States merely agreed to try to improve the balance of payments and thereby increase the value of the dollar. Under "Trade Measures," Japan made commitments to increase imports, whereas the United States did not—in turn—promise to increase exports. Finally, under the "Review Procedures," both governments agreed to open the Japanese market, but there was no mention of U.S. import quotas on steel, color televisions, or many other industrial and agricultural products, or of the export prohibition on Alaskan oil.

While the Ushiba-Strauss joint communiqué identified the problems that were to be jointly resolved, the division of responsibilities was unequal. Consequently, the agreement reinforced the siege mentality of many Japanese officials and put Japan on the defensive in the upcoming trade negotiations.

Following the agreement the Japanese government introduced a number of economic measures to promote economic growth. The Bank of Japan cut the discount rate, and long-term interest rates, including the prime rate, subsequently fell, also. Furthermore, a seven-point economic stimulus plan was adopted which included: acceleration of public-works spending, expansion of government-financed housing loans, encouragement of private-sector investment in plants and equipment, creation of public-works jobs in areas hard hit by the recession, and relief for industries with structural problems.[14] Export-limiting and import-promoting measures were also taken, and at the Bonn summit meeting in July 1978, Japan pledged to attain a 7 percent real economic growth rate in FY 1978, limit the total volume of exports to the FY 1977 level, and double its official development assistance over a three-year period. It also promised to adopt a supplementary stimulus package, if needed. (It was needed and adopted in September 1978.)

Reality, however, turned out to be different. Japanese growth was not so rapid as predicted: the annualized rate for the first quarter of FY 1978 was only 4.1 percent; and the current-account surplus continued to grow, reaching over $8 billion for the first half of calendar year 1978. Despite the sharp appreciation of the yen, the trade and current-account surpluses continued to grow because, while export volumes were negatively affected (depressing the economy), their dollar value was rising.[15]

The Japanese government had no choice but to revise its economic outlook for FY 1978. The original projection of a 7 percent increase in real output (12 percent in nominal terms) was retained, but the expected rise in consumer prices was lowered from 6.8 percent to 4.9 percent, and the estimated change in wholesale prices was revised from a 2.7 percent increase to a 1.5 percent decline. In addition, the projections for the current- and trade-account surpluses were raised from $6 to $13.2 billion, and from $13.5 to $20.5 billion, respectively.[16]

The resulting increase in tensions required a cabinet-level exchange of views. When Finance Minister Murayama and his entourage met with Treasury Secretary Blumenthal, Federal Reserve Chairman Miller, and Under Secretary of Treasury Solomon on September 24, 1978, the differing views on the macroeconomic policy were the focal point of the discussion. Mr. Murayama wanted to talk to Secretary Blumenthal about the implications of three issues: (1) the decline in Japanese export, and increase in import volumes, and the decrease of the trade surplus (measured in yen), as well as of the economic growth rate from the initially projected 7 percent to 5.7 percent; (2) the overvaluation of the yen by approximately 20 percent, primarily because of short-term speculative and psychological factors (To remedy such distortions, the Japanese expected cooperative moves similar to the currency swap agreement between the United States and the Federal Republic of Germany); and (3) the specific measures the United States planned to take to curb inflation and to promote exports.

In the ensuing discussion, Secretary Blumenthal expressed his hope that the Japanese would achieve 7 percent growth and restore trade balances, as measured in both dollars and volume. He emphasized the belief that Japan should promote manufactured imports by lifting the still-existing protectionist measures and by passing on to consumers the benefits of the yen appreciation so that the United States could export more. Mr. Blumenthal then went on to say that current changes in the exchange rate reflected basic problems that had to be solved in order to stabilize foreign-exchange rates and calm speculators. He explained that the United States viewed the Japanese position in the "Tokyo Round" (MTN) as tough and not forthcoming and that the execution of a swap agreement would be very difficult as long as Congress regarded Japan as protectionist. Moreover, he pointed out, the administration would seek new legislation to cut government expenditures and intended to ask management and labor to comply with the wage and price standards. Also, within the limits of the GATT rules, the administration planned new financial measures designed to interest U.S. firms in exporting. Finally, Mr. Blumenthal also asked Japan to help curtail official export financing subsidies and expressed his desire to explore this issue at the October 1978 OECD meeting.

Mr. Murayama did not challenge Mr. Blumenthal on the first two points, but categorically rejected the U.S. request on export subsidies. He argued that Japan had always respected the existing OECD guidelines on which an agreement had just been reached; therefore, it would not be wise to engage in another lengthy discussion of the same issue. Furthermore, since interest-rate levels and currency strengths differ, establishing a single export-credit guideline would not be easy. Finally, Mr. Murayama explained that the entire subject called for expert knowledge, that is, studies and consultations with MITI. In pointing this out, the finance minister clarified the fact that he could not make a decision without consulting his bureaucracy. In response, Secretary Blumenthal assured Mr. Murayama that he was not asking for a decision, but only wanted the finance minister to understand that the existing guidelines were insufficient and incapable of preventing excessive competition in export financing.

When Finance Minister Murayama explained the measures Japan took to please the United States, Mr. Blumenthal did not express any satisfaction, primarily because he was skeptical of Japanese intentions. He still believed that Japan maintained protectionist measures, even though Mr. Murayama claimed exactly the opposite. Although Mr. Blumenthal perceived Japan as being tough and uncooperative, Mr. Murayama was very proud of Japan's MTN initiatives and advance concessionary offers. He firmly believed that there was ample evidence to prove Japan's concessions to be larger than those offered by the United States and the European community. (It is important to note that several high Japanese officials believed that by offering voluntary concessions in advance, they had made a mistake because the United States and Europe did not appreciate the offer made in the traditional spirit of *Giri* and *Ninjo*).[17]

When Mr. Murayama asked the United States to help stabilize the yen-dollar exchange rate, Mr. Blumenthal rejected his request, saying that basics should be remedied first because, otherwise, Congress would not want to cooperate on this matter. From the Japanese point of view, this was discrimination, because the United States agreed to execute a currency swap agreement with the Federal Republic of Germany. (Ironically, the United States eventually had to ask Japan to help defend the dollar when the rescue measures were launched on November 1, 1978.)

The communication gaps and misperceptions that produced friction over the macroeconomic policy can be illustrated by this meeting. Secretary Blumenthal, for example, did not explain to—let alone consult with—the Japanese about U.S. policy plans. While in principle, U.S. adminstrations may intend to inform allies about policy plans, in reality, they frequently fail to do so. This might be attributable to the U.S. style of leadership, which does not necessarily involve consultation with followers. Although such leadership takes less time than the consensual decision-making process of the Japanese, it is also more vulnerable to inconsistency and lack of cooperation by followers.

In contrast, the Japanese finance minister immediately suggested consultation with MITI and expert analysis of the problems. This implied a bottom-up, participative, decision-making approach in which all affected parties have an opportunity to present their views and to agree on a course of action. Although it is slow, such a process may prevent major errors of policy formulation.

Another significant feature of the Blumenthal-Murayama meeting was the difference in the background of the two cabinet members. Mr. Blumenthal, holder of a Ph.D. in economics and an expert on trade, possessed the needed expertise. In contrast, Mr. Murayama, although a former top-level MOF career official, was a generalist. Because his background was in the area of taxation, he was able to respond spontaneously and effectively only to the problem of export-financing subsidy.

A follow-up attempt to retard the intensification of frictions was made by Undersecretary of State for Economic Affairs Cooper and Deputy Foreign Minister Miyazaki in Washington in early October.

At the beginning of the meeting, Mr. Cooper immediately announced that a 7 percent economic growth rate and a substantial reduction in the current-account surplus would be important not only to Japan, but also to the rest of the world. He was followed by other members of the U.S. delegation, who requested that Japan change its economic orientation from exports to domestic consumption, and use the benefits of the dollar depreciation to reduce import prices. The Americans also expressed skepticism about the effectiveness of Japan's emergency imports of uranium, aircraft, and other products, and called them "bookkeeping" operations.

The U.S. delegates then expressed hope for a significant improvement in the U.S. trade account for 1979 due to a gradual recovery of the world economy, the effects of the declining dollar, lower than previously expected energy imports, lower inflation, and greater emphasis on export promotion. Thus, the top economists of the Carter administration were convinced as early as the fall of 1978 that the U.S. trade account would significantly improve in 1979, although they did not specifically say so during the discussions.

Following Mr. Miyazaki's visit, additional discussions were held by Japanese Vice-Finance Minister Sagami and Treasury Undersecretary Solomon. Mr. Solomon, like others before him, urged the Japanese to achieve a 7 percent growth rate and to reduce the current-account surplus, and warned that if Japan failed to achieve either one of these goals, antagonism in the United States could increase. He worried about the political implications of pressures on the dollar and expressed pessimism concerning the Japanese emergency import measures because he doubted that they changed the basics and because he was afraid that they would decrease long-term imports. Finally, Mr. Solomon suggested that Japan improve its external balances through increasing economic assistance programs, importing more grain from the United States, and opening up government procurement to foreign firms.

Although the weak U.S. dollar, inflation, and external imbalances were no less the responsibility of the United States than of other countries, Mr. Solomon's guest did not challenge the U.S. position. Because Japanese negotiators avoid open confrontation, Mr. Sagami did not assert that the United States was equally responsible for curbing inflation, strengthening the dollar, and restoring the trade balance through fiscal and monetary discipline. Such culturally conditioned behavior, however, did not mean that he agreed with Mr. Solomon, who may have mistaken the minister's nonchallenging attitude for consent.

As the year 1978 drew to an end, it became apparent that, despite stimulative measures, the Japanese economy had been growing at a rate much slower than 7 percent. By November, most MOF officials were skeptical about the target and pointed out that since nearly 40 percent of expenditures were generated through borrowing, the use of further fiscal measures was limited. In addition, due to the stimulative measures, inflation picked up again.

Nevertheless, non-Japanese economists—including those in the international organizations—continued to believe that the Japanese economy should grow faster than 5 or 6 percent. From the Japanese point of view, they were wrong, because they ignored the structural changes that the Japanese economy had experienced between 1960 and 1970, such as the persistent excess capacity in the textile and shipbuilding industries. Why, under these circumstances, only the Japanese economy should continue to grow rapidly, remained an annoying puzzle to most officials in Tokyo.

At the Bonn summit conference, the 7 percent target was accepted by Japan, primarily to help reduce the trade- and current-account surpluses. Thus, from the viewpoint of the Japanese economic policy formulators, as long as the external imbalances were narrowed—regardless of the measures—domestic economic growth should have been of no concern to anybody but the Japanese. Japan should have been allowed to find its own pace, one that was compatible with an acceptable rate of inflation, unemployment, and other domestic economic factors.

The Japanese could not understand why U.S. officials—especially such highly regarded economists as Richard Cooper, Anthony Solomon, and Henry Owen—insisted that Japan live up to its growth commitment. Cooper even argued that Japan should grow domestically at a 9 percent annual rate because the external sector's growth rate was sharply declining due to surging imports and sluggish exports. To the Japanese policy formulators, this seemed like a confusion of ends and means because the real end was to reduce Japan's trade- and current-account surplus, and the 7 percent growth rate was supposed to be only the means to this end. In other words, the United States continued to urge Japan to grow at a 7 percent rate, while Japanese officials grew increasingly more doubtful about the rationality of such a demand.

However, Prime Minister Fukuda also stubbornly continued to insist on 7 percent growth. When high-level MOF officials, emphasizing its irrational nature and probable negative effects on inflation and budgetary deficits, tried to persuade him to yield, he called them incompetent and uncommitted. Mr. Fukuda, an adept, former high-level MOF-career official, of course, knew what he was demanding. But credibility, spirit, determination, and commitment transcended his pragmatic considerations: trying to do his best until the very end was more important to him than the achievement of his goal. He did this because according to Japanese cultural norms, doing one's best—even if the goal cannot be achieved—is considered to be an ultimate virtue. In contrast, being half-committed is not acceptable, even if the objective is achieved. Thus, whether they supported him or not, the Japanese understood the reasons for Mr. Fukuda's actions. Subconsciously, Mr. Fukuda himself, of course, also expected the international community to appreciate his efforts, although he never said so publicly.

As time went on and the Japanese economy grew much more slowly than the government projected, U.S. policy formulators became increasingly more annoyed and frustrated with the widening gap between the government's claims and reality. In the pragmatic U.S. culture, though attitudes are important, the achievement of goals is more important. Accordingly, while Mr. Fukuda was understood in Japan, U.S. policy formulators began to talk about Japanese insincerity. Simply put, integrity—understood as deeds matching words—is one of the highest virtues in U.S. culture; in contrast, unyielding determination, even if unsuccessful, is more highly valued in Japan.

U.S. scholars like Lawrence Krause and Robert Solomon of the Brookings Institution—who know Japan well—asked why the FY 1978 forecast could not be changed, since it was unrealistic.[18] The United States, they argued, recognizing the fallibility of most predictions, revised forecasts as frequently as quarterly or even monthly. Therefore, Americans would not understand Japanese insistence on the target; as a result, tensions between the two countries would increase.

Through arduous efforts, MOF officials eventually persuaded Prime Minister Fukuda to announce that the Japanese economy would not be able to achieve 7 percent growth. This happened shortly before Mr. Fukuda, to continue as prime minister, had to be reelected as president of the LDP at the party convention in early December. Most Japanese considered Mr. Fukuda's reelection a foregone conclusion, but to everyone's surprise, through a very complex political process, Masayoshi Ohira upset Mr. Fukuda. MOF officials now had to ask Mr. Ohira to announce the abandonment of the 7 percent growth rate.

On December 8, in his first press conference as prime minister, Mr. Ohira announced that Japan was abandoning the 7 percent growth target because it was difficult to achieve.[19] To underline his point he added that " 'setting a goal . . . and driving madly toward it is not realistic.' "[20]

The Carter administration's reaction was immediate and sharp. Frustrated by the continuing Japanese trade surplus, worn out by the difficult bilateral negotiations, and, in 1979, concerned with congressional acceptance of the MTN agreement, President Carter sent Prime Minister Ohira a strongly critical letter in which he expressed regret that Japan had abandoned the growth target and urged—despite the prevailing skepticism even among U.S. officials—that the prime minister continue working toward the goal in FY 1978.[21] The letter had most likely been drafted by Ambassador Owen in consultation with Richard Cooper and Anthony Solomon, and it was interpreted by the Japanese, though probably erroneously, as a threat that unless Japan reduced the trade surplus with the United States, President Carter might not attend the Tokyo economic summit scheduled for June 1979.[22]

Concerned that Mr. Ohira might change Mr. Fukuda's cooperative policies, the Carter administration reminded Japan of its international responsibilities. A high State Department official, for example, expressed his fear that Mr. Ohira, as a former MOF official, was probably too domestically oriented and inward-looking.[23] The abandonment of such an important international pledge as the 7 percent growth-rate target at such an inopportune time could not be explained otherwise. U.S. officials, however, were mistaken. As a matter of fact, Mr. Ohira was one of the most internationally versed Japanese politicians, having attended numerous multilateral meetings as a minister of finance and having served as the chairman of the Finance Minister's Conference (the Group of 10), the most authoritative and influential international group dealing with world monetary and trade affairs. U.S. officials did not realize that the renunciation of the 7 percent growth target was decided through the bureaucratic policy formulation process, and only with Mr. Fukuda's grudging agreement. Mistakenly, they attributed the abandonment to the change in prime ministers, the same way that policy changes in the United States can be attributed to the election of a new president. Thus, not realizing that in Japan bureaucratically determined policies can easily survive cabinet changes, the Carter administration reacted excessively. As could be expected, the Japanese saw the strong U.S. reaction as another expression of pressure.

Recognizing the importance of good U.S.-Japan relations, Prime Minister Ohira explained to President Carter that Japan's inability to achieve 7 percent growth was attributable to external factors such as a strong yen. Nevertheless, the new Ohira administration was still committed to a growth rate of more than 6 percent, as well as to the reduction of the current-account surplus for FY 1979.

In February 1979, Prime Minister Ohira send Ambassador Yasukawa to the United States to explain his economic policies and to assess the political climate in Washington. The mission was also supposed to eliminate misunderstandings before the Carter-Ohira summit meeting scheduled for May.

Mr. Yasukawa, a former Japanese ambassador to the United States, replaced Mr. Ushiba as minister for external economic affairs in the new Ohira administration. He was a close friend of the prime minister and was known to reflect his views. Naturally, this gave his mission added significance.

He met with several high officials of the Carter administration, among others, with Vice-President Mondale, Undersecretary of State Cooper, Charles Schultze, chairman of the President's Council of Economic Advisers, and Ambassador Owen who, the Japanese believed, played an important role in formulating President Carter's letter to Prime Minister Ohira. The U.S. officials told Mr. Yasukawa that in order to avoid congressional pressure and to have the 1979 MTN agreement eventually approved, Japan must maintain a relatively high growth rate and reduce its current-account surplus through various import promoting measures, including an adjustment in the exchange rate. More specifically, during the talks with various officials Mr. Yasukawa was told that Japan should: (1) accelerate the reduction of tariffs; (2) include NTT in the MTN government procurement code and create an open bidding system; (3) simplify product standards, inspections, and other import related procedures; and (4) liberalize leather and tobacco imports. As usual, the responsibility for all of these recommendations fell on Japan, but not on the United States; there was no reciprocity of obligations.

When Ambassador Yasukawa eventually met STR Strauss, the U.S. official explained that he had almost given up hope of persuading Congress to accept the Japanese explanations, although he had supported some of the Japanese views. He feared that Japan would realize the significance of the current trade frictions only after a harsh congressional reaction, and complained that the abandonment of the 7 percent growth rate would further accelerate Japanese exports and curb imports. He also added that he lost the support of such important members of Congress as Senators Bentsen, Ribicoff, and Javits.

When Ambassador Yasukawa reported to Prime Minister Ohira that the U.S. attitudes toward Japan had been much more severe than he expected, his remarks caused a great uproar in Japan. They encouraged Japanese newspapers to play on the "U.S. pressure" theme and, thus, to report an ever-increasing "U.S. frustration." The prime minister and the Japanese public were shocked by Mr. Yasukawa's assessment and by the press reports about U.S. displeasure.

Thus, Ambassador Yasukawa unintentionally increased Japanese anxiety by expressing the "more-than-expected" shock he experienced during his U.S. mission. Mr. Yasukawa's attitude can be explained only by assuming that he had probably underestimated U.S. anger, and therefore, was not prepared for what awaited him.

This, of course, is a common danger in special delegations reporting about another nation's concerns. To be truly effective, the Yasukawa delegation should have assessed the degree of frustration that had existed in the United States in the past, and the direction such frustration was taking, and not what it found in relation to its own expectations, which could have been based on erroneous information.

This is not to say that U.S. officials, Congress, and the mass media were not pressuring Japan. The strategy of U.S. officials, in particular of STR Strauss, of using the threat of congressional action (or inaction) to pressure the Japanese, is well illustrated by the congressional hearings on U.S.-Japan trade in early 1978. The hearings were held on February 1, 1978, by Senator Ribicoff, then chairman of the Subcommittee on International Trade of the Senate Finance Committee. The administration was represented by STR Strauss who, having just completed the Ushiba-Strauss joint communiqué, acted like a triumphant general returning from a victorious battle. It was obvious that as the former chairman of the Democratic Party he still had great influence over the Democratic majority of the Senate.[24]

In his opening speech, Ribicoff expressed his anxiety to hear about Strauss' recent consultations with Japan:

> We are most anxious, Mr. Strauss, to hear about the recent consultations with Japan. Last year, Japan ran up an $8 billion trade surplus with the United States. They also ran up a current-account surplus of over $11 billion.
>
> Mr. Strauss has tried to address these problems and has tried to achieve a better trading relationship with Japan . . .[25]

Following Senator Ribicoff, Senator Roth also made a statement that reflected a typical Capitol Hill view. He argued that although Japan was the most important U.S. ally in Asia, it had been so protectionist that the United States had to bargain hard and apply pressure. More specifically, he emphasized:

> Very frankly, I have been disappointed in Japan's foreign economic policies and performance, especially this past year. The Japanese have been beneficiaries of the liberal trade policies of the United States, but it has been highly protectionist at home . . .
>
> What the American people want from Japan is . . . the same access to Japanese markets as the Japanese have to ours . . .
>
> . . . we must continue to bargain hard and apply pressure on Japan to make the changes that are needed.[26]

In response, Mr. Strauss stated that his talks with Japan culminated in the January 13 Ushiba-Strauss joint communiqué, which "—if substantially implemented—could redefine the economic relationship between the United States and Japan."[27] Later, when asked about the agreement, he answered that "We've made a rather dramatic breakthrough in terms of a course of conduct,"[28] which he must have honestly believed. However, he also recognized the remaining problems and observed:

> The ultimate value of these consultations depends largely on what we do to follow through on our efforts . . .
> If we neglect this aspect, in my judgment we will end up with a few minor trading concessions at best. If we follow up properly, we may, together, Congress and the executive branch, have truly brought about a major, positive step forward in our international trade posture for the benefit of every American and, indeed, the world.[29]

Thus, a joint executive-congressional follow-up to the just-concluded negotiations was set. In a similar vein, Mr. Strauss stressed how helpful Capitol Hill pressures were in gaining concessions from Japan:

> My experience was that those men from the Hill who had been in Japan for the 30 days prior to the time I was there were exceedingly helpful. The very day we were negotiating, Senator Kennedy, for example, happened to be coming back from China. He made a tough speech in Tokyo and it was meaningful.
> It helped us in those negotiations, and we used it . . .
> . . . the pressures I feel, I would like the Japanese to feel, and the Germans to feel, and the European Community generally, everybody to feel some of the pressures from the Congress that I feel.[30]

Congressional suspicions about Japan's intentions were expressed by Senator Hathaway, who addressed Mr. Strauss by saying:

> Now, you have been quoted in the press as saying that the agreement reached in Tokyo was a dramatic breakthrough . . .
> These promises on the part of the Japanese Government are similar to those made in 1971 . . .
> When these promises were made, the United States had a $3.2 billion trade deficit with Japan. It has now reached approximately $9.5 billion, and it appears to be growing. So much for the promises from our trading partners.
> . . . we are now hearing that Japan will soon tell the U.S. President why they cannot live up to their January promises. Thus, 1971 seems to be repeating itself.[31]

U.S. officials in both the legislative and executive branches believed that Japan would either renege on its promises or procrastinate to achieve minimum compliance. Most of these Americans failed to consider the Japanese decision-making style, which emphasized consensus, and, therefore, could be very time-consuming, sometimes producing only limited or temporary results. Therefore, Americans were apt to blame the unsatisfactory outcomes on political weakness or deliberate delaying tactics. They believed that they had to resort to pressure.

However, as pointed out before, already in 1978–1979, but even now during the 1980s, many Japanese openly resent such congressional pressure. As a matter of fact, the "very specific suggestions" of Mr. Strauss and Congress that Japan must achieve a 7 percent economic growth rate and must reduce the current-account surplus by a certain deadline angered officials in some domestically oriented ministries, as, for example, MOF, so much that they openly accused the United States of interfering in domestic matters. According to the "Wise Men's Report":

> American pressure has been most resented and least effective where it has been regarded as intruding upon "domestic issues" as in the 1977–78 effort by American officials to secure Japanese agreement to certain macroeconomic targets.[32]

Thus, during all of 1978 and part of 1979 U.S. and Japanese policy formulators held opposing views on the macroeconomic policy questions raised by the differing international and domestic interests of the two countries. U.S. officials believed that Japan did not live up to its international responsibilities, while the Japanese maintained that they had done as much as they could reasonably be expected to do. Nevertheless, once the conflict was settled—chiefly through the Carter-Ohira meeting in May 1979—it did not recur again. This seems to indicate that even the most protracted U.S.–Japan trade conflicts may be, at least partially, settled through top-level negotiation channels.

THE INCIDENT OF THE IMPORT QUOTAS ON CITRUS AND BEEF

While all of the trade policy formulation incidents discussed in this book shed light on the Japanese policy formulation process, perhaps none of them illustrates better the long-lasting sense of frustration that has developed on both sides of the Pacific than the disagreement over the import quotas on citrus and beef.[33]

Ever since the dispute began in 1977 (and it is still going on in 1983), the United States viewed the Japanese import limitations on these two agricultural products as symbols of the "closed" Japanese market. On the other hand, the Japanese see the U.S. position not only as unreasonable, but, at times, even as hypocritical.

Japan is the world's largest importer of agricultural products, and the United States is Japan's foremost supplier. In 1981, for example, the United States exported a total of $6.5 billion worth of agricultural commodities to Japan.[34] Of this amount, about $279 million represented beef and veal and approximately $416 million citrus fruits.[35] This was around 60 percent of all the beef and 40 percent of all the citrus fruits the United States exports worldwide.[36]

While—as reported by the U.S. Department of Agriculture—in 1982 U.S. farm exports to Japan were somewhat lower, Japan was still by far the United States' most important market. Table 5-1 presents the value of U.S. farm exports by destination for the year 1982.

Nevertheless, as pointed out before, U.S. policy formulators focus on the Japanese agricultural quotas—which are against GATT rules—as symbols of the closed Japanese market and of the "unfair practices" of Japanese trade policy.

Given the above-mentioned statistics, most Japanese cannot understand why U.S. trade officials continue to attach such importance to the quotas. Of course, there are compelling domestic reasons for the United States to pressure Japan on agricultural matters. In comparison to the manufacturing sector, the agricultural industry has long been more export-oriented. In FY 1982, for example, agricultural exports accounted for 20 percent of all U.S. exports, earning about $39 billion.[37] Two of every five acres of harvested cropland produce for the export market, and the United States dominates world markets in several major agricultural products such as coarse grain and soybeans. The United States is also a major exporter of meat, poultry, fruit, and vegetables. But even so, the trade potential in citrus and beef with Japan—given a completely free access to the Japanese market—amounts to only a small proportion of the total trade between the two countries. Thus, the

Table 5-1.   U.S. Farm Exports by Destination, 1982 (in billions of dollars)

Country	1982 Exports
Japan	$ 5.5
Netherlands	3.0
Soviet Union	1.9
Canada	1.8
South Korea	1.6
China	1.5
Spain	1.5
Federal Republic of Germany	1.4
Mexico	1.2
Taiwan	1.2

Source: *New York Times*, 21 February, 1983, p. D4.

elimination of the quotas would not even make a dent in the U.S. bilateral trade deficit. Furthermore, as long as the United States also restricts beef and citrus imports and maintains regulations barring the sale of Japanese mandarin oranges to all but six states, it is very hard for most Japanese to understand why Americans insist on viewing only Japan as a closed market for these two items.[38]

The political and social reasons for the Japanese insistence on the citrus and beef import quotas have been discussed in the previous chapter. By now, they should be reasonably well known and understood even outside Japan, although many Japanese are not quite convinced that Americans have fully appreciated the extent to which this domestic political problem burdens the Japanese government, which is partially responsible for the farmers' plight.

Because some years ago the government had directed a shift from growing rice to raising cattle and harvesting fruits such as Mikan (mandarin oranges), many of Japan's farmers often go through a difficult period caused by overproduction of Mikan and certain other products. Beef cattle farmers are also frequently in trouble because of excess supplies and weak demand.

Thus, Japanese citrus and cattle farmers are—to some extent—victims of the government's policy. Mikan growers are particularly hard hit, having invested a considerable amount of borrowed money in the construction of greenhouses for Mikan trees. The Ministry of Agriculture, Forestry and Fisheries (MOAFF) suggested that farmers equip these greenhouses with heating systems to advance Mikan harvesting by one or two months, from September–October to July–August, because the earlier Mikan obtains a much higher price. To increase demand, some farmers were even persuaded to install cooling systems to color Mikan. In view of the energy price hikes, the need for such facilities was questionable, but farmers had already made the investment under the guidance of the government.

Under these circumstances, highly competitive U.S. oranges represent a major threat to the Japanese Mikan farmers, and MOAFF still feels guilty enough to try to protect them from the consequences of its policy.[39] Because at the time of the 1977–1978 conflict few U.S. officials were informed of this dilemma in detail, they were upset by the citrus quota limiting U.S. exports.

To make matters worse, Japanese politicians are hard pressed by the desperate Mikan farmers who formed an association to oppose the liberalization of imports. The pressures are additionally intensified by the sectionalism among the different ministries, particularly MOAFF, MOFA, and MITI. The farmers and MOAFF insist that they should not be sacrificed on the altar of trade frictions caused by excessive export of manufactured goods. But MOFA and MITI share the view that Japan should not provide justification for U.S. protectionism, an action that could be fatal, just because of a small amount of citrus imports. Because of the traditionally strong sectionalism of the Japanese bureaucracy, it is impossible for any of the competing ministries to coordinate the dispute effectively at the administrative level.

What is true for citrus also proves true for beef. The Japanese soon discovered that the United States maintained restrictive quotas for beef from Australia, New Zealand, and Argentina, yet insists upon the liberalization of Japanese beef import in accordance with the principles of free trade.

It is interesting to note that from the beginning the citrus and beef import quota incident closely paralleled the events of the macroeconomic policy conflict, although the participants differed.

The Carter administration's major efforts to open up the Japanese market to U.S. agricultural exports began in September 1977 when a delegation from the STR's office went to Japan to disucss the MTN negotiations. During the follow-up, subcabinet-level consultations, which concentrated on the increasing trade imbalance between the two countries, U.S. officials restated their specific citrus and beef import demands.

Japan was not responsive. MOAFF officials argued that they could not eliminate orange and beef import quotas because of overproduction and a lack of demand. The negative Japanese response disappointed U.S. officials who feared that continued trade tensions might harm overall relations and increase anti-Japan sentiments, thereby promoting protectionist moves against the MTN agreement. So, they decided to present another set of even more specific demands to get a response. Some Japanese officials, particularly in MOFA, agreed with this strategy, because they believed that only such demands could influence the hardcore, proagriculture interest groups. But the move turned out to be counterproductive because some high MOF and MOAFF officials resented the U.S. strategy, which they viewed as an excessive intervention into Japan's domestic economy.

From the beginning of the dispute, U.S. officials believed that while oranges and beef imports were economically insignificant, it would look good to Congress if the United States could obtain concessions. A special STR mission headed by General Counsel Rivers was sent to Tokyo to make it clear to the Japanese how important concessions were for the congressional approval of the MTN agreement. In other words, U.S. negotiators used the "displeasure of Congress" argument in the same manner as they did during the macroeconomic policy dispute.

Shortly after General Counsel Rivers left Tokyo, Prime Minister Fukuda reshuffled his cabinet, and in its first meeting established an intracabinet unit called the "Economic Ministers Group" (*Keizai Kakuryo*

Kaigi). This clearly indicated that the effective coordination of Japan's agricultural trade policy among the different ministries required political leadership at the highest level of government.

While efforts at the highest level of the Japanese government resulted in an offer that the Japanese hoped would be accepted, the domestic reaction to the offer was swift and powerful. Alarmed by the rapid move toward import liberalization, about 40 Diet members organized a "Beef Caucus" (Parliamentary League for the Promotion of Livestock Industry) and adopted a resolution strongly opposing any changes in the agricultural import procedures. Caucus membership quickly grew to 200, and a separate "Fruit Caucus" (Fruit Promotion Parliamentary League) of 150 Diet members was organized.

As usual, increasing Japanese resistance only heightened U.S. pressure. For example, STR Strauss—in a meeting with a visiting LDP delegation—stated that:

> Should Japan fail to make an appropriate response to the latest U.S. demands . . . an anti-Japanese import-control bill would be passed by Congress and Japanese products would be pushed out of the U.S. market within 90 days.[40]

U.S. farmers and their supporters continued to press for the total elimination of Japan's quotas, arguing that such a move would benefit not only the agricultural industry, but all Americans. Members of Congress had already been aroused by the bilateral talks and were therefore very alert to the symbolic importance of citrus and beef. As could be expected, Mr. Strauss and other U.S. officials believed that to ensure congressional approval of the MTN agreement major Japanese concessions were required.

Congress was exerting very strong pressure on Japan. While the conflict was intensified by erroneous press reports in both Japan and the United States, much misleading information was published by U.S. congressional committees in the form of special reports.

From the Japanese point of view, the "Jones Reports" were the most influential and misleading because they were prepared over a short period of time by researchers with vested political interests and relatively modest resources.[41]

The reports were commissioned because of the growing trade imbalance during 1977 and 1978. Concern was heightened by the negotiations that culminated in the Strauss-Ushiba joint communiqué of January 1978. Several members of Congress, alarmed by the publicized trade imbalance, insisted that Congress insure the implementation of the communiqué.

Member of Congress James Jones of Oklahoma was the driving force behind this effort. He became interested in U.S.-Japan trade when he tried to expand the Japanese market for Oklahoma beef in 1977. Mr. Jones feared that U.S. anger at the growing trade deficit with Japan could produce a protectionist movement in the United States. Recognizing that the Strauss-Ushiba joint communiqué would be fulfilled only through congressional pressure, he proposed the formation of a task force to monitor implementation of the agreement.

The task force on U.S.-Japan trade was appointed by Congressman Charles Vanik, chairman of the Subcommittee on Trade of the House Ways and Means Committee in April 1978. Its goals were to "monitor the implementation of the Strauss-Ushiba Agreement of January 13, 1978, and to advise the subcommittee on U.S.-Japan trade problems."[42] One staff member saw the task force as having two additional goals, namely, " 'to give a kick in the butt to the U.S. bureaucracy enforcing the agreement and to do the same to the Japanese.' "[43]

The final report prepared by the task force became one of the most influential publications on U.S.-Japan trade. Led by Mr. Jones, its authors included Rep. Abner Mikva (D.-Ill.) and Rep. Bill Frenzel (R.-Minn.). But before it was released on January 2, 1979, the task force issued an interim report on August 9, 1978, which also raised several controversial issues.

The interim report stated that the task force was "seriously concerned about the lack of any progress in the Trade Facilitation Committee [TFC]. Since the task force's creation in April, not a single new case has been resolved in the TFC. . . . The typical Japanese response has been either to provide technical counterarguments of questionable plausibility or to claim that the problem is not susceptible to 'simple solution.' "[44] Although the report acknowledged "the inability of both [U.S.] government and industry to place greater priority on exports,"[45] it was convinced that the Japanese would not do anything without constant pressure. It emphasized that "the consistent roadblocks and delays thrown up to trade liberalization, particularly in beef and citrus, continue to provide an important source of frustration and a symbol of the trade problems between our two countries."[46] Such arguments increased pressures on Japan to an extent that most Japanese could not understand. In particular, they wondered why the United States focused on items that made up a relatively insignificant part of the total bilateral billion trade deficit.

While in general, the final Jones report did contribute to a better understanding of the bilateral trade problems, it also disseminated erroneous information about Japan, thereby intensifying the trade conflict. In spite of this, the Japanese government responded with only a six-page summary of critical comments developed by the various ministries. This short paper was distributed to Japanese policy formulators only two months after the final Jones report was published and was not readily available to other interested parties. Many Japanese officials were frustrated that in addition to its limited distribution, the summary paper did not address, much less challenge, most of the controversial claims. This tepid Japanese response is a good illustration of the passive siege mentality prevailing in the government bureaucracy as well as of the negative consequences such a mentality has on the trade policy formulation process.

Because it pointed out alleged problems in U.S.-Japan trade relations, and called for congressional pressures, the report had a significant impact on Japanese policy formulators and businessmen. However, while it charged Japan with unfair trade practices, the report ignored similar problems on the U.S. side, such as the "Buy American" requirements and U.S. import quotas on beef from Australia, New Zealand, and Argentina.

Nevertheless, the Jones reports provided some useful insights. First of all, they showed that the U.S. Congress participated not only in trade policy formulation but also in trade negotiations, thus enabling Congress to pressure Japan both speedily and effectively. But the authors also confirmed the fact that congressional members and their staffs were less informed than officials from the executive branch were. Members of Congress obtained much of their information from business and labor lobbyists who continued to refer to past Japanese restrictions when making their cases on Capitol Hill.

The reports also revealed that the Japanese government was the only de facto negotiator. This handicap was complicated by the government's ineffectiveness in meeting the well-organized and persistent attacks by the U.S. Congress because officials were, in principle, required to be far more reserved and cautious than politicians were. In fact, it was almost impossible for them publicly to denounce or criticize either the U.S. or Japanese legislature. The Japanese were also limited because they lacked an effective negotiating coordinator, such as the STR; consequently, when congressional criticism was directed simultaneously at such diverse ministries as MITI, MOF, or MOAFF, the government could not develop a coherent set of timely responses.

Finally, the Japanese response to the report showed that neither the government nor the Diet had put anything convincing on paper to publicly influence trade negotiations. While, as pointed out before, the government, at least, circulated a short response, Diet members merely responded to the pressure from their constituencies but did not publish any formal position papers or studies to convey their point of view to the Americans.

Japanese farmers, however, were very active in defending their interests. Led by the national organization Zenchu, they pressured Japanese policy formulators through individual visits with Japan's chief negotiators, mass demonstrations, and aggressive articles in their newspaper (*Nihon Nogyo Shimbun*). They warned politicians that they would never forget any "sell-out" of their interests.

The negotiation style of the U.S. officials offended Japanese sensibilities more than, for example, during the macroeconomic policy incident. Always very concerned about the formalities of international relations, the Japanese were very upset by the "open" and "honest" negotiation approach of the U.S. officials. What STR General Counsel Rivers may have viewed as a "forthright" presentation of the U.S. position during his initial visit, the Japanese saw as unacceptable "bullying" by a "schoolmaster" who presumed to lecture them about what was right for their country. STR Strauss' tactic of briskly breaking off negotiations whenever it served his purpose—while, undoubtedly accepted negotiation ploys in the United States and Western Europe—struck many Japanese as arrogant, ill-mannered, and uncalled for. Such widely divergent views on what constitutes a mutually acceptable approach to international negotiations has, of course, long plagued U.S.-Japan trade relations.

The initial stage of the import quota conflict was eventually settled around the end of 1978.[47] Japanese citrus and beef producers acquiesced in the settlement, apparently satisfied that they had prevented full liberalization. Spokesmen for the U.S. citrus and beef industries were also satisfied and subsequently endorsed the MTN agreement, which U.S. negotiators were afraid they would not endorse unless convinced that the settlement served their interests.

During the second half of 1979, the trade frictions between the United States and Japan subsided, and for a while economic relations between the two countries were tranquil. Improvements in the bilateral trade balance, the "GAO Report," the shift of the mass media's attention from trade to energy matters and, in particular, the summit meeting between President Carter and Prime Minister Ohira in May 1979 were the major reasons for the substantially improved economic relations.[48]

But it was just a matter of time before the citrus and beef quota problems surfaced again. As soon as the bilaterial trade balances between 1979–1981 indicated a continual increase in the U.S. deficit, U.S. policy formulators again focused on the quotas as symbols of the "closed Japanese market."

It must be pointed out, however, that during these recurring periods of verbal jousting more and more Americans began to appreciate the domestic political dilemma the Japanese government faces with respect to agricultural imports. An article published in the *New York Times* in early 1982 is a case in point:

No guns have been brandished nor shots fired, but a "bloodless war," as one Government official put it, is raging in Japan.

At odds in the battle are the nation's two most powerful political constituencies: the business community and the agricultural lobby. It is big business, especially representatives of export-dependent manufacturing industries, versus small farmers—the most efficient sector of the Japanese economy against the least efficient.

The conflict shows that while Japan may be more tightly knit than most Western nations, it by no means speaks with one voice. Nor is its Government immune to the claims of special-interest groups or the realities of partisan politics.[49]

Nevertheless, when halfway through 1982 it became clear that the bilateral trade surplus of Japan for the year would be around 20 billion dollars, the issue again erupted. Negotiations over the citrus and beef quotas held in Hawaii in October 1982 were eventually suspended and the mass media in both countries had a field day publishing the real or alleged statements of past and present policy formulators concerning the gravity of the conflict.[50] As Japan's former chief negotiator and ambassador to the United States, Nobuhiko Ushiba put it:

Recent statements in Washington and Tokyo appear to presage a new round of acrimonious trade conflict between Japan and the United States. Heated debate is becoming an almost annual occurrence, eroding the good will and the ability to cooperate between the two largest market economies.

Suspension of negotiations in Hawaii in October over Japan's agricultural quotas, especially for beef and citrus fruits, illustrates some mistakes both sides have been making. Neither beef nor citrus is a "big ticket" item in the overall Japan-U.S. trade balance, but they are symbolically important to both countries. To Americans, they are a visible market barrier, and symbolic of what they regard as an unwillingness of the Japanese to take politically courageous acts to make their market as open as the American market. To the Japanese farmer organizations, they are symbolic of the willingness of the Japanese government to protect the welfare of Japan's farming community, which sees itself under increasing siege from much cheaper foreign imports.[51]

As pointed out in the previous chapter, during the preparation of Prime Minister Nakasone's visit to Washington in January 1983, Japanese policy formulators followed the ancient tradition of putting together an appropriate *Miyage* (gift) for President Reagan. They were also very busy ensuring that no unpleasant confrontation would mar the meeting of the two heads-of-state. Well before the prime minister left Tokyo for Washington, they announced that Japan intended to reduce or eliminate entirely import duties on 47 farm commodities and 28 industrial products and to expand import quotas for a half dozen farm items, such as fruit puree and noncitrus fruit juice.

While the preparations were taking place, Japan's farmers, under the leadership of Zenchu, made themselves heard again. In early January 1983, they organized the largest profarm and anti-U.S. demonstration seen in Japan in years. They also submitted a petition to the Japanese government demanding that import quotas for, among others, citrus and beef, be retained. Thus, the Japanese government was caught again in the old dilemma; how to respond to U.S. pressure without antagonizing the powerful farm lobby. Not surprisingly, it decided to placate the farmers by promising not to give in to U.S. demands and the United States by trying to explain that its farm dilemma has the same political significance in Japan as the protection of the automobile industry has in the United States. It also offered other trade liberalization measures.

Thus, at the time of this writing the citrus and beef quota conflict not only remains unresolved, but continues as the focal point of U.S.–Japan trade conflicts whenever the U.S. side wants to launch an attack on Japan's trade policies. The quotas serve as a convenient target; they are protectionist, they are contradicting GATT rules, they have been the subject of U.S. complaints and pressure for many years. Furthermore, in spite of some minor adjustments, the Japanese have been quite intransigent about their elimination. Consequently, there appears to be a standstill in the debate and what both sides can at best hope for is that in spite of the occasionally inflammatory rhetoric and actions, the dispute will not get out of control over the next few years. No doubt, some day Japan will have to eliminate the quotas. But the decision as to when that day has arrived is for the Japanese to make; the quotas represent a domestic political dilemma; therefore, only domestic political measures reached through the consensual decision-making process can eliminate them. No amount of U.S. pressure can change this. Therefore, the United States should not exaggerate the symbolic importance of the quotas. It should also realize that only after the current U.S.-Japan agreement on these products expires on March 31, 1984, will the Japanese government be able to even discuss the gradual elimination of these quotas over the long run.

Of course, the Japanese must also realize that their increasingly hardening attitude toward U.S. pressures concerning citrus and beef quotas should not be allowed to degenerate into a rigid and uncompromising position.

Only if both sides realize that this ongoing conflict is beginning to threaten the basic elements of an important and beneficial alliance and trading relationship will they be able to reach a satisfactory solution.

THE INCIDENT OF GOVERNMENT PROCUREMENT

During the 1977–1979 MTN negotiations of the code for government procurement,[52] the United States asked Japan to open up the purchases by Nippon Telephone and Telegraph Company (NTT) to competitive bidding. The Japanese refused on the grounds that most telephone monopolies of the world use the same closed, negotiated-contract system as NTT does.

As a public monopoly, NTT had the sole authority to approve the use of communications equipment manufactured by any company, Japanese or foreign. As could be expected, NTT's policies favored domestic suppliers and substantially limited the purchase of imported telephone equipment. Technical specifications were based on design, rather than performance, and favored products were supplied by a small group of domestic companies known as the "NTT family," to which foreign firms were not admitted.

The U.S. balance of trade in the category of telecommunication products with Japan was quite negative. The deficit went from approximately $3,321 billion in 1978, to $2,786 billion in 1979, $2,991 billion in 1980, and $4,601 billion in 1981.[53]

Even though the United States sold only slightly more to Europe than to Japan, Americans resented the Japanese surpluses, because—to their view—the imbalances represented another example of the "unfair" Japanese trade practices. This, combined with the initially intransigent Japanese position, set the stage for an acrimonious debate between the two trading partners.

In July 1978, when serious discussions of the government procurement code began, Japan offered to open the procurement practices of only central government ministries, such as the Ministry of Finance or Transportation, which would have created a market potential of about $3.5 billion for foreign firms. This was well below the offer of the Europeans or Americans, who wanted to provide business opportunities of over $10 billion to foreign companies.

In order to bridge the gap between the Japanese, U.S., and European offers, the United States asked Japan to include in its offer the purchases of major public corporations, including, among others, the Nippon Telephone and Telegraph (NTT), the Japan National Railway (JNR), and the Japan Tobacco Monopoly Corporation.

In the early stages of the dispute, the United States was interested in NTT only because of the amount of its purchases, not because of the high-technology equipment it procured. In other words, NTT was seen as the corporation in the Japanese government whose purchasing power was large enough to increase Japan's offer sufficiently.

The Japanese government did not include NTT in its initial offer chiefly because it did not directly control the corporation and because the European Community (EC) did not include similar corporations in its offer, either. This upset the United States because from its point of view, the Japanese government should have been able to direct NTT, a public corporation created by law in 1952, with 100 percent government ownership.

U.S. officials, however, misunderstood the relationship between the government and NTT's management. When NTT was established, it was given all the responsibility for operating the nation's telephone, telegraph, and other communications services. The Ministry of Posts and Telecommunications was given supervisory control over NTT, but this authority allowed the ministry to issue only broad guidelines. Specific operational decisions, particularly in the area of procurement, were in the hands of NTT's management. In time the company developed into a giant corporate bureaucracy that the government could not control. Its relationship with the "family" of NTT companies was continually strengthened by the annual *Amakudari* of numerous company executives into responsible positions of the "family" companies. The resulting close relationship is one of the major reasons that the NTT bureaucracy has strongly resisted government pressures to open up procurement to foreign companies. Unfortunately, initially, U.S. negotiators did not sufficiently appreciate these circumstances, and consequently, perceived the nonresponsiveness of the Japanese government as deliberate procrastination and reluctance to cooperate.

Congressional attention quickly focused on the issue that U.S. senators identified as another symbol of Japan's closed market. Soon, outbursts and frustration were common in both the United States and Japan. The dispute became interwoven with the preparations for two summit meetings scheduled for mid-1979—the Carter-Ohira summit in May and the Tokyo seven nation summit in June.

The unique characteristics of the Japanese trade policy formulation process made matters worse. Lacking a central trade negotiator (like the STR in the United States), and because MOFA was in charge of the MTN negotiations, the responsibility of maintaining liaison with NTT during the dispute was naturally given to MOFA. The foreign service officials, however, were handicapped in their efforts to deal with the company in two ways. First, they had no domestic constituency; their clients, in fact, were abroad rather than in Japan. Second, because of the highly technical nature of the dispute, MOFA lacked the necessary expertise. For example, MOFA could not challenge NTT's claim that technical considerations prohibited competitive bidding.

Thus, in the summer of 1978, the Japanese government was unable to honor the United States' request that NTT be included in the discussions of the government-procurement code. As a result, NTT's management, which had nothing to do with the multilateral trade negotiations, was not really aware of the seriousness of the emerging conflict. In the early stages of the dispute, MOFA may have also conveyed the wrong message to NTT by assigning only middle-level officials (section chiefs and below) to the case. MOFA's admonitions that it should help to successfully conclude the MTN were too weak to overcome management's independence and internal politics.

The Japanese reluctance to respond to U.S. demands quickly increased pressure. Two groups, the Department of Commerce's "U.S.–Japan Trade Facilitation Committee," and the "Task Force on U.S.-Japan Trade" of the House Ways and Means Committee, began to examine NTT's procurement practices.

In November 1978, members of the congressional task force went to Japan to examine alleged trade barriers. There, they asked NTT's management to expand procurement of its high technology to include more foreign firms, particularly to include those from the United States. The meeting, however, was a disaster. The members of Congress were offended because on the day they were scheduled to meet with NTT's President Akigusa, he was unavailable. Although NTT officials explained that he had been unexpectedly summoned to the Diet, the task force members were skeptical and felt that they had been deliberately snubbed. Unfortunately, while the U.S. delegation was still in Japan, Mr. Akigusa was reported to have said that the only thing NTT would buy from the United States would be " 'mops and buckets.' "[54] Whether or not Mr. Akigusa really said this remains unclear, but the effect of the reported statement was electric in that it conveyed a condescending and unyielding attitude.

The task force's reaction to this episode was predictable. Its report, issued in January 1979, included the observation that:

> We could detect no sign that the NTT officials were making any plans to amend their "Buy Japan" policies or to cooperate in making access to the non-NTT interconnect market easier. The interview with NTT officials was one of the low points of our visit in Japan.[55]

The report also stated that "NTT does not appear to have any awareness of the incredibly serious trade problems between our two nations or that NTT procurement policies in particular are one of the sorest points in our bilateral trade."[56] Referring to the overall imbalance in the telecommunications trade, they added: "Since telecommunications is one of the industries 'of the future,' this type of one-sided and unfair trade competition is particularly serious."[57]

The report recommended that the U.S. government either change NTT's procurement practices or find ways to retaliate. It warned that the task force would "raise the issue of ways to encourage the opening of the Japanese telecommunications market during the drafting of the MTN Government Procurement Code implementing legislation,"[58] which STR Strauss planned to submit to Congress in 1979.

As a result of the report, NTT and its procurement practices were strongly criticized in the United States. This generated considerable resentment in Japan, particularly among some of the MOFA officials who had been involved with the case. Most of them believed that NTT is not symbolic of Japan's "closed market," because almost all other telephone systems in the developed world use purchasing methods similar to NTT's.

In December 1978, a U.S. trade delegation and a group of U.S. telecommunications executives arranged for another meeting in Tokyo with government and NTT officials. The discussions focused on NTT's possible purchase of non-Japanese switching equipment, earth stations, and other sophisticated telecommunication products. Sources close to the meeting later reported that NTT rejected all such demands.

Shortly afterwards, STR Strauss sent a letter to Japanese government officials to restate his conviction that any international trade agreement involving the United States and Japan must include the Japanese telephone company and other public corporations. He argued that:

> The position of the United States is that the inclusion of Nippon Telephone and Telegraph under the code is an important contribution which Japan should make to the total MTN package, . . .
> I firmly believe that the failure to include NTT is inconsistent with our mutual objectives and interests and contrary to the principles of our national objectives.[59]

Meanwhile, several other events interfered with the resolution of the NTT dispute. For one thing, because of the long and difficult MTN discussions, particularly the just-concluded agricultural negotiations, STR officials had grown increasingly more frustrated, believing that the painfully slow and difficult talks had yielded only meager results. From the U.S. point of view, Japan's negotiations consisted of conscious delaying tactics aimed at wearing down the opponent ("as one STR official put it, 'they try to frustrate the hell out of you until you do something irresponsible' ").[60] So U.S. officials feared that the same situation, compounded by the difficulties of congressional approval, would arise during the NTT talks.

As pointed out before, throughout most of 1978, the United States' negotiators focused on NTT's procurement volume and the effect its inclusion could have on Japan's overall government procurement offer. However, beginning in late 1978 and early 1979, the U.S. negotiators became more interested in the technological content of NTT's purchases.

In January 1979, U.S. officials explained that while major telecommunications equipment did not have to be placed under an open-bidding system immediately, and while NTT's purchase of office equipment and supplies was not a problem, Japan had to allow all new products developed by U.S. firms to compete through open bidding. In addition, all terminal and other accessory equipment had to be immediately procured under open bidding.

The United States presented these demands to Takashi Yasukawa, Japan's representative for the "Tokyo Round" negotiations in Washington. Officially, the Japanese continued to maintain that NTT procurement could not be opened, but Mr. Yasukawa carried back the impression to Tokyo that the Americans were very concerned and that the fate of the MTN Agreement depended on a settlement. For the talks to be successfully concluded, Japan's offer would have to be increased to between $7–8 billion.

It was at this time that the chairman of the Joint Economic Committee, Senator Bentsen, threatened Japan with an import surcharge. Although Bentsen's statement was not specifically related to the NTT issue, it was a good indication of the kind of leverage Congress provided to U.S. negotiators.

In the meantime, some MOFA officials began to argue—as they usually do—that something had to be done before U.S. pressure and frustration became too intense. But more important than the efforts by MOFA officials was the increasing concern among Japan's top political leadership about the continuing resistance of NTT's management. MITI Minister Esaki even criticized the company in the Diet.

Eventually the government agreed that some concessions would have to be made by NTT. This was a very important move, because while the government's decision did not indicate how far it was willing to go to placate U.S. demands, it signaled to NTT and its supporters that their case was weakening. Unfortunately, the U.S. side did not seem to properly appreciate this decision in the context of the Japanese trade policy formulation process. If they had done so, they could have seen that this decision represented the beginning of the end for NTT.[61]

Without the benefit of this insight the U.S. side increased pressure on Japan. When Ambassador Ushiba presented the government's new offer—which now amounted to about $5 billion in procurement opportunities—to STR Strauss, the U.S. official abruptly terminated the talks after only one day. This, together with the treatment he received from other U.S. officials, offended Mr. Ushiba so deeply that he returned to Tokyo.

Thus the mixture of U.S. pressure and delayed Japanese response together with the mutual inability to appreciate each other's positions and sensibilities led to a blowup. Although evidence suggests that STR Strauss acted the way he did to impress Congress, most Japanese, unfamiliar with U.S. domestic politics, did not know this and were left with bitter feelings toward the "rude" Americans.[62]

The talks collapsed as two deadlines were approaching; thus, a resolution of the NTT dispute was imperative. First, the conclusion of the MTN agreement was scheduled for April 1979. The other important deadline was the U.S.–Japan summit meeting scheduled for the first week in May 1979. As mentioned before, summit meetings with the United States are critical events in Japan's political life. A discussion of the NTT conflict and a possible capitulation by Prime Minister Ohira to U.S. demands at the highest level could have gravely damaged him at home.[63]

Thus, eventually the government instructed NTT to substantially increase both the quality and the quantity of its foreign procurement offer. NTT's president accepted the government's demands and immediately thereafter resigned his position in the traditional Japanese fashion, because as the head of NTT he failed to coordinate properly.

However, when even this new offer was rejected by STR Strauss, the Japanese—for the first time—reacted differently. They were incensed by what they considered to be unreasonable U.S. demands and pressures. A major U.S. newspaper reported that top Japanese officials

. . . have been uncharacteristically blunt in conversations with American reporters, insisting that the U.S. demands are unreasonable and claiming that they amount to direct intervention in domestic affairs.[64]

In a hastily arranged emergency cabinet meeting, the government reached the consensus that it could no longer give in to U.S. demands. Once informed of this decision, STR Strauss changed his strategy and proposed that if Japan fully liberalized NTT's procurement practices by 1985, the United States would go along with Japan's latest offer. While from a U.S. point of view this was a fully acceptable quick "course correction," the Japanese could not immediately respond to it. The inflexibility inherent in the consensual bureaucratic decision-making process made this impossible. Therefore, as on several occasions before, U.S. negotiation strategies combined with an unwillingness to appreciate the plodding nature of the Japanese trade policy formulation process intensified an already bruising conflict. While STR Strauss, in light of the Japanese concern about the summit expected a quick Japanese response, he failed to realize that even under the greatest of pressures the Japanese bureaucracy may move very slowly. As a consequence, only a few days before Prime Minister Ohira's visit to Washington, the NTT conflict remained unresolved.

Members of Congress were apparently even less aware of the situation because they bitterly attacked not only the Japanese government but also personally the prime minister.[65] Not realizing that in Japan even the prime minister is limited by the consensual trade policy formulation process, they deeply embarrassed Ohira who could not respond.[66]

Through a compromise, the NTT conflict was eventually settled shortly before the prime minister's arrival in Washington. The summit took place on schedule and without any problems. NTT procurement practices, however, remained at the center of U.S.–Japan trade relations well after the 1979 compromise agreement. Because NTT's bureaucracy was slow in untangling its close relationship with the company "family" of suppliers, U.S. pressure for quicker action was beginning to increase again in 1982. As a *Business Week* article put it:

> Never has the glare of publicity been so bright at Japan's Nippon Telegraph and Telephone Public Corp. as it has in recent months. Accustomed to running its communications monopoly out of public sight as a close-knit, inbred bureaucracy, the government-owned telephone giant has suddenly become the main symbol in the U.S. drive to open Japanese high-technology markets to foreign suppliers. American executives are zeroing in on NTT because it is the heart of an information processing market that is second only to that of the U.S.[67]

The article also contains the implication that unless NTT's management responds quickly to U.S. demands, congressional pressure—fueled by business circles—could be severe in the near future. More delays by NTT to fully open its procurement to U.S. companies could promote the passage of some type of "local content" legislation aimed at the Japanese automobile industry. In other words, according to the article the stage was set for an eventual replay of the trade conflict cycle involving high-technology products in general and NTT's procurement practices in particular.

The likelihood of such a development was increased by the statements made at a conference of U.S. high-technology producers in Washington in early February 1983. Robert W. Gavin, chairman of Motorola, Inc., strongly attacked the Japanese. According to a report by the *Washington Post*

> . . . he (Gavin) thinks the Japanese are conducting a sustained campaign to reduce the United States to a position of dependence in the electronics industry.[68]

William C. Norris, chairman of Control Data Corporation, argued that

> . . . the way to deal with this Japanese threat is to throw them out of the American research laboratories where they acquire so much of their knowledge.[69]

In describing the attitude of the top executives of the U.S. high-technology industry, the article pointed out that

> These leading figures in the high-technology establishment, who were in Washington for a conference on high-technology industries and public policy sponsored by Government Research Corp., showed no inclination to be conciliatory about what they regard as unfair competitive tactics by their Japanese counterparts.[70]

Mr. Gavin was also reported to have argued that because the Japanese do not believe that the United States is willing to confront their "extreme protectionism," they are "targeting" the American high-technology industries to become dependent on Japan.[71]

The conference was well timed. Mr. Gavin's and Norris' statements made shortly before the new Congress began its 1983 hearings on international trade were bound to inflame passions on Capitol Hill and to stimulate joint congressional, industry, and administration efforts to pressure Japan.

Thus, through its focus on NTT, the U.S. side planned to continue its criticism of the "generally closed" Japanese high-technology market in spite of the fact that NTT's procurement practices are the exception and not the rule. In connection with this, it must be pointed out that the arguments of the U.S. high-technology industry frequently sound hollow to the Japanese, because a number of U.S. companies have, for instance, received the approval of the Justice Department for joint research and development. While such an arrangement is not quite a cartel, it is not something one usually finds in openly competitive industries. Most U.S. high-technology industries also benefit by increased defense spending; from a Japanese point of view, the U.S. defense budget looks like a lucrative source of industry subsidies.[72]

The agreement concerning easier access by U.S. companies to high-technology trade and investment opportunities and research projects sponsored by the Japanese government and reached in early February 1983 is a hopeful sign that both governments are beginning to take a more measured approach toward the resolution of the problem. It is now up to the industry representatives to also lower their voices and to discuss the matter less emotionally, because otherwise the issue may again quickly erupt into a bitter trade conflict.

ADDITIONAL OBSERVATIONS

The three incidents illustrate the manner in which Japanese trade policy is formulated and how the various forces influence this process. The conflict over the restraints on Japanese automobile exports to the United States during 1980–1981, by and large, reflected the same forces.[73] Contrasting international and, in particular, domestic economic interests generated the concerns that eventually evolved into a conflict. As usual, the United States exerted pressure and the Japanese resisted such pressure for quite some time, partly because their automobile industry was well informed about the respective trade debate in the United States through its "listening posts." Industry executives knew that many Americans objected to restraints on Japanese exports on the grounds that they would worsen inflation, reduce consumer choice, and perpetuate managerial and labor inefficiency in the industry. As pointed out in Chapter 4, this knowledge for the first time enabled the Japanese automobile industry to resist its government's pressures for accommodation.

As could be expected, the Japanese delay and resistance were met by increased congressional pressure, which received a great deal of publicity in both the U.S. and Japanese mass media. After a lengthy and acrimonious debate, the Japanese government and automobile industry reached a compromise and eventually an agreement was reached with the Americans as well.

The conflict was caused by a sharp increase in exports of Japanese automobiles to the United States during the late 1970s. Due to their fuel efficiency, good quality, and competitive prices, Japanese automobiles sold well. By 1980, exports reached approximately $10 billion—nearly the total trade surplus Japan had with the United States that year. For a variety of reasons, the U.S. automobile industry was not well prepared to meet the Japanese competition; thus, it sought protection.

The United Automobile Workers (UAW) and the Ford Motor Company appealed to the International Trade Commission (ITC). The ITC, however, ruled that the U.S. auto manufacturers faced problems, because they failed to foresee consumer preferences, national energy policies, and inordinately high wages.[74] Despite the ITC's decision that Ford was not entitled to protection, the auto industry and labor continued to lobby together.

The Reagan administration was divided over the automobile industry's demand for protection. USTR Brock, for example, did not take a position for quite some time. However, eventually the president decided to oppose the protectionist demand and sent an appropriate signal to Capitol Hill. The administration also announced that it would not officially ask Japan to take any restrictive measures, although informally it implied that such measures would be welcome.

On April 29, 1981, two days before the Japanese announced "voluntary" retraints, USTR Brock visited Tokyo to inform the Japanese government of the acceptability of the Japanese measures by the supporters of U.S. protectionist legislation. While in Tokyo, Brock called Senators Bentsen, Danforth, Dole, and Long to hear their recommendations for the size of a Japanese export quota and the duration of the "voluntary" restraints. The senators, Brock, and the White House came to terms, and their recommendations were carried out and quietly promulgated. In short, the Reagan administration made all the appropriate political moves to convince the Japanese of the necessity to initiate "voluntary" restraints and, at the same time, to maintain its free-trade stance toward the rest of the world.

When on May 1, 1981, the Japanese government announced its program of "voluntary" restraints, protectionist pressures in the United States eased. According to the agreement, Japan was to limit the number of automobiles exported to the United States from 1.8 million in 1980 to 1.68 million in 1981 and to undertake certain restrictive measures for 1982 and 1983, respectively. The question that remained unanswered, however, was how "voluntary" the Japanese measures could have been if they had been made under continual pressure from the United States— and despite strong resistance from Japanese manufacturers.

Although the increasing 1981 bilateral trade imbalance signaled new problems, for a time trade relations were tranquil. However, when Assistant Secretary of State for Economic and Business Affairs Robert Hormats attended the Shimoda Bilateral Conference in September 1981, he warned that unless the Japanese took effective measures to reduce the trade imbalance, new conflicts between the two countries would be unavoidable. High-level officials of the American embassy in Tokyo conveyed the same message to MITI, MOFA, and MOF officials. The Japanese officials—although they understood the importance of the U.S. warning—failed to act, as they had done before. Not surprisingly, their inaction invited increasing U.S. pressure, in particular from Congress.

If the Japanese had properly recognized their increased international role, they would not have waited until U.S. frustration over the trade imbalance had again become so intense that nearly a dozen different "reciprocity" and "local content" bills were introduced in both the House and the Senate. Not surprisingly, the stagnating economy, unemployment, and the fact that 1982 was a congressional election year made U.S. politicians very sensitive to complaints from constituents. Former Congressman Brodhead (D-Michigan) and others, for example, have explained that they could not face the thousands of unemployed workers in their districts unless they could direct their anger at some visible target such as the Japanese, whose bilateral trade surplus stood out among all the other economic indicators and whose manufactured products were flooding the U.S. market.[75] As usual, this political strategy was encouraged by the traditionally passive Japanese response to such moves on Capitol Hill.

While protectionist sentiments were rising in Congress, the administration also became very concerned over the lack of response to its supply-side economics. Although it realized that only a restructuring of the United States' industries could help the nation regain its overall international competitiveness, it also needed some "visible" short-term measures that might offer some hope to improve the balance of trade. The "opening" of foreign markets—in particular, for agriculture and the high-technology and service industries in which U.S. firms are still very competitive—therefore, had a certain appeal.

During all of this time the Japanese press acted as usual. According to a *New York Times* report:

> In the United States, trade issues are often relegated to specialists, but in Japan, which depends on trade for its economic survival, it is a subject of broad general interest and constant concern.
>
> For example, when congressional hearings were held in Washington a few weeks ago on American-Japanese relations, reports about the testimony on trade frictions by Reagan Administration officials dominated the front pages of Japanese newspapers. In the United States, by contrast, the press for the most part ignored the hearings.[76]

The Japanese ministries also continued their jurisdictional disputes, thereby hampering the consensual decision-making process. When, for example, USTR Brock in the fall of 1981 sent a letter to the then MITI Minister Tanaka concerning possible Japanese trade measures and congressional responses, MOFA was offended that the letter was addressed to MITI. Thus, because the Japanese government could not respond to the letter in time, the Reagan administration was impelled to go to Congress to defend its trade policies without having heard the Japanese point of view. Had the Japanese responded to the Brock letter, the administration could at least have let it be known to Congress that it was engaged in negotiations with the Japanese to reduce the trade imbalance. Instead, the members of Congress availed themselves of a splendid opportunity to introduce their various "protectionist" bills. These bills, naturally, were described in detail in the Japanese mass media, and by the spring of 1982 "U.S. pressure" and the impending "trade-war" between the two countries again dominated the news in Tokyo.

Once the Japanese government realized the extent of U.S. frustration, several high officials were sent to Washington to survey the situation. In January 1982, MITI Minister Abe visited the United States to attend the Trilateral Conference, which was also attended by USTR Brock and by representatives from the EC and Canada. In late February, senior-ranking Diet Member Esaki led a group of several LDP Diet members to Washington to present Japanese measures to help alleviate the trade problems. The measures, however, disappointed not only U.S. policy formulators and business circles, but also the public at large, which read in the newspapers about the "inadequate Japanese offer." This deeply disappointed Mr. Esaki, who like Ambassador Yasukawa in 1979, was surprised by the degree of frustration he found in the United States.

During the 1982 bilateral negotiations, the Japanese again failed to take initiatives through which they could have placed themselves on the offensive. They also failed to understand that U.S. officials (sometimes even those in the top echelons of the executive branch) may use a diversified line of arguments—some manifestly protectionist—during negotiations or in public statements, as long as the administration's overall policy adheres to the principle of free trade. Furthermore, they were not aware of the diversity of views expressed by members of Congress; nor did they realize that these views do not represent official policy unless translated into legislation. Thus, Japanese policy formulators were very suspicious of U.S. intentions. Unfortunately, such misperceptions have created confusion in Tokyo, thereby reducing the effectiveness of the Japanese government's responses.

Beginning in late 1982 and early 1983, concern about the fate of the automobile agreement—which was scheduled to expire on March 31, 1983—was increasing in both the United States and Japan. Although in 1981 and 1982 Japanese market shares were higher than planned under the agreement, by and large, the restraints worked.[77] The U.S. automobile industry took advantage of the two-year respite and updated its plants. It introduced a variety of new, fuel-efficient automobiles that included the latest technology and were of a better quality than the automobiles manufactured during the 1970s. Furthermore, by the spring of 1983 domestic car sales increased and the economy began to slowly improve, though the industry (and the rest of the economy) was still plagued by a very high rate of unemployment.

The leaders of the U.S. automobile industry believed that in view of the increasing protectionism on Capitol Hill and throughout the country, the Japanese exporters would eventually "voluntarily" extend the agreement, at least for another year. They argued that the Japanese must increase the value of the yen and eliminate the "subsidies" through which they promote automobile exports. Both industry and UAW leaders believed that unless they acted, Congress would eventually pass a "local content" legislation that would stop the "unfair" practices of Japanese automobile manufacturers.

Douglas Fraser, president of the UAW, explained the objective of the "local content" bill as follows:

> It would encourage Toyota and Datsun and Honda to build plants here and create jobs for auto workers, steelworkers, rubber workers, aluminum workers, and would strengthen the whole industrial base of America, including our high-technology industries. We estimate that it would save or open up about a million new jobs. This really is an investment program rather than an attempt to restrict the sales of foreign cars.[78]

Mr. Fraser also offered advice to the Reagan administration concerning its trade policy toward Japan:

> It's a wonder to me why we haven't done some retaliating ourselves when I see all of the severe limitations that are placed by Japan upon our citrus fruits, our beef and tobacco, and, for a while, telecommunications. We couldn't even bid in that market.
>
> What we need to do is to talk bluntly and frankly with the Japanese so that they will begin to take us seriously. I think the whole push behind domestic-content legislation will help Trade Representative Brock in his negotiations.[79]

While U.S. manufacturers and labor leaders were preparing the ground for "blunt" and "frank" talks, the Japanese—as always—remained passive and, by and large, silent. Although some policy formulators and industry representatives mentioned the gradually improving U.S. sales figures during late 1982 and early 1983 as possibly eliminating the need for an extension, during USTR Brock's visit to Tokyo in mid-February 1983 the Japanese agreed to extend the agreement at the level of 1.68 million cars until March 31, 1984. The Americans pressed hard for a two-year extension—pointing out that 1984 would be a presidential election year, which would make a discussion of another extension difficult—but the Japanese categorically rejected the idea.

Also during mid-February of 1983, General Motors and Toyota announced their agreement to jointly produce a subcompact car in the United States. This was the first time that GM—the dominant producer in the U.S. market—turned to a foreign manufacturer for assistance in producing cars in the United States. The joint venture was viewed by numerous industry observers as a concession to Japan's reputation for superior quality and higher production efficiency. From the Japanese point of view, the venture was expected to reduce the trade tensions between the two nations and, in particular, to forestall pressures for "local content" legislation in Congress.

At about the same time, the Japanese also announced that they had agreed to limit exports of videotape recorders, color television tubes, color television sets, automobiles, and selected machine tools to the European Economic Community. All of these decisions were reached under strong pressures from the United States and the EEC in an effort to forestall the protectionist measures that both trading partners continually implied before and during the negotiations.

PRIME MINISTER NAKASONE'S VISIT TO WASHINGTON

As discussed in Chapter 4, summit meetings are important events in Japanese politics. The visit of the new Japanese prime minister, Yasuhiro Nakasone, to the United States in January 1983, however, became even more important due to the rapid increase of trade tensions between the two countries.

Nakasone came into office in November 1982 after a bruising political battle within the LDP. Thus, time was very short to prepare the visit; nevertheless, through his personal efforts, the Japanese succeeded in putting together an appropriate selection of *Miyage*. The prime minister offered, among other things, to ease import restrictions on tobacco, chocolate, biscuits, and other products. He also initiated a study of customs inspection procedures and promised to strengthen Japan's military role as well as authorized Japanese firms to sell military technology to the Americans.

While preparations were taking place in Tokyo, pressure was growing on the administration in Washington to exact even more trade concessions. An editorial in *Business Week* is a good summary of the viewpoint that had emerged in congressional and business circles:

> When Prime Minister Yasuhiro Nakasone shows up in Washington for a visit with President Reagan later this month, he had better have some meaningful trade concessions in his briefcase. The Reagan Administration is finding free trade harder and harder to defend against a rise of protectionist sentiment in Congress. Many lawmakers feel that one of the best arguments for protectionist measures is Japanese trade prac-

tices, such as pushing exports to pick off one U.S. market after another while shielding domestic markets from U.S. companies.[80]

While there was nothing new in this and similar editorials, the generally harsh tone prevailing in the U.S. mass media and among members of Congress as well as the open hostility of numerous business and labor union leaders did not bode well for the visit.

However, Nakasone's personal style and the proclivity of Americans to associate a change in political leadership and style with a change in policy made the visit a public relations success. Joseph Kraft, the respected columnist of the *Washington Post* wrote:

> A favorite American explanation for the trivialization [of trade issues] features the inscrutable Orient. The theory is that Japanese leaders do not move till they have a consensus. Lacking a consensus on export restrictions, they sit mute in meetings or even fall asleep. That leaves the working out of issues to a bureaucracy that specializes in trivia.
>
> Nakasone, an outsider in Japanese politics, whose maneuvering for the top job earned him the sobriquet "weathervane," is plainly an exception to the rule. After his elevation on November 24, he acted before the bureaucrats could begin to get hold of him, to answer known American complaints.[81]

The notion that a Japanese prime minister—if he really wants to—can change the nation's trade policy overnight and thereby satisfy most U.S. demands unfortunately is still fairly widespread in the United States. It reflects the popular "can do" attitude that characterizes Americans but is alien to the Japanese who do not want their leaders to get too far ahead of the consensus, particularly on such politically sensitive issues as trade and defense. Furthermore, while personal style is very important in the United States, it plays a lesser role in Japan, where adherence to traditions is still a widely accepted norm.

While Mr. Nakasone undoubtedly had made a game effort to come to a better understanding with the United States on most major trade issues, even he could not offer any concessions on such politically touchy problems as the citrus and beef quotas, which carry great symbolic importance in the United States. This, together with the very high expectations that his visit to Washington created, puts Mr. Nakasone into a difficult position. If he cannot deliver on his promises within a "reasonable" period of time, (determined by the domestic economic and political realities in the United States during 1983-1984), his visit may have done more harm than good to U.S.–Japan relations. Disappointed Americans may strengthen their image of the "insincere" and "evasive" Japanese and exert new pressures to obtain what they believe Mr. Nakasone promised but failed to deliver.

The stakes in the eventual outcome of the visit are very high, not only for the two nations involved, but also for the rest of the world. The United States and Japan dominate international trade. While President Reagan and the prime minister had no difficulties in agreeing that their two countries share an obligation to revitalize the world economy by resisting protectionism and promoting free trade, practicing what they preach is going to be the real test for both of them, in particular for Mr. Nakasone. As an insightful *Wall Street Journal* article put it:

> Politically, attitudes already have begun to change in Japan. There is more widespread recognition now than a year ago, for example, that U.S. economic troubles are serious. And more Japanese seem aware that Japan must do more to open up its markets or risk undermining the entire world trading system. But the process is a slow one. And Japanese special-interest groups aren't known for having any broader vision than their U.S. counterparts.[82]

Indeed, as soon as Mr. Nakasone had completed his visit to Washington, the Japanese mass media and some members of the Diet took a very strong exception to his trade- and, in particular, defense-policy plans.[83] According to some political observers, his defense-policy stance may have cost him a lot of the support he needs to realize his trade policy goals as outlined during his Washington visit. Others argued that he may have gone too far too quickly in endorsing a plan of action that the bureaucracy and the nation are not yet fully prepared to accept.

THE "CLOSED" JAPANESE MARKET

Throughout the discussed incidents and well into the present time, a key element of Japanese trade policy always had to be response to the U.S. and Western European charge that the Japanese market is "unfairly closed" to foreign competition. The general passivity of Japanese trade policy formulators combined with the vehemence of this charge is a major factor leading to misunderstandings, the now familiar "pressure-slow response" trade relations cycle and, ultimately, the major trade conflicts between Japan on the one hand and the United States and Western Europe on the other hand.

As mentioned in the previous chapters, until the early 1970s, Japan's industrialization strategy was—to a large extent—based on the protection of the domestic markets and the subsidization of selected growth industries. However, once this strategy was successful and a number of Japanese industries became internationally competitive, partially in response to outside pressure and partially in response to government decisions and industry demands, the protectionist devices were gradually dismantled. Admittedly, some protectionist measures, (i.e., citrus and beef quotas) cannot be eliminated for political reasons even today. But such limited restrictions are not unique to Japan.

While the Japanese market restrictions were eliminated over the years, U.S. and European policy formulators and, in particular, business circles continued to use the "closed market" argument, because it served their purpose. Using outdated statistics and arguments, they could place pressure on their governments to demand further measures of the Japanese even if and when such measures no longer served any legitimate aims and amounted to interference in Japanese domestic matters. When, in time, they accepted the fact that among all industrialized nations Japan has some of the lowest tariffs, they focused on the assumed nontariff barriers many of which are in reality traditions rooted in the nation's unique social and cultural history over which the government has no control.

The extent to which the lagging appreciation of change and the misunderstanding of Japan's social and cultural fabric resulted in unfairly increased pressures can be well illustrated by the background and eventual findings of the U.S. General Accounting Office (GAO) Report published at the height of the U.S.–Japan trade conflict in 1979.[84]

In December 1978, a time when many misunderstandings between the United States and Japan prevailed, Senator Lloyd Bentsen, chairman of the Joint Economic Committee of the Congress asked the General Accounting Office to prepare a comparative report on the trade policies of the two countries, with particular emphasis on tariff and nontariff obstacles to U.S. exports. The report was published on September 21, 1979.

Before the report was published, Senator Bentsen, a well-known free trader, who believed that the Japanese market had been unfairly closed, took a tough attitude toward Japan. During late 1978 and early 1979, he made a series of speeches that criticized the Japanese government for allegedly blocking U.S. access to Japanese markets. While there is no reason to believe that STR Strauss orchestrated every "Bentsen blast" at the Japanese during 1978-1979, it appears that the "get-tough" tone of those pronouncements was welcomed, if not inspired, by Strauss. Indeed, Senator Bentsen's request for the GAO report, the study's fact-finding potential notwithstanding, was designed to keep the pressure on the Japanese during the final phase of the "Tokyo Round" talks. Not surprisingly, during the state visit of Prime Minister Ohira in May 1979, Senator Bentsen delivered a strong speech on the Senate floor. Although he also criticized the United States' economic performance, his main purpose was to attack Japan's closed market.

In his press release of October 8, 1979, Senator Bentsen introduced the GAO Report as "one of the most extensive and detailed studies ever made of trade relations between the United States and Japan."[85] He then added that although it contained some notable exceptions the report showed a decrease in Japan's protectionist measures.

The senator explained that the report contained information that the United States should have obtained much earlier. He argued that:

> We should not, however, look at our trade relations with Japan as nothing more than a series of problems. There are lessons to be learned for our own economy in studies such as this one produced by the GAO, . . .
>
> Just as the Japanese trade offensive over the past two decades has contributed to our trade problems, it provides some guidelines for the future conduct of American trade policy, . . .
>
> We need to place more emphasis on exports and on policies that will make our exports more competitive on the world market. . . .[86]

The significance of the GAO Report was threefold: first, because trade conflict between the two countries had become a persistent strain on U.S.–Japan relations, Congress was finally concerned enough to request a fair and comprehensive study of the problem; second, the GAO Report corrected numerous misperceptions about Japanese policies; and third, the report comprehensively organized the causes, problems, and recommendations as a basis for negotiations and further research.

In its comparative analysis of the two economies, the GAO found "striking differences in 'export consciousness' "[87] between the two countries. Japan's commercial policy, the study claimed, "rests on identifying industries with strong export potential and providing them with support."[88] In the United States, on the other hand, there is no coordinated analysis of export potential on an industry-by-industry basis, so that labor-intensive and high-technology industries are treated equally. The net effect, the report concluded somewhat gloomily, was that "Japan encourages its strong industries; the United States protects its weak ones."[89]

Regarding domestic markets, the report noted that Japan had for a long time provided layers of protection to its industries, while continuing to expand exports. But it also noted that trade policies had been substantially liberalized since the 1960s, resulting in reduced tariffs and the elimination of many nontariff barriers. The problem, the report observed, was that both the United States and Japan suffered from a perceptual lag concerning changes:

> . . . attitudes on both sides of the Pacific have been slow to adjust to the new circumstances. American businessmen still remember the frustra-

tion of earlier attempts to penetrate the Japanese market. Similarly, mid-level Japanese Government officials, responsible for administering the new approach, frequently operate as if there were no new commercial policy.[90]

The report concluded that "most of these Japanese barriers are now dismantled, but mental attitudes change more slowly."[91]

Western European trade policy formulators and business interests have over the years argued in the same fashion as their U.S. counterparts. Whenever a F.R.G. or French company failed to successfully enter the Japanese market, charges of "protectionism" and "unfairness" abounded throughout Western Europe.

However, the more objective and less emotionally involved Western European observers are now also beginning to admit that these charges are, by and large, unfounded because they are based on long outdated views of the Japanese market.[92] A leading F.R.G. businessman stationed in Tokyo, for example, stated with respect to Japan's supposedly "unfair" trade barriers that ". . . the greatest trade barrier is in the heads of the managers of the Federal Republic."[93] As reported in the same *Der Spiegel* article, a study on Japanese trade barriers sponsored by the Commission of the European Economic Community and involving Japan-based European firms found that ". . . . The firms' managers believe that there is nothing more the Japanese government can do to open up markets; it is up to the firms themselves to solve the problems and to become successful."[94] However, the same managers also observed that success in the Japanese market requires more experience and effort than success in any European market. The "right" product with the "right" promotion is not enough for success, because what is needed is

> . . . many visits to Japan. One has to find competent people with whom a business can be built up together, and to whom one can give understanding, patience, flexibility, trust, and an exceptionally high degree of support. Naturally, this requires some time, money, strong nerves, and a good sense to choose the right partner. The time required to do all of this is very long.[95]

Other European managers who know Japan well point out that competition in its markets is exceptionally hard and that average products that the Japanese can produce in the same quality at a lower cost undoubtedly have little chance for survival. However, technically superior or very well-designed products that meet the Japanese consumers' needs can become ". . . exceptionally successful."[96]

The most recently published study on the nature of the Japanese market was sponsored by the Tokyo-based "U.S.–Japan Trade Study Group" whose membership consists of government and business representatives from both countries.[97] The research for the study was done by McKinsey Company, the U.S. management consulting firm.

The study is important for two reasons; first, because it dispels a lot of myths about the Japanese market widely held in the United States. Second, because it was done by a U.S. organization, it cannot be dismissed as an attempt to distort its findings in favor of Japan. One of the study's major conclusions is particularly noteworthy:

> Evidence suggests that exporters and investors are being needlessly discouraged by misleading assumptions about Japan's business prowess and domestic market entry problems.[98]

Furthermore, they also point out:

> Evidence suggests that among the greatest hurdles U.S. firms face in Japan is the gap between headquarters expectations and the marketplace realities. Real and significant barriers to success in many cases have stemmed from a foreign corporation's failure or inability to recognize and accommodate: (1) the Japanese market's inordinate size, complexity, special needs and conditions; (2) traditional Japanese business customs, practices and approaches to business relations.[99]

The authors also emphasize that Americans place too much emphasis on the size of the merchandise trade deficit while not paying any attention to the nonmerchandise sources of income benefiting the United States as, for example, the licensing royalties in the high-technology, proprietary soft-drink concentrates, records, printed materials, and film markets.[100] They believe that the current-account and import penetration measures are more appropriate and less inflammatory indicators of the state of U.S.–Japan trade relations:

> . . . The trade balance, as noted, is but one index. Another measure is the percent of goods imported in terms of Japan's total GNP. . . . Although U.S. imports account for a little less than 2 percent (actually 1.9 percent), this figure is almost 50 percent greater than Japan's penetration (1.3 percent) in the United States.[101]

Fanueil Adams, chairman of Mobil Oil Corporation's Japanese subsidiary, declared in the press conference introducing the study in Tokyo in early March 1983 that the U.S. government's insistent demands that Japan "open" its markets have greatly contributed to the misunderstandings and tensions between the two nations:

> To be so noisy about the demands perpetuates in the United States a growing atmosphere of resentment and bitterness that makes it seem to

someone who doesn't know about Japan that it's a hopeless place to do business, and that simply isn't true.[102]

Finally, it is important to clarify another misunderstanding about the nature of the Japanese market. During the spring of 1983 U.S. policy formulators strongly criticized MITI's policy of organizing recession-hit industries as, for example, shipbuilding and cotton spinning, into production cartels for the purpose of reducing capacity without a competitive struggle. Such action is based on a 1978 law that allows temporary production cartels.

The measure is not aimed at imports, and it should also be noted that it has created a bitter controversy between MITI and Japan's Fair Trade Commission, which opposes all cartels, including temporary ones aimed at capacity reduction. MITI, however, strongly believes in the necessity of such arrangements and argues that in recessionary times every country, including the United States, tries to apply measures to protect some of its "sick" industries, at least on a temporary basis.[103] As a matter of fact, some MITI officials take the view that U.S. criticism of the temporary production cartels is unjustified interference in Japan's domestic economy. Be that as it may, it should be noted that even such temporary domestic production cartels are very controversial in Japan and that the government does not speak with a single voice on the issue.

CONCLUDING REMARKS

The selected incidents of Japanese trade policy formulation discussed in the context of U.S.–Japan trade relations illustrate the interplay of the various forces influencing the process. Each of the incidents involved differing international and domestic economic interests that were intensified by misunderstandings caused by unique political, social, and cultural characteristics.

In the macroeconomic policy incident, the United States pressured Japan to achieve a 7 percent growth rate, in spite of the limited economic rationality of such a demand. Because of the history of U.S.–Japan political and economic relations, the Americans believed that the pressure was necessary to convince the reluctant Japanese of their international economic responsibilities. While historically, such a strategy had always worked, during the macroeconomic policy conflict, it became apparent that the Japanese now resent and resist such tactics.

The Blumenthal-Murayama cabinet-level meeting in late September 1978 illustrates some of the sources of the misunderstandings between the two countries. The U.S. secretary, a trade specialist, and the Japanese minister, a generalist appointed chiefly on the basis of legislative tenure, were hindered both by language barriers and disparate leadership roles. Mr. Murayama, in particular, was handicapped because he lacked the authority to make decisions without consulting his bureaucracy.

The misunderstandings were then deepened by the behavior of Japanese Prime Minister Fukuda. In accordance with his country's cultural norms, Mr. Fukuda persisted in pursuing the 7 percent growth rate long after its realization had become not only impossible, but undesirable. U.S. officials, raised in a pragmatic culture, misinterpreted Mr. Fukuda's attitude, concluding that he was evasive at best, and insincere at worst. The official abandonment of the growth target by his successor, Prime Minister Ohira, intensified the problems. Although the new policy was actually the result of a lengthy bureaucratic process of consensual decision-making, whose conclusion coincided with the change in prime ministers, U.S. officials, attributing the change to Mr. Ohira, were irritated.

The Yasukawa mission, designed to clarify the misunderstandings between the two countries, did not help. U.S. officials were not receptive to Mr. Yasukawa's arguments and cited potential congressional displeasure as one of the major reasons for their nonresponse. The Japanese government, negotiating alone because the Diet lacked the resources and opportunity to become directly involved, responded ineffectually to U.S. pressures.

The citrus and beef import quotas incident was also intensified by mutual misunderstandings. While the Japanese restrictions undoubtedly violate free-trade principles, their elimination would not have substantially improved the trade balance between the two countries. The U.S. side, however, viewed the import quotas as symbols of Japan's closed market and, therefore, emphasized their elimination or, at least, immediate reduction. But Japanese domestic politics, the decentralization of trade policy formulation, and the sectionalized bureaucracy made the negotiations long, difficult, and, from the U.S. perspective, frustrating.

The NTT-procurement incident was even more intense than the citrus and beef conflict had been. In the absence of policy coordination between MOFA and the Ministry of Posts and Telecommunication, the Japanese were forced to respond slowly to the United States. But U.S. officials, remembering the frustrating agricultural negotiations, as well as other cases, and ignoring the relationship between the Japanese government and publicly owned corporations, assumed that Japan was insincere and evasive.

During the lengthy negotiations, Congress pressured U.S. officials to escalate their demands to the point that required a cabinet-level response by the Japanese. Such a response is rare in Japan, and if it happens, it involves a great deal of time because it has to be preceded by the consensual bureaucratic decision-making process. However, once the decision is made, it cannot be changed easily, and this decreases the flexibility of Japanese negotiators.

In addition, MITI and MOFA used the argument of U.S. pressure to justify their own sectional interests; further, U.S. officials also believed that by reinforcing MITI and MOFA's arguments, a settlement could be reached more quickly.

All throughout the incidents, the Japanese style of negotiating exacerbated misunderstandings and tensions. The slow consensual decision-making process, the passive siege mentality, the inadequate delegation of authority, bureaucratic sectionalism, the risk-avoidance behavior of bureaucrats, a decentralized trade policy, and a nonresponsive negotiating stance all severely handicapped mutual understanding. U.S. officials were frustrated and angry, believing that Japan intentionally sabotaged their structured approach to negotiations. As a result, a pattern of events was frequently repeated: once a dispute began, U.S. pressure was followed by a delayed Japanese response, which increased U.S. frustration and pressure. This, in turn, forced the Japanese resentfully to concede. The resentment incubated and triggered nationalistic outbursts, which, in turn, fueled the trade conflicts. The Americans did not appreciate Japanese concessions, which were usually too little and too late. Thus, even when they deserved it, the Japanese did not get any credit, and their poor image among Americans was confirmed or, more precisely, reconfirmed. U.S. business interests cashed in on the resulting suspicions and lobbied Congress for even more pressure on the Japanese.

The dispute over Japanese automobile exports to the United States and the continuation of the citrus-beef import quota and high-technology conflict during the 1980s followed a similar pattern because they were influenced by the same—previously discussed—forces. Furthermore, Americans—as they are wont to do—again associated a change in political leadership with an immediate large-scale change in Japanese trade policy, which does not bode well for the trade relations between the countries over the next year or two, because Prime Minister Nakasone cannot possibly deliver what the United States expects of him. Thus, in spite of some progress on certain issues, eventual U.S. disappointment, frustration, and anger is inevitable.

Finally, U.S. and Western European trade policy formulators, politicians, and business interests must take a less emotional and more factual account of the Japanese market. While some protectionist measures undoubtedly continue to exist, they are small in number and limited to certain special segments of the economy. The Japanese market as a whole is as "open"—although more competitive and quality-conscious—as the U.S. or Western European markets. High-quality products, meeting the Japanese consumers' expectations and well marketed, are bound to succeed.

NOTES

1. The United States is Japan's most important trade partner. Therefore, Japanese trade policy toward the United States is central to the understanding of the trade policy formulation process.

2. For a detailed chronological discussion of the macroeconomic policy incident see, I. M. Destler and Hisao Mitsuyu, "Locomotive on Different Tracks: Macroeconomic Diplomacy, 1977–1979," in Coping with U.S.-Japanese Economic Conflicts, eds. I. M. Destler and Hideo Sato (Lexington, Mass.: D.C. Heath, 1982), pp. 243–69. The following discussion is partially based on Destler's and Mitsuyu's contribution.

3. U.S. Department of Commerce, Bureau of the Census, Statistical Abstract of the United States: 1979, 100th ed. (Washington, D.C.: Government Printing Office, 1979), p. 920.

4. U.S. Congress, Joint Economic Committee, The 1980 Joint Economic Report (Washington, D.C.: Government Printing Office, 1980), p. 66.

5. The Japanese fiscal year begins April 1 and ends March 31 of the following year. For wholesale price index figures, see U.S.–Japan Trade Council, Yearbook of U.S.-Japan Economic Relations 1978 (Washington, D.C.: U.S.–Japan Trade Council, 1979), p. 114.

6. Destler and Mitsuyu, "Locomotives on Different Tracks," p. 248.

7. Leon Hollerman, "Locomotive Strategy and U.S. Protectionism: A Japanese View," in Japan and the United States: Economic and Political Adversaries, ed. Leon Hollerman (Boulder, Col.: Westview Press, 1980), p. 193.

8. Ibid.

9. In talks with Treasury Secretary W. Michael Blumenthal and Undersecretary of State Richard Cooper at the end of 1977, Ambassador Ushiba was warned that the essential problem was "that Japan's $8 billion to $10 billion current-account surplus, added to the oil cartel's $40 billion surplus,. . . [was] creating an unwieldy debt burden for the deficit countries." Hobart Rowen, and Art Pine, "U.S. Officials Are Pessimistic Over Results of Trade Talks," Washington Post, 14 December, 1977, p. Cl.

10. ". . . U.S. Vice-President Walter Mondale warned that 'economic tension between Japan and the United States is getting extremely serious' because of the trade surpluses.

" 'Prime Minister (Takeo) Fukuda promised at the London summit conference (in May) that Japan would reduce its trade surplus, but actual developments don't show it,' Mr. Mondale told visiting Japanese politicians in Washington.

"He added that domestic pressure (in the United States) is getting stronger' for protectionism despite U.S. government efforts to keep 'an open trade policy." "Japanese Move to Stem Inflow of U.S. Dollars," Wall Street Journal, 18 November, 1977, p. 20.

11. "Traditionally, Japan—with an eye on potential inflation—limits deficit financing to 30 percent of its national budget." See Hobart Rowen, "Japan to Change Deficit Financing Limit, Trade Official Says," Washington Post, 16 December, 1977, p. A16.

12. For examples of U.S. pressure tactics, see Greg Conderacci, "U.S.-Japan Trade

Talks Seen Producing Important Results but No Final Answers," *Wall Street Journal*, 12 December, 1977, p. 4. Also, Hobart Rowen, and Art Pine, "Trade Proposals Offered by Japan Rejected by U.S.," *Washington Post*, 13 December, 1977, p. A1.

13. See text of Ushiba-Strauss joint communiqué in U.S. Congress, House Committee on Ways and Means, *Task Force Report on United States-Japan Trade*, Committee Print 95-110, 95th Cong., 2d sess. (Washington, D.C.: Government Printing Office, 1979), pp. 70–72.

14. U.S.–Japan Trade Council, *Yearbook 1978*, p. 2.

15. Beginning in January and throughout the 12 months of 1978, the dollar value of Japan's exports rose over those of the previous year, by 19.5, 26.8, 22.9, 14.5, 26.7, 21.7, 15.1, 23.6, 31.2, 20.9, 21.3, and 13.3 percent, in the 12 consecutive months; while in volume terms for the same period, Japan's exports rose 3.8, 11.6, and 7.0, but then continued to decline over those of the previous year, beginning with a decline of 5.7 in April, and then declines of 0.8, 1.6, 7.6, 4.3, + 0.7, 6.4, 3.2, and 4.6 percent in the following months. U.S.-Japan Trade Council, *Yearbook 1979*, pp. 115–16.

16. U.S.–Japan Trade Council, *Yearbook 1978*, p. 24.

17. According to this tradition, the Japanese consider an advance offer as a means of obtaining a cooperative attitude, that is, maximum counteroffers but minimum additional demands. When the United States and the EC accepted the Japanese offer, but assumed that the negotiations would start from there, the Japanese were, naturally, deeply disappointed.

18. During discussions in Washington in 1978.

19. On Dec. 12, the Economic Planning Agency officially estimated that Japan's FY 1978 real economic growth rate would only be 6 percent (U.S.–Japan Trade Council, *Yearbook 1978*, p. 25).

20. Destler and Mitsuyu, "Locomotives on Different Tracks," p. 258.

21. See U.S.–Japan Trade Council's, *Yearbook 1978*, p. 25; and their *Yearbook of U.S.–Japan Economic Relations 1979*, (Washington, D.C.: U.S.–Japan Trade Council, 1980), pp. 21–22.

22. "Sources labeled grossly exaggerated 'a story published February 10 that said President Carter, in a letter to Prime Minister Ohira, had threatened to cancel his appearance at a midyear Tokyo economic summit if Japan did not reverse its course on trade.' " Hobart Rowan, "Cut Surplus, Japan Warned," *Washington Post*, 15 February, 1979, p. F1.

23. During a discussion in Washington, D.C., in mid-Dec. 1978.

24. Mr. Strauss himself stated during an interview: "I suspect that the strongest thing that I've brought to this job is an understanding of Capitol Hill—the fact that I have pretty good instincts on just how far to go to keep them growling but not biting, . . ." "World Trade: 'Steps in the Right Direction' " (Interview with Robert S. Strauss, Special Representative for Trade Negotiations), *U.S. News and World Report*, 13 March, 1978, p. 48.

25. U.S. Congress, Senate, Committee on Finance, *United States/Japanese Trade Relations and the Status of the Multilateral Trade Negotiations*, 95th Congress, 2d session, 1979 (Washington, D.C.: Government Printing Office, 1979), p. 7.

26. Ibid., pp. 7, 8.

27. Ibid., p. 8.

28. "World Trade: Steps in the Right Direction," p. 47.

29. Senate Finance Committee, *United States–Japanese Trade Relations*, p. 12.

30. Ibid., p. 22.

31. Ibid., p. 23.

32. *Report of the Japan–United States Economic Relations Group*, p. 101.

33. For a detailed chronological discussion of this incident during 1977–1978, see Hideo Sato, and Timothy J. Curran, "Agricultural Trade: The Case of Beef and Citrus," in *Coping with U.S.-Japanese Economic Conflicts*, eds. I. M. Destler, and Hideo Sato, pp. 121–83. The following section is partially based on their contribution.

34. *Yearbook of U.S.-Japan Economic Relations 1981* (Washington, D.C.: Japan Economic Institute of American, 1981), Table 38 Appendix B.

35. *U.S. Foreign Agricultural Trade Statistical Report, Calendar Year 1981: A Supplement to Foreign Agricultural Trade of the United States* (Washington, D.C.: International Economic Division, Economic Research Service, U.S. Dept. of Agriculture, April 1982).

36. Ambassador Mike Mansfield, "The Indispensable Relationship," an address delivered to the Southeast U.S.–Japan Association Conference in Nashville, Tennessee, on 17 September, 1982. (Tokyo: United States Information Service, American Embassy, 1982), p. 5.

37. Bureau of Public Affairs, "Agriculture in U.S. Foreign Economic Policy" (Washington, D.C.: Department of State, January 1983), p. 1.

38. See the "Meat Import Act" and the prohibition on importing Japanese mandarin oranges into the United States except for Alaska, Hawaii, Washington, Montana, Idaho, and Oregon.

39. In describing the efforts of the Japanese government to switch small-scale rich farmers to the production of citrus fruits, with a result of surplus oranges and falling prices, at the time of the 1977–1978 conflict, a U.S. magazine article stated that "For the Japanese government to compound these difficulties by suddenly opening the market to cheaper U.S. oranges would seem a betrayal." David Pauly, and Rich Thomas, "Battle of the Oranges," *Newsweek*, 18 September, 1978, p. 73.

40. Sato and Curran, "Agricultural Trade: The Case of Beef and Citrus," p. 142.

41. House Committee on Ways and Means, *Task Force Report 1979*. The report was published in an interim and final version.

42. Ibid., p. 1.

43. Timothy J. Curran, "Politics and High Technology: The NTT Case," in *Coping with U.S.-Japanese Economic Conflict*, eds. I. M. Destler, and Hideo Sato (Lexington, Mass.: D.C. Heath, 1982), p. 200.

44. House Committee on Ways and Means, *Task Force Report 1979*, p. 60.

45. Ibid., p. 61. The Task Force wrote: "A report by an independent consulting firm done recently for the Treasury Department suggests many high ranking U.S. businessmen may have inaccurate perceptions of competitive opportunities in Japan."

46. Ibid.

47. *See* "U.S.-Japan Accord," *New York Times*, 6 December, 1978, p. D8.

48. U.S. Comptroller General, *United States–Japan Trade: Issues and Problems* (Washington, D.C.: General Accounting Office, 1979). This so-called "GAO Report" was a balanced and fair review of the trade relations between the two countries. It should also be noted that during the fall of 1980 the second so-called "Jones Report" was also published. In contrast to the first two (the interim and final) reports, the second report was notably objective. It also contributed to a better understanding of the trade problems in both the United States and Japan. *See* U.S. Congress, Committee on Ways and Means, *United States–Japan Trade Report*, Committee Print 96–98, 96th Congress, 2nd sess. (Washington, D.C.: U.S. Government Printing Office, 1980).

49. Steve Lohr, "Business vs. Farmers in Japan," *New York Times*, 5 May, 1982, p. D1.

50. See, among others, Alan Wm. Wolff, "Shape Up, Japan," *New York Times* 17 January, 1983, p. A20. Mr. Wolff was Deputy STR between 1977–1979.

51. Nobuhiko Ushiba, "Let's Lower Our Voices," *Washington Post* 9 December, 1982, p. A29.

52. For a detailed chronological discussion see Timothy J. Curran, "Politics and High Technology: The NTT Case," in *Coping with U.S.-Japanese Economic Conflict*, eds. I. M. Destler, and Hideo Sato (Lexington, Mass.: D.C. Heath, 1982), pp. 185–241.

53. *Yearbooks of U.S.-Japan Economic Relations 1980 and 1981* (Washington, D.C.: Japan Economic Institute of America, Inc., [1981 and 1982]), Tables 38 and 39.

54. Curran, "Politics and High Technology," p. 201.

55. House Committee on Ways and Means, *Task Force Report 1979*, p. 33.

56. Ibid.

57. Ibid.

58. Curran, "Politics and High Technology," p. 202. The counterpart of the NTT in the United States is American Telegraph and Telephone Company, "a private corporation that invites bids from whatever source it chooses, principally 'from its subsidiaries over which it has exclusive control.' " Leon Hollerman, "Notes," in *Japan and the United States: Economic and Political Adversaries*, ed. Leon Hollerman (Boulder, Col.: Westview Press, 1980), p. 224.

59. Leonard Curry, "Strauss Pressing Japan to Include Phone Firm in Trade Agreement," *Washington Star*, 30 December, 1978, p. B6.

60. Curran, "Politics and High Technology," p. 202.

61. See Henry Kissinger's statement concerning this problem even at the highest levels of the U.S. government on p. 69, Chapter 4.

62. Curran, "Politics and High Technology," pp. 217–18.

63. One official said, " 'The last thing we want is for him [Prime Minister Ohira] to go to Washington with a messy affair like government procurement still unresolved after all these months of talks.' " Henry Scott Stokes, "Japan Plans Trade Issue Concession," *New York Times*, 23 April, 1979, p. 1.

64. William Chapman, "Japan Refuses to Expand Concessions on Trade," *Washington Post*, 26 April, 1979, p. A35.

65. Curran, "Politics and High Technology," p. 228.

66. See Henry Kissinger's observations on the futility of pressuring an individual Japanese politician on p. 70, Chapter 4.

67. "High-Technology Gateway," *Business Week* 9 August, 1982, p. 40.

68. "Beleaguered U.S. Electronics Makers Want Hard Line Against Japanese," *Washington Post*, 3 February, 1983, p. C11.

69. Ibid.

70. Ibid.

71. Ibid.

72. In 1982, Houdaille Industries, Inc., a machine-tool manufacturer filed a petition under Section 103 of the Internal Revenue Act of 1971 demanding that the president deny a 10 percent tax credit to any U.S. company that buys capital goods from a country whose industries benefit from cartel arrangements or subsidies. The petition claimed that Japan's high-technology industries benefit from such practices while the Americans do not. In April 1983, the administration denied the petition.

73. Therefore, the discussion of this incident is shorter than the discussion of the other three incidents.

For a detailed chronological discussion of events see Gilbert R. Winham, and Ikuo Kabashima, "The Politics of U.S.–Japanese Auto Trade," in *Coping with U.S.-Japanese Economic Conflicts*, eds. I. M. Destler and Hideo Sato (Lexington, Mass.: D.C. Heath, 1982), pp. 73–119.

74. In contrast to the U.S. automobile workers who received an average of about $20 per hour, the Japanese workers' hourly wages ranged between $10–$11.

75. In discussions in Washington, D.C., in 1982.

76. Steve Lohr, "Tokyo Must Also Weigh Domestic Political Issues," *New York Times*, 27 March, 1982, p. 32. Not surprisingly, the U.S. press also continued to use the "unfair Japanese" theme in its trade reports.

77. Because the agreement limited the Japanese to a certain number of cars in a shrinking market, their market share turned out to be larger than expected.

78. "Pro and Con: Require U.S. Parts in Foreign Cars?" *U.S. News and World Report*, 7 February, 1983, p. 47.

79. Ibid.

80. "A New U.S. Weapon for Defending Free Trade," *Business Week*, 17 January, 1983, p. 138.

81. Joseph Draft, "The Inscrutable West," *Washington Post*, 23 January, 1983, p. C7.

82. Art Pine, "U.S. Officials, Impressed by Nakasone, Wonder How He Will Fare Back in Japan," *Wall Street Journal* 24 January, 1983, p. 28.

83. Tracy Dahlby, "Nakasone's Frank Remarks Threaten Support in Japan," *Washington Post* 23 January, 1983, p. 1.

84. Comptroller General, *United States–Japan Trade 1979.*

85. U.S. Congress, Joint Economic Committee, "Bentsen Releases GAO Study on U.S.–Japan Trade; Protectionism Remains a Factor Though Diminishing," Press Release, 8 October, 1979 (Typewritten).

86. Ibid.

87. Comptroller General, *United States-Japan Trade*, p. ii.

88. Ibid., p. iii.

89. Ibid.

90. Ibid., p. 2.

91. Ibid., p. 190.

92. "It takes Time and Strong Nerves," *Der Spiegel*, No. 1, 1983, pp. 80–86.

93. Ibid., p. 80.

94. Ibid., p. 81.

95. Ibid.

96. Ibid.

97. McKinsey & Company, Inc., and the U.S.-Japan Trade Study Group, *Japan Business Obstacles and Opportunities* (New York: Wiley, 1983).

98. Ibid., p. xiii.

99. Ibid., p. xiv.

100. Ibid., p. 2.

101. Ibid., pp. 4–5.

102. *Wall Street Journal*, 16 February, 1983, p. 35.

103. See, for example, the "voluntary" Japanese automobile export restrictions and the role the U.S. government played in establishing them.

6

GENERAL CONCLUSIONS AND RECOMMENDATIONS

Due to the lack of a central trade policy formulating entity, as well as the absence of official coordination mechanisms, Japan's trade policy formulation is marked by slowness and dissension. Bureaucratic sectionalism, promoted by lifetime employment and a high degree of organizational loyalty—in combination with the consensual decision-making process—make Japanese trade policy formulation appear uncoordinated, sluggish, and nonresponsive. Given the constraints of the Japanese political and bureaucratic system, coordination must take place through interministerial negotiations.

Trade policy formulating power basically resides with the career bureaucracy. Carefully chosen, trained, and surrounded by an aura of respect, career bureaucrats employed for life are the closest advisors of the politically appointed ministers, most of whom obtained their positions because of parliamentary tenure. Therefore, functionally, the Japanese career officials are more analogous to the U.S. political appointees or the elite French career officials than the U.S. civil servants.

Among the ministries, MITI plays the central trade policy formulating role. It has strong influence over and good contracts with the domestic manufacturing and distribution industries; thus, it has direct access to the information needed for the development of effective trade policies. However, MITI's role in international trade negotiations is limited, because by law only MOFA can represent Japan internationally. Yet MOFA is also limited because it does not have MITI's contacts with domestic industry and lacks the technical expertise required to negotiate, for example, high-technology matters. MOF occupies a special position in the trade policy formulating hierarchy because its authority in trade policy is limited to matters affecting tariffs and the service industries (banking, security, insurance). However, because of its control over the budgetary process, MOF's direct influence is immense. MOAFF is a domestically oriented ministry possessing authority only over agricultural matters and is inclined to foster protectionism. Nevertheless, since, for example, in the U.S.–Japan trade conflicts agricultural issues play an important role, MOAFF's influence on trade policy can, at times, be considerable. As can be expected, because of such a division of authority, Japan's trade policy formulation is plagued by frequent jurisdictional disputes, particularly between MITI and MOFA.

The MITI, MOFA, MOF, and MOAFF committees of the Japanese Diet participate in the discussions of trade matters. However, because of the nature of the parliamentary system, the majority party—through its control over the executive branch and the Diet—influences those committees. Additionally, the lack of qualified supporting staff reduces the influence of these committees on trade policy formulation and negotiations.

Within such an institutional framework, the rather passive Japanese trade policy formulation process usually begins with the recognition of differing international and domestic economic interests between Japan and its trading partners. These differing interests develop into conflicts because of contrasting trade policy formulation processes, the varying nature of influencing factors, and the resulting misunderstandings. Additional misunderstandings intensify the conflicts, in particular, because Japan and its trading partners view the other side's unique characteristics not as differences that need to be understood, but as qualities that must be resisted. In this respect, for example, U.S.–Japan trade relations do not seem to have changed since Commodore Perry and Consul Harris first went to Japan in the nineteenth century.

What seems to be ignored by all sides is that while nations are allies and friends, they will continue to encounter differing international and domestic economic interests. Therefore, they must seek to understand these differing interests and better appreciate and accept each other's unique ways of managing their political, social, and economic systems.

It is particularly important that Americans and Europeans appreciate the changing outlook for Japan's economy. The world economic slowdown and the resulting protectionism in Japan's major markets are potentially very damaging. Exports, a mainstay of the economy, are growing slowly, and in 1982, the trade surplus, for example, declined by 21.2 percent, and both exports and imports were reduced by 8.7 and 7.9 percent, respectively.[1] The coming years promise to be sluggish for both the domestic and the world economy. While even under such conditions the Japanese economy is probably going to perform better than the economies of most other highly industrialized nations, compared to past performance the expectations for 1983–1984 and the years beyond are modest. Table 6-1 presents a summary overview of the relevant statistics as reported by Japan's Economic Planning Agency:

Table 6-1.   Real GNP and Export Growth, 1970–1984

Fiscal Year	Real GNP Growth	Export Growth
1970-80 Average	5.3%	11.1%
1981	4.5%	16.6%
1982	3.3%	15.3%
1983 (Estimated)	3.1%	1.6%
1984 (Estimated)	3.4%	3.3%

Source: *Wall Street Journal* 1 February, 1983, p. 38.

To this must be added the heavy import dependence of the country for nearly all key raw materials, the perhaps terminally depressed state of major domestic industries, such as shipbuilding, petrochemicals, and aluminum as well as the increasing competition from the newly industrialized countries of Taiwan, South Korea, and others which are penetrating traditional Japanese markets both at home and throughout the world. Finally, the government deficit has reached an all-time high; in 1982 it amounted to 5.6 percent of GNP (in comparison, the much talked about U.S. deficit is around 4 percent of GNP).[2] To reduce the deficit Prime Minister Nakasone announced belt-tightening measures, which, among others, include reductions in government loans, public works, and the freezing of social security spending.

Thus, while the Japanese economy is expected to expand during the remainder of the 1980s, the impressive double-digit rates of annual growth experienced during the 1970s are a thing of the past. Such a development combined with persistent protectionism throughout the world is likely to leave its mark on Japanese trade policy formulation.

During the 1980s, the rest of the world in general, but the United States and Western Europe in particular, can expect a much more assertive Japan than in the past. Especially, the new generation of Japanese career officials is tired of having Japan blamed for the United States and Europe's real or imagined economic problems. Not influenced by the World War II-related guilt feelings of their elders, the younger generation views the relentless criticism of Japan as "scape-goating" at best and "unjustified interference in domestic matters" at worst. More internationally minded and thus, better informed, they are likely to be more outspoken in defending the interests of their country. Of course, this is not to suggest that the basic institutional arrangements, policy formulating traditions, and behavioral practices can and will be changed overnight. The social and political consensus that is necessary for such changes takes a long time, and, in the meantime, Japanese trade policy is still formulated by a generation of officials and political leaders who are influenced by the pre-1980 views of Japan and the world.

RECOMMENDATIONS

As the discussion of the trade policy formulating incidents has shown, Japan's major trade conflicts are with the United States. The handling of these conflicts by the world's first and second most important economic power affects the economic well-being of not only these two countries, but also of the rest of the world. Consequently, the following recommendations are addressed to both the United States and Japan in the belief that by establishing more cordial trade relationships they could make a major contribution to the reestablishment of free trade throughout the world.

In light of the previous discussions, it is almost axiomatic to argue that in both countries the international sensitivity of the policy formulators must be improved. This can best be done through early education in international relations, so that future generations can understand the high degree of economic interdependence that characterizes the world today. Increased international awareness is particularly necessary in the United States, where the "large country mentality" is still widespread. Although the United States is still the most powerful country in the world, only through increased sensitivity to the needs and unique characteristics of other nations can the United States maintain its position of leadership.

Similar educational efforts must also be made in Japan, where the dominant "small country mentality" must be replaced with a new appreciation of Japan's political and economic importance in the world. Japanese economic and, in particular, trade policies must be appreciated by the Japanese as key elements of the international economic order.

By way of educational efforts, medium- and long-term exchanges of students, academicians, government officials, and legislative staffs should be promoted in both countries. To fully appreciate each other's unique cultural characteristics, such exchanges should last at least three to five years, although an increase in short-term, ad hoc visits would also be desirable.

Additionally by way of education, U.S. government officials and business representatives should place more emphasis on the study of the Japanese language. While learning Japanese is undoubtedly difficult, a systematic and comprehensive effort must be undertaken to better understand Japanese society and culture through language. Only through direct communication can Americans expect to appreciate Japanese thought processes and traditions. By the same token, Americans should not underestimate the difficulty that the Japanese have with English. Although many Japanese officials read and speak English fairly well, they do not necessarily understand the nuances of American English, particularly during tense negotiations.

While both the Japanese government and Japanese business firms have been regularly sending junior officials and executives to U.S. universities, they should begin sending midlevel officials and executives with long professional experience. Such individuals could be placed in U.S. "think-tanks" to review and analyze with their U.S. counterparts the relationships between the two countries. This could be particularly useful to those Japanese career officials who are locked into the seniority system of their "closed," hierarchical bureaucracy whose values they have internalized over the years.

The direct exchange of information between the two countries must also be improved. Both U.S. and Japanese government departments or ministries and agencies, unversities, research institutes, and legislative committees should continually be supplied with current information. In particular, the Japanese must improve their efforts in this regard because views of their country in the United States are more distorted than vice versa. The Japanese must understand that as long as their economic policies in general and their trade policies in particular undergo change, as rapidly as they have until now, current information is a must to prevent misunderstandings. Joint research efforts between U.S. and Japanese scholars, and between government departments, agencies, and legislative groups, together with the establishment of a joint data bank in Washington and Tokyo, could be an effective way to promote the exchange of information. As matters stand, much useful information is not only duplicated by the various institutions of the two countries, but sometimes is not even known to exist and, therefore, remains unused.

Premature leaks of information by the press frequently intensify trade conflicts to the detriment of both countries. To prevent this from happening in the future, both the U.S. and Japanese governments should establish more effective channels of communication and consultation. While the creation of the "Wise Men's Group" was a step in the right direction, more needs to be done. The Japanese, for example, could make relevant information more readily available to foreign correspondents in Tokyo.

Both countries, but in particular Japan, should make better use of the back channels of communication. Although Japanese business firms maintain a broad informational network in Washington, the Japanese government has not yet gained a full appreciation of the usefulness of these channels. By using such channels the Japanese government could overcome the uncertainties generated in the United States by the often conflicting information emanating from various Japanese ministries engaged in jurisdictional disputes. MOFA especially needs to become more flexible; it should no longer insist on the diplomatic channel as the only authorized means of exchanging information, and it should better prepare its officials to deal with economic matters.

As far as the organizational aspects of the two goverments are concerned, while it may be desirable to establish a Department of International Trade in the United States, it is the Japanese who should immediately review and reorganize the process involved in the formulation of their international trade policy. To this end, the Japanese government should establish a small, USTR-type agency, attached to the prime minister's office, and guarantee its independence by being staffed with permanently assigned officials. Such a specialized and independent agency could oversee and coordinate the formulation of trade policy and, in particular, develop an overall strategy of settling bilateral disputes with the United States in a multilateral context, that is, through the GATT. This could help resolve trade conflicts within the framework of the generally accepted principles of international trade and could, therefore, replace the emotionally charged process of bilateral negotiations.

In both the United States and Japan, the administrative practices involved in the formulation of trade policy should also be improved. In the United States, political appointees should rely more on career officials in developing and implementing trade policies. This could increase institutional memory, provide for greater consistency in trade policy, and reduce the time needed by political appointees to acquaint themselves with their assignments. Efforts should be made to motivate—by more frequent promotions—able career officials and to involve them in policy formulation, as they already know what most political appointees initially have to learn. The resultant bottom-up flow of information would enable political appointees to spend more time analyzing the differing U.S. and Japanese international and domestic economic interests that generate trade conflicts.

In Japan, the administrative practice of valuing domestic experience more than international experience should be changed. It is a waste of valuable human resources to continue this bureaucratic tradition. Nor is it in the country's best interest that career officials who prove themselves in domestic matters formulate trade policies and undertake trade negotiations, rather than career officials who accumulate valuable international experience through foreign assignments. Therefore, the Personnel Agency should introduce a merit evaluation system that rewards international experience.

It is particularly important that, in the future, the trade policy formulating officials and the international negotiators of both countries pay more attention to differences in decision-making styles. Americans must be fully aware of the Japanese bottom-up, consensual decision-making process, which can be only as fast as the slowest ministry. Even a Japanese minister must always consult his bureaucracy; therefore, policy and negotiation delays are not the result of carefully designed tactics, but of uniquely Japanese ways of reaching decisions. On the other hand, Japanese officials must understand that, even if a U.S. administration makes a formal commitment, Congress may prevent or, at least, delay the implementation of the decision. This is not the result of duplicity, but of the U.S. top-down, quick-slow decision-making process, as well as of the unique form of U.S. government. Furthermore, the Japanese also must understand that members of Congress frequently introduce bills only for the purpose of impressing their constituents with their strong stance on trade issues. Most bills introduced in Congress do not stand a chance of becoming incorporated into the law of the land.

The Japanese must understand that it is the constitutional division of power that makes it possible for any U.S. administration to simultaneously work together with Congress and the various interest groups while still maintaining a free-trade stance toward the rest of the world, even if Congress proposes to introduce strong protectionist legislation as, for example, the "reciprocity" and "local content" bills.

The Japanese need to realize that while all recent U.S. administrations have effectively used the "congressional threat" argument in negotiations with Japan, in the end they have always resisted the highly protectionist measures that Congress and the various interest groups wanted legislated. The pressures placed on the administrations to support such legislation is always formidable, particularly during the early 1980s when it became clear that most of the United States' basic industries were in trouble aggravating an already unbearable employment situation.

To maintain an essentially free-trade stance under such circumstances is difficult. Nevertheless, President Reagan in his 1983 "State of the Union" message and subsequent interviews has steadfastly maintained that he believes in free trade and, in principle, ". . . would veto protectionist legislation."[3] In reference to Prime Minister Nakasone's difficult domestic political situation, he also indicated that he understood its nature:

. . . I also believe in quiet diplomacy. Once you start front-paging every-thing you are going to do, well, then you put the people you're dealing with in a kind of political corner, where they can't appear to be backing down. Prime Minister Nakasone, with great political courage, did a re-markable job in moving back tariffs.[4]

Indeed, U.S. officials should practice quiet diplomacy. In particular, during U.S.–Japan trade negotiations, they should refrain from applying pressure on their Japanese counterparts. In view of the Japanese decision-making process, as well as of the domestic political conditions, U.S. officials should be more patient and should realize that continuous pressure places pro-American Japanese governments on the defensive at home. As mentioned several times earlier, the Japanese mass media are, for historical reasons, always ready to exaggerate even the smallest sign of U.S. pressure. In the resulting highly charged emotional atmosphere, Japanese government officials and negotiators find it difficult to re-spond to even the most reasonable U.S. expectations. In particular, Americans should not pressure individual officials, who, even if they wished to, cannot make commitments on the spot and are only embar-rassed by such demands.

On the other hand, Japanese officials must overcome their tradi-tional "siege" mentality and not mistake the structured U.S. negotiatory approach for pressure. Instead of recoiling when presented with U.S. demands and expectations, they should reciprocate by clearly stating their own agenda. Finally, the Japanese should speak up more frequently in multilateral fora and present their side of the conflicts to the interna-tional community. Such a strategy might generate a better understand-ing of Japanese concerns and expectations.

While the implementation of these recommendations would not im-mediately minimize U.S.–Japan trade conflicts, failure to—at least—consider them can only create more problems in the future. This is neither in the interest of the two nations, nor the rest of the world; there-fore, the recommendations should be taken seriously by both sides.

NOTES

1. Steve Lohr, "1982 Trade Surplus Off 21.2% in Japan," *New York Times*, 20 January, 1983, p. D17.
2. *Business Week*, 15 November, 1982, p. 16.
3. *Business Week*, 14 February, 1983, p. 122.
4. Ibid.

BIBLIOGRAPHY

Adams, John. *The Contemporary International Economy: A Reader*. New York: St. Martin's Press, 1979.

Akamatsu, Paul. *Meiji 1868: Revolution and Counter-Revolution in Japan*. Translated. New York: Harper and Row, 1972.

Alderson, George, and Everett Sentman. *How You Can Influence Congress*. New York: E. P. Dutton, 1979.

Allen, G. C. *How Japan Competes: An Assessment of International Trading Practices with Special Reference to "Dumping."* Lansing, Mich.: The Institute of Economic Affairs, 1978.

Amano, Akihiro, and Fukutaro Watanabe. *Kokusai Keizairon: Riron to Seisaku No Gendaiteki Tenkai* [International Economics: Contemporary Development of Theories and Policies]. Tokyo: Yuhikao, 1980.

Ando, Yoshio. *Nippon Keizai Seisakushi Ron*, vols. I and II [The History of Japan's Economic Policy]. Tokyo: Tokyo University Press, 1976.

Armstrong, John A. *The European Administration Elite*. Princeton, N.J.: Princeton University Press, 1973.

Austin, Lewis, ed. *Japan: The Paradox of Progress*. New Haven: Yale University Press, 1976.

Baldwin, Robert E., and David A. Kay "International Trade and International Relations." In *World Politics and International Economics*, edited by C. Fred Bergsten and Lawrence B. Krause, pp. 99–131. Washington, D.C.: The Brookings Institution, 1975.

Barnds, William J., ed. *Japan and the United States: Challenges and Opportunities*. New York: New York University Press, 1979.

Bauer, Raymond A., and Kenneth J. Gergen, eds. *The Study of Policy Formation*. New York: The Free Press, 1968.

Benedict, Ruth. *The Chrysanthemum and the Sword: Patterns of Japanese Culture*. 1946 reprint ed. New York: The New American Library, 1974.

Bergsten, C. Fred. *The Dilemmas of the Dollar*. New York: New York University Press, 1975.

_____. *The International Economic Policy of the United States: Selected Papers of C. Fred Bergsten, 1977–1979*. Lexington, Mass.: D. C. Heath, 1980.

_____. *Managing International Economic Interdependence: Selected Papers of C. Fred Bergsten, 1975–1976.* Lexington, Mass.: Lexington Books, 1977.

_____. *Toward a New World Trade Policy: The Maidenhead Papers.* Lexington, Mass.: D. C. Heath, 1975.

Bergsten, C. Fred, and Lawrence B. Krause, eds. *World Politics and International Economics.* Washington, D.C.: The Brookings Institution, 1975.

Bergsten, C. Fred, Robert O. Keohane, and Joseph S. Nye. "International Economics and International Politics: A Framework for Analysis." In *World Politics and International Economics*, edited by C. Fred Bergsten and Lawrence B. Krause, pp. 3–36. Washington, D.C.: The Brookings Institution, 1975.

Bhagwati, Jagdish N., ed. *International Trade: Selected Readings.* Cambridge, Mass.: The MIT Press, 1981.

Blake, David H., and Robert S. Walters. *The Politics of Global Economic Relations.* Englewood Cliffs, N.J.: Prentice-Hall, 1976.

Blaker, Michael K. *Japanese International Negotiating Style.* New York: Columbia University Press, 1977.

_____, ed. *The Politics of Trade: U.S. and Japanese Policymaking for the GATT Negotiations.* New York: Columbia University Press, 1978.

_____. "Probe, Push and Panic." In *The Foreign Policy of Modern Japan*, edited by Robert A. Scalapino, pp. 55–101. Berkeley: University of California Press, 1977.

Block, Fred L. *The Origins of International Economic Disorder.* Berkeley: University of California Press, 1977.

Boltho, Andrea. *Japan: An Economic Survey, 1953–1973.* London: Oxford University Press, 1975.

Bozeman, Barry. *Public Management and Policy Analysis.* New York: St. Martin's Press, 1979.

Bryan, Greyson. *Taxing Unfair International Trade Practices.* Lexington, Mass.: D. C. Heath, 1980.

Brzezinski, Zbigniew. *The Fragile Blossom: Crisis and Change in Japan.* New York: Harper and Row, 1972.

Burnham, Walter Dean, and Martha Wagner Weinberg. *American Politics and Public Policy.* Cambridge, Mass.: The MIT Press, 1978.

Campbell, John C. "Contemporary Japanese Budget Politics." New York: Columbia University Ph.D. Dissertation, 1973.

Carlson, Jack, and Hugh Graham. *The Economic Importance of Exports to the United States*. Washington, D.C.: Center for Strategic and International Studies, 1980.

Caves, Richard E., and Ronald W. Jones, *World Trade and Payments: An Introduction*. 2d ed. Boston: Little, Brown, 1977.

Cleaver, Charles Grinnell. *Japanese and Americans: Cultural Parallels and Paradoxes*. Minneapolis: University of Minnesota Press, 1976.

Cline, William R., Noboru Kawanabe, T.O.M. Kronsjo, and Thomas Williams. *Trade Negotiations in the Tokyo Round: A Quantitative Assessment*. Washington, D.C.: The Brookings Institution, 1978.

Cohen, Jerome. *Pacific Partnership: United States–Japan Trade: Prospects and Recommendations for the Seventies*. Lexington, Mass.: D. C. Heath, 1972.

Cohen, Stephen D. *The Making of United States International Economic Policy*. New York: Praeger, 1977.

Craig, Albert M. "Functional and Dysfunctional Aspects of Government Bureaucracy." In *Modern Japanese Organization and Decision-Making*, edited by Ezra F. Vogel, pp. 3–32. Berkeley: University of California Press, 1975.

_____, ed. *Japan: A Comparative View*. Princeton, N.J.: Princeton University Press, 1979.

Curran, Timothy J. "Politics and High Technology: The NTT Case." In *Coping with U.S.–Japanese Economic Conflicts*, edited by I. M. Destler and Hideo Sato, pp. 185–241. Lexington, Mass.: D. C. Heath, 1982.

Curtis, Gerald T. "The Tyman Oil Development Project and Japanese Foreign Policy." In *The Foreign Policy of Modern Japan*, edited by Robert A. Scalapino, pp. 147–173. Berkeley: University of California Press, 1977.

Denison, Edward F. *Accounting for Slower Economic Growth: The United States in the 1970s*. Washington, D.C.: The Brookings Institution, 1979.

Destler, I. M. *Making Foreign Economic Policy*. Washington, D.C.: The Brookings Institution, 1980.

_____. "United States Trade Policymaking During the Tokyo Round." In *The Politics of Trade: U.S. and Japanese Policymaking for the GATT Negotiations*, edited by Michael Blaker, pp. 15–73. New York: Columbia University Press, 1978.

Destler, I. M. and Hisao Mitsuyu. "Locomotives on Different Tracks: Macroeconomic Diplomacy, 1977–1979." In *Coping with U.S.–Japanese Economic Conflicts*, edited by I. M. Destler and Hideo Sato, pp. 243–269. Lexington, Mass.: D. C. Heath, 1982.

Destler, I. M. and Hideo Sato. *Coping with U.S.–Japanese Economic Conflicts*. Lexington, Mass.: D. C. Heath, 1982.

Destler, I. M., Haruhiro Fukui, and Hideo Sato. *The Textile Wrangle: Conflict in Japanese–American Relations, 1969–1971*. Ithaca, N.Y.: Cornell University Press, 1979.

Destler, I. M., Hideo Sato, Priscilla Clapp, and Haruhiro Fukui. *Managing an Alliance: The Politics of U.S.–Japanese Relations*. Washington, D.C.: The Brookings Institution, 1976.

DeVos, George A. "Apprenticeship and Paternalism." In *Modern Japanese Organization and Decision–Making*, edited by Ezra F. Vogel, pp. 210–27. Berkeley: University of California Press, 1975.

Diebold, William, Jr. *Industrial Policy as an International Issue*. New York: McGraw-Hill, 1980.

Doi, Takeo. *The Anatomy of Dependence*. Tokyo: Kodansha, 1970.

Dore, Ronald P., ed. *Aspects of Social Change in Modern Japan*. Princeton, N.J.: Princeton University Press, 1967.

Douglass, Gordon K., ed. *The New Interdependence*. Lexington, Mass.: D. C. Heath, 1979.

Dowdy, Edwin. *Japanese Bureaucracy: Its Development and Modernization*. Melbourne: Cheshire, 1973.

Dower, John W. *Origins of Modern Japanese State: Selected Writings of E. H. Norman*. New York: Pantheon, 1975.

Drucker, Peter F. "Economic Realities and Enterprise Strategy." In *Modern Japanese Organization and Decision-Making*, edited by Ezra Vogel, pp. 228–48. Berkeley: University of California Press, Ltd., 1975.

Economic Policy Council of U.N.—U.S.A. *Trade Policy Issues: Global Structural Changes and the U.S. Economy*. New York: United Nations, 1980.

Emmerson, John K. *The Japanese Thread: A Life in the U.S. Foreign Service*. New York: Holt, Rinehart and Winston, 1978.

Endo, Shokichi. *Nippon Keizei No Gunzo: Jitsuryoku Shudan No Shiso To Kodo* [Power Elites in Japanese Economy: Thoughts and Behaviors of Powerful Groups]. Tokyo: Gakuyo Shobo, 1975.

Franck, Thomas M., and Edward Weisband. *Foreign Policy by Congress*. New York: Oxford University Press, 1979.

Fujihara, Kotatsu. *Kanryo: Nihon No Seiji Wo Ugokasu Mono* [Bureaucrats: Those Who Influence Japanese Politics]. Tokyo: Kodansha, 1964.

Fukui, Haruhiro. "The GATT Tokyo Round: The Bureaucratic Politics of Multilateral Diplomacy." In *The Politics of Trade: U.S. and Japanese Policymaking for the GATT Negotiations*, edited by Michael Blaker, pp. 75–169. New York: Columbia University Press, 1978.

_____. *Party in Power: The Japanese Liberal Democrats and Policy-making*. Berkeley: University of California Press, 1970.

_____. "Policy-Making in the Japanese Foreign Ministry." In *The Foreign Policy of Modern Japan*, edited by Robert A. Scalapino, pp. 3–35. Berkeley: University of California Press, 1977.

Galbraith, John K. *The New Industrial State*. Boston: Houghton Mifflin, 1967.

George, Alexander L. *Presidential Decisionmaking in Foreign Policy: The Effective Use of Information and Advice*. Boulder, Col.: Westview Press, 1980.

Gibney, Frank. *Japan: The Fragile Superpower*. New York: Norton, 1975.

Goldwin, Robert A. *Bureaucrats, Policy Analysts, Statesmen: Who Leads?* Washington, D.C.: American Enterprise Institute, 1980.

Gordon, Robert J., and Jacques Pelkmans. *Challenges to Interdependent Economies: 1980s Project/Council on Foreign Relations*. New York: McGraw-Hill, 1979.

Greene, Fred. *Stresses in U.S.–Japanese Security Relations*. Washington, D.C.: The Brookings Institution, 1975.

Grossack, Irvin M. *The International Economy and the National Interest*. Bloomington: Indiana University Press, 1979.

Halloran, Richard. *Japan: Images and Realities*. New York: Random House, 1969.

Harris, Townsend. *The Complete Journal of Townsend Harris*. 2d ed., rev. Rutland, Vt. and Tokyo, Japan: Charles E. Tuttle, 1959.

Hayashi, Shintaro, and Fukutaro Watanabe. *Kokusai Keiza Kyooshitsu* [Study of International Economy]. Tokyo: Yuuhikaku, 1973.

Heady, Ferrel. *Public Administration: A Comparative Perspective*. 2d ed., rev. and expanded. New York: Marcel Dekker, 1979.

Heclo, Hugh. *A Government of Strangers: Executive Politics in Washington*. Washington, D.C.: The Brookings Institution, 1977.

Hirschmeier, Johannes, and Albert Dewald. *Nishi Doitsu To Nippon: Tozai Yuutosei Shakai No Hikaku* [West Germany and Japan: Comparison Between Eastern and Western Elites]. Tokyo: Toyoo Keizai Shimpoo Sha, 1979.

Hitchner, Dell G. and Carol Levine. *Comparative Government and Politics*, 2d ed. New York: Harper and Row, 1981.

Hollerman, Leon, ed. *Nippon Gaiko No Zahyoo* [The Axes of Japan's Diplomacy]. Tokyo: Chuo Koron, 1979.

_____ et al., eds. *Nichibei Kankei Shi*. 4 vols. [History of the U.S.–Japan Relations]. Tokyo: Tokyo University Press, 1972.

Ichiroo, Murakawa. *Seisaku Kettei Katei: Gyoosei Kikoo Series No. 121* [Policy-formulation Process: Administrative Structure, Series No. 121]. Tokyo: Kyooiskusha, 1979.

Iizuka, Koji. *Nippon No Seishinteki Huudo* [Japanese Spiritual Ecology]. Tokyo: Iwanami Shoten, 1952.

Ike, Nobutaka. *Japanese Politics: Patron Client Democracy*. 2d ed. New York: Knopf, 1972.

Institute for Contemporary Studies. *Tariffs, Quotas and Trade: The Politics of Protectionism*. San Francisco: Insitute for Contemporary Studies, 1978.

Iriye, Akira, ed. *Mutual Images: Essays in American–Japanese Relations*. Cambridge, Mass.: Harvard University Press, 1975.

Itoh, H. *Japanese Politics—An Inside View*. New York: Cornell University Press, 1973.

Jervis, Robert. *Perception and Misperception in International Relations*. Princeton, N.J.: Princeton University Press, 1976.

Johnson, Chalmers. "MITI and Japanese International Economic Policy." In *The Foreign Policy of Modern Japan*, edited by Robert A. Scalapino, pp. 227–79. Berkeley: University of California Press, 1977.

Johnson, Haynes. *In the Absence of Power: Governing America.* New York: Viking, 1980.

Kahn, Herman. *The Emerging Japanese Super State: Challenge and Response.* Englewood Cliffs, N.J.: Prentice-Hall, 1970.

_____. *World Economic Development: 1979 and Beyond.* New York: Morrow Quill Paperbacks, 1979.

Kahn, Herman, and Thomas Pepper. *The Japanese Challenge.* New York: Harper and Row, 1979.

Kaplan, Eugene J. *Japan: The Government-Business Relationship: A Guide for the American Businessman.* Washington, D.C.: Department of Commerce, 1972.

Kaplan, Morton A., and Kimihide Mushakoji. *Japan, America, and the Future World Order.* New York: Free Press, 1976.

Kase, Hideaki, James Abegglen, and Garrett Scalera. *Trilogue: Hachijuu Dai Nichi Bei Keizai Wo Yomu: Nippon Keizai No Tsuyomi To Yowami* [Trilogue: Outlook of the U.S.–Japan Relations in the 1980s: Strength and Weakness of the Japanese Economy]. Tokyo: Tokuma Shoten, 1979.

Kato, Hidetoshi. *Hakaku Bunka He No Shikaku* [An Angle for Comparative Culture]. Tokyo: Chuokoron, 1968.

Kawai, Kazuo. *Japan's American Interlude.* Chicago: University of Chicago Press, 1960.

Kelley, Robert. *The Cultural Pattern in American Politics.* New York: Knopf, 1979.

Kindleberger, Charles P. *Economic Response: Comparative Studies in Trade, Finance and Growth.* Cambridge, Mass.: Harvard University Press, 1978.

Kissinger, Henry. *American Foreign Policy.* 3d ed. New York: W. W. Norton, 1977.

_____. *Years of Upheaval.* Boston: Little, Brown, 1982.

Kojima, Kazuo. *Hooritsu Ga Dekiru Made* [Process of Making a Law]. Tokyo: Kk Gyosei, 1979.

Kojima, Kiyoshi. *Japan and a New World Economic Order.* Boulder, Col.: Westview Press, 1977.

Komiya, Ryuutaro. *Gendai Nippon Keizai Kenkyuu* [Study of Current Japanese Economy]. Tokyo: Tokyo University Press, 1975.

Krause, Lawrence B., and Sueo Sekiguchi, eds. *Economic Interaction in the Pacific Basin.* Washington, D.C.: The Brookings Institution, 1980.

Krauss, Melvyn B. *The New Protectionism: The Welfare State and International Trade.* New York: New York University Press, 1978.

Kubo, Akira. *Higher Civil Servants in Postwar Japan: Their Social Origins, Educational Backgrounds, and Career Patterns.* Tokyo: Kodansha, 1967.

Kyooikusha, ed. *Gaimu Shoo.* [The Ministry of Foreign Affairs]. Tokyo: Kyooikusha, 1979. Administration Series No. 104.

———, ed. *Naikau Sorifu.* [Office of the Prime Minister]. Tokyo: Kyooikusha, 1979. Administration Series No. 101.

———, ed. *Norinsuisan Shoo.* [The Ministry of Agriculture, Forestry, and Fishery]. Tokyo: Kyooikusha, 1979. Administration Series No. 107.

———, ed. *Ohkura Shoo.* [The Ministry of Finance]. Tokyo: Kyooikusha, 1979. Administration Series No. 105.

———, ed. *Tsusan Shoo.* [The Ministry of International Trade and Industry]. Tokyo: Kyooikusha, 1979. Administration Series No. 108.

Laszlo, Ervin, and Joel Kurtzman, eds. *The Structure of the World Economy and Prospects for a New International Economic Order.* New York: Pergamon Press, 1980.

Lebra, Takie S. *Japanese Patterns of Behavior.* Honolulu: The University Press of Hawaii, 1976.

Leveson, Irving, and Jimmy W. Wheeler, eds. *Western Economies in Transition: Structural Change and Adjustment Policies in Industrial Countries.* Boulder, Col.: Westview Press, 1980.

Levine, Solomon B. and Kawada, Hisashi. "Human Resources." In *Japanese Industrial Development.* Princeton, N.J.: Princeton University Press, 1980.

Lewis, W. Arthur. *The Evolution of the International Economic Order.* Princeton, N.J.: Princeton University Press, 1977.

Lineberry, Robert L. *Government in America: People, Politics and Policy.* Boston: Little, Brown, 1980.

Maruyama, Masao. *Thought and Behavior in Modern Japanese Politics.* London: Oxford University Press, 1963.

May, Judith V., and Aaron B. Wildavsky. *The Policy Cycle*. Beverly Hills, Calif.: Sage Publications Inc., 1978.

McKinsey & Company, Inc., and U.S. Japan Trade Study Group. *Japan Business Obstacles and Opportunities*. New York: Wiley, 1983.

Minear, Richard H. *The Past: The Root from Isolation; vol. 1 of Through Japanese Eyes Series*. New York: Praeger, 1974.

Ministry of Finance. *Okurasho No Kiko* [The Organization of the Ministry of Finance]. Tokyo: Okura Zaimu-Kyokai, 1974.

Ministry of Foreign Affairs. *Waga Gaikoo No Kinkyoo, 1979* [Current Report on Japan's Diplomacy for 1979]. Tokyo: Ministry of Foreign Affairs, 1979.

Ministry of International Trade and Industry (Research Group for Overseas Investment in U.S.). *Taibei Tooshi No Jittai To Kankyo* [Actuals of Environments for Overseas Investment in the U.S.]. Tokyo: Diamond Inc., 1978.

Mitchell, Douglas D. *Amaeru: The Expression of Reciprocal Dependency Needs in Japanese Politics and Law*. Boulder, Col.: Westview Press, 1976.

Mochizuki, Kiichi. "Government-Business Relations in Japan and the United States. A Study in Contrasts." In *U.S.–Japanese Economic Relations*, edited by Diane Tasca, pp. 85–93. New York: Pergamon Press, 1980.

Morley, James W., ed. *Prologue to the Future: The U.S. and Japan in the Post-Industrial Age*. Boston: D. C. Heath, 1974.

Moulder, Frances V. *Japan, China and the Modern World Economy*. Cambridge, England: Cambridge University Press, 1979.

Myer, Armin H. *Assignment: Tokyo: An Ambassador's Journal*. New York: Bobbs-Merrill, 1974.

Nachmias, David. *Public Policy Evaluation: Approaches and Methods*. New York: St. Martin's Press, 1979.

Nakane, Chie. *Japanese Society*. Berkeley: University of California Press, 1970.

Neuman, William L. *America Encounters Japan: From Perry to MacArthur*. Baltimore: The Johns Hopkins Press, 1963.

Nippon, Kanzei Kyokai. *Boeki Nenkan, 1979* [Annals of International Trade, 1979]. Tokyo: Nippon Kanzei Kyokai, 1979.

Nippon Keizai Shimbun. *Tokyo Round No Subete: Hachijuunen Dai No Booeki Rule* [All About Tokyo Round: Trade Rules in the 1980s]. Tokyo: Nippon Keizai Shimbun, 1979.

_____ . *Tokyo Shijoo No Shooki Tachi: Yen Wo Ayatsupu Soobashi No Mure* [Small Devils in Tokyo Foreign Exchange Market: Group of Speculators to Manipulate the Yen]. Tokyo: Nippon Keizai Shimbun, 1979.

Nussbaum, B., Edward M. Mervosh, Jack Kramer, Lenny Glynn, Lewis Berman, William Wolman, and Lewis H. Young. (The Business Week Team), *The Decline of U.S. Power (and What We Can Do About It)*. Boston: Houghton Mifflin, 1980.

Odaka, Kunio. *Toward Industrial Democracy: Management and Workers in Modern Japan*. Cambridge, Mass.: Harvard University Press, 1975.

Odawara, Kenichi. *Ooinaru America Byoo* [Great American Disease]. Tokyo: Toyoo Keizai Shimpoo Sha. 1980.

Ohkura Zaimu Kyookai, Inc., ed. *Ohkura-shoo No Kikoo* [The Organization of the Ministry of Finance]. Tokyo: Ohkura Zaimu Kyookai, 1980.

Ohyama, Hiroto. *Nichibei Keizai Masatsu: Semari Kuru Kiki Wo Do Kaiki Suruka* [Japanese–U.S. Frictions: How to Avoid Forthcoming Crises]. Tokyo: Diamond, 1980.

Orfield, Gary. "Congressional Policy-Making: The Basic Patterns." In *The Congressional System: Notes and Readings*. 2d ed., edited by Leroy N. Rieselbach, pp. 368–91. North Scituate, Mass.: Duxbury Press, 1979.

Ozawa, Terutomo. *Multinationalism, Japanese Style: The Political Economy of Outward Dependency*. Washington, D.C.: The Brookings Institution, 1976.

Pascale, Richard T., and Anthony G. Athos. *The Art of Japanese Management*. New York: Simon and Schuster, 1981.

Passin, Herbert, ed. *The United States and Japan*. Englewood Cliffs, N.J.: Prentice-Hall, 1966.

Passin, Herbert, and Akira Iriye, eds. *Encounter at Shimoda: Search for a New Pacific Partnership*. Boulder, Col.: Westview Press, 1979.

Pastor, Robert A. *Congress and the Politics of U.S. Foreign Economic Policy, 1929–1976*. Berkeley: University of California Press, 1980.

Patrick, Hugh, ed. *Japanese Industrialization and Its Social Consequences*. Berkeley: University of California Press, 1976.

Patrick, Hugh, and Henry Rosovsky, eds. *Asia's New Giant: How the Japanese Economy Works*. Washington, D.C.: The Brookings Institution, 1976.

Pempel, T.J. *Patterns of Japanese Policymaking: Experiences from Higher Education.* Boulder, Col.: Westview Press, 1978.

Pempel, T.J., ed. *Policymaking in Contemporary Japan.* Ithaca, N.Y.: Cornell University Press, 1977.

Peters, Charles. *How Washington Really Works.* Reading, Mass.: Addison-Wesley, 1980.

Putnam, Robert D. *The Comparative Study of Political Elites.* Englewood Cliffs, N.J.: Prentice-Hall, 1976.

Reischauer, Edwin O. *Japan: Past and Present.* 3d ed. New York: Knopf, 1964.

_____. *The Japanese.* Cambridge, Mass.: Harvard University Press, 1977.

_____. *The Japanese.* 10th printing. Cambridge, Mass.: Harvard University Press, 1980.

_____. *United States and Japan.* Cambridge, Mass.: Harvard University Press, 1957.

Richardson, Bradley M. "Policymaking in Japan: An Organizing Perspective." In *Policymaking in Contemporary Japan,* edited by T. J. Pempel, pp. 239–68. Ithaca, N.Y.: Cornell University Press, 1977.

_____. *Political Culture in Japan.* Berkeley: University of California Press, 1974.

Riesman, David, and Evelyn Thompson Riesman. *Conversations in Japan.* New York: Basic Books, 1967.

Rohlen, Thomas P. *For Harmony and Strength: Japanese White Collar Organizations in Anthropological Perspective.* Berkeley: University of California Press, 1974.

Rosen, Steven J., and Walter S. Jones. *The Logic of International Relations.* 3d ed. Cambridge, Mass.: Winthrop Publishers, 1980.

Rubin, Barry. "How Others Report Us: America In The Foreign Press." *The Washington Papers. VII,* 65. Beverly Hills and London: Sage Publications, 1979.

Sakakibara, Eisuke. *Nippon Wo Enshutsu Suru Shin Kanryoo Zoo* (The Image of New Bureaucrats Representing Japan). Tokyo: Yamate Shobo, 1977.

Samson, G.B. *The Western World and Japan.* New York: Vintage Books, 1949.

Sato, Hideo and Timothy J. Curran. "Agricultural Trade: The Case of Beef and Citrus," In *Coping with U.S.–Japanese Economic Conflicts*, edited by I. M. Destler and Hideo Sato, pp. 121–83. Lexington, Mass.: D. C. Heath, 1982.

Scalapino, Robert A. *The Foreign Policy of Modern Japan.* Berkeley: University of California Press, 1977.

Seidensticker, Edward. *This Country, Japan.* Tokyo: Kodansah International, Ltd., 1979.

Sengoku, Tamotsu and Atsuko Toyama. *Hikaku Nipponjin Ron* [Comparative Japanese]. Tokyo: Shogakukan, 1973.

Sheiner, Irwin. *Modern Japan: An Interpretative Anthology.* New York: Macmillan, 1974.

Shiels, Frederick L. *Tokyo and Washington.* Lexington, Mass.: Lexington Books, 1980.

Shinkai, Yoichi, Hiroshi Niida, and Takashi Negishi. *Kindai Keizaigaku* [Modern Economics]. Tokyo: Yuhikaku, 1979.

Shively, W. Philips. *The Craft of Political Research*, 2d ed. Englewood Cliffs, N.J.: Prentice-Hall, 1980.

Shultz, George P., and Kenneth W. Dam. *Economic Policy Beyond the Headlines.* New York: W. W. Norton, 1977.

Solomon, Richard H., ed. *Asian Security in the 1980s: A Time of Transition.* Santa Monica, Cal.: Rand Corporation, 1979.

Spannier, John, and Joseph Nogee. *Congress, The Presidency and American Foreign Policy.* New York: Pergamon Press, 1981.

Stewart, Edward C. *American Cultural Patterns: A Cross Cultural Perspective.* Society for Intercultural Education, Training and Research, n.p., n.d.

Strauss, Anselm. *Negotiations: Varieties, Contexts, Processes, and Social Order.* San Francisco: Jossey-Bass, 1979.

Tamarin, Alfred. *Japan and the United States: Early Encounters, 1791–1860.* New York: Macmillan, 1970.

Tasca, Diane, ed. *U.S.–Japanese Economic Relations: Cooperation, Competition and Confrontation.* New York: Pergamon Press, 1980.

Thayer, Nathaniel B. *How the Conservatives Rule Japan.* Princeton, N.J.: Princeton University Press, 1969.

Thorp, Willard L., ed. *The United States and the Far East.* 2d ed. Englewood Cliffs, N.J.: Prentice-Hall, 1962.

Tsuji, Kiyoaki. *Nippon Kanryoo Sei No Kenkyuu* [Study of Japanese Bureaucracy]. Tokyo: University of Tokyo Press, 1969.

_____. *Shinpan Nippon Kanryoo-Sei no Kenkyuu* (Study of Japanese Bureaucracy. New ed.). Tokyo: Tokyo Daigaku Shuppan Kai, 1976.

Tsuneishi, Warren M. *Japanese Political Style.* New York: Harper and Row, 1966.

Tsurumi, Yoshi. *The Japanese Are Coming.* Cambridge, Mass.: Ballinger, 1976.

Tsurutani, Taketsugu. *Political Change in Japan.* New York: David McKay, 1977.

Vogel, Ezra F. *Japan as Number One: Lessons for America.* Cambridge, Mass.: Harvard University Press, 1979.

_____. *Japan's New Middle Class.* Berkeley: University of California Press, 1967.

_____, ed. *Modern Japanese Organization and Decision-Making.* Berkeley: University of California Press, 1975.

Ward, Robert E. *Japan's Political System.* 2d ed. Englewood Cliffs, N.J.: Prentice Hall, 1978.

Weinstein, Franklin B., ed. *U.S.–Japan Relations and the Security of East Asia: The Next Decade.* Boulder, Col.: Westview Press, 1978.

Weiss, Leonard. *Trade Liberalization and the National Interest.* Washington, D.C.: Center for Strategic and International Studies, 1980.

Wildavsky, Aaron. *Budgeting: A Comparative Theory of Budgetary Processes.* Boston: Little, Brown, 1975.

Williams, Robin M. *American Society: A Sociological Interpretation.* 3d ed. New York: Knopf, 1970.

Winham, Gilbert R. and Ikuo Kabashima. "The Politics of U.S.–Japanese Auto Trade." In *Coping with U.S.–Japanese Economic Conflicts,* edited by I. M. Destler and Hideo Sato, pp. 73–119. Lexington, Mass.: D. C. Heath, 1982.

Wu, Yuan-li. *U.S. Foreign Economic Policy: Politico-Economic Linkages.* Stanford, Cal.: Stanford University Press, 1980.

Yamamura, Kiharu. *Ohkura Kanryo No Fukushuu* [Revenge by the Ministry of Finance Officials]. Tokyo: Kohshoboo, 1979.

Yasuhara, Kazuo. *Ohkura Sho (Gyossei Kikoo)* [The Ministry of Finance: Administrative Series No. 3]. Tokyo: Kyooikusha, 1976.

Yeager, Leland B., and David G. Tuerck. *Foreign Trade and U.S. Policy: The Case for Free International Trade.* New York: Praeger, 1976.

Yoshino, M. Y. "Emerging Japanese Multinational Enterprises." In *Modern Japanese Organization and Decision-Making,* edited by Ezra F. Vogel, pp. 146–66. Berkeley: University of California Press, 1975.

_____. *The Japanese Marketing System.* Cambridge, Mass.: The MIT Press, 1971.

_____. *Japan's Managerial System.* Cambridge, Mass.: The MIT Press, 1968.

Yoshitake, Kiyoshi. *An Introduction to Public Enterprise in Japan.* Tokyo: Nippon Hyoron Sha, 1973.

Yoshitomi, Masaru. *Gendai Nippon Keizai Ron: Sekai Keizai No Henbo To Nippon* [Current Japanese Economy: Changing World Economy and Japan]. Tokyo: Toyoo Keizai Shimpoo Sha, 1978.

Young, Alexander K. *The Soso Shoshai: Japan's Multinational Trading Companies.* Boulder, Col.: Westview Press, 1979.

Zucker, Seymour, et al. (Business Week Team). *The Reindustrialization of America.* New York: McGraw-Hill, 1982.

Newspapers

Bentsen, Lloyd. "The Reluctant Unmaking of a Free Trader." *Washington Star,* 9 February, 1981, p. A11.

"Beleagured U.S. Electronics Makers Want Hard Line Against Japanese." *Washington Post,* 3 February, 1983, p. C11.

"Black and White: U.S. News is Big News in Japan, but the Angle Always Seems the Same." *Wall Street Journal,* 9 December, 1982, p. 1.

"Brock Irked by Reaction to Proposed Joint Talks." *Japan Times,* 23 November, 1981, p. 1.

Chapman, William. "Japan Refuses to Expand Concessions on Trade." *Washington Post,* 26 April, 1979, p. A35.

Conderacci, Greg. "U.S.–Japan Trade Talks Seen Producing Important Results But No Final Answers." *Wall Street Journal,* 12 December, 1977, p.4.

Curry, Leonard. "Strauss Pressing Japan to Include Phone Firm in Trade Agreement." *Washington Star,* 30 December, 1978, p. B6.

Dahlby, Tracy. "Plans to Boost Japan's Defenses Shrink in Bureaucratic Cauldron." *Washington Post,* 6 February, 1981, p. A25.

_____. "Nakasone's Frank Remarks Threaten Support in Japan." *Washington Post,* 23 January, 1983, p. 1.

Farnsworth, Clyde H. "Trade Offer By Japan Rejected." *New York Times,* 26 April, 1979, p. 4.

Higashi, Chikara. "Why Should Nissan, Toyota Invest in U.S.?" *Japan Times,* 15 June, 1980, p. 3.

Ishii, Ken. "Japan Shuffles Along to the Familiar Tune." *International Herald Tribune,* 7 December, 1981, p. 6.

"Japanese Move to Stem Inflow of U.S. Dollars." *Wall Street Journal,* 18 November, 1977, p. 20.

"Japan's Proposals to Cut Its Tariffs Covers 318 Items." *Wall Street Journal,* 15 December, 1977, p. D5.

Kanabayashi, Masayoshi. "Japan Sets Plan to Cut Surpluses In Its U.S. Trade." *Wall Street Journal,* 7 December, 1977, p. 3.

Kraft, Joseph. "The Inscrutable West." *Washington Post,* 23 January, 1983, p. C7.

Lachica, Eduardo. "Will The U.S. Improve Its Trade Ties with Japan?" *Asian Wall Street Journal,* 22 October, 1981, p. 4.

Lawrence, Richard. "Surcharge Proposal Rejected." *Journal of Commerce and Commercial,* 26 January, 1979, p. 1.

Lehner, Urban C., "U.S. Firms' Market Penetration in Japan is Much Deeper Than Thought, Study Shows." *Wall Street Journal,* 16 February, 1983, p. 35.

Lohr, Steve. "Business vs. Farmers in Japan." *New York Times,* 5 May, 1982, p. D1.

_____. "Japan Sees Use for Trade Threats." *International Herald Tribune,* 14 October, 1981, p. 9.

_____. "1982 Trade Surplus Off 21.2% in Japan." *New York Times,* 20 January, 1983, p. D7.

_____. "Tokyo Must Also Weigh Political Issues." *New York Times*, 27 March, 1982, p. 32.

Malcolm, Andrew H. "New Plan By Japan to Promote Imports Aims to Cut Surplus." *New York Times*, 22 April, 1978, p. 25.

Parry, Robert. "Japanese Lowering Barriers." *Washington Post*, 8 October, 1979, p. D13.

Pine, Art. "U.S. Officials, Impressed by Nakasone, Wonder How He Will Fare Back in Japan." *Wall Street Journal*, 24 January, 1983, p. 28.

Rowen, Hobart. "Cut Surplus, Japan Warned." *Washington Post*, 15 February, 1979, p. F1.

_____. "Japan's Ohira Arrives for First Visit with Carter, Key Trade Issue is Muted." *Washington Post*, 1 May, 1979, p. A8.

_____. "Japan to Change Deficit Financing Limit, Trade Official Says." *Washington Post*, 16 December, 1977, p. A16.

_____. "Japan–U.S. Trade Talks Fruitless." *Washington Post*, 8 September, 1978, p. F1.

_____. "Japan Warns of Retaliation in Multilateral Trade Talks." *Washington Post*, 5 October, 1978, p. F3.

_____. "Still No Deal But Japanese Feel Better." *Washington Post*, 9 September, 1978, p. B3.

_____. "Strauss Warns of Retaliation By U.S. to 'Buy Japan' Policy." *Washington Post*, 28 April, 1979, p. A14.

_____. "U.S. Congressmen Warn of Japanese Drive." *International Herald Tribune*, 24–25 December, 1981, p. 9.

Rowen, Hobart, and Art Pine. "Trade Proposals Offered by Japan Rejected by U.S." *Washington Post*, 13 December, 1977, p. A1.

_____. "U.S. Officials Are Pessimistic Over Results of Trade Talks." *Washington Post*, 14 December, 1977, p. C1.

Samuelson, Robert J. "Japan's Choices: Act or Be Acted Upon," *Washington Post*, 13 December, 1977, p. D7.

Seaberry, Jane. "Learning to Walk Softly, Speak Softly: Bill Brock Changes His Style." *Washington Post*, 19 April, 1981, p. F1.

Shapiro, Isaac. "Second Thoughts About Japan." *Wall Street Journal,* 5 June, 1981, p. 24.

Sneider, Richard L. "American Pressure on Japan." *Wall Street Journal,* 7 March, 1980, p. 16.

Stokes, Henry Scott. "Japan Plans Trade Issue Concession." *New York Times,* 23 April, 1979, p. 1.

Taylor, Walter, and Lisa Myers. "Haig Tells Hill White House Fails to Consult." *Washington Star,* 24 March, 1981, p. A5.

_____. "Haig Loses White House Policy Fight." *Washington Star,* 25 March, 1981, p. A6.

"U.S. Congressmen Urge Open Market." *Japan Times,* 12 January, 1982, p. 1.

"U.S. Criticizes Japan Trade Plan, Calls It 'Considerably Short of What is Necessary' " *Wall Street Journal,* 13 December, 1977, p. 3.

"U.S. Farm Exports by Destination, 1982." *New York Times,* 21 February, 1983, p. D4.

"U.S.–Japan Accord." *New York Times,* 6 December, 1978, p. D8.

Ushiba, Nobuhiko. "Let's Lower Our Voices." *Washington Post,* 9 December, 1982, p. A29.

Wolff, Alan Wm. "Shape Up, Japan," *New York Times,* 17 January, 1983, p. A20.

Periodicals

Abegglen, J., and T. Hout. "Facing Up to the Trade Gap with Japan." *Foreign Affairs* (Fall 1978): 146–68.

"A New U.S. Weapon for Defending Free Trade." *Business Week,* 17 January, 1983, p. 138.

Bendor, Jonathan. "A Theoretical Problem in Comparative Administration." *Public Administration Review* 36 (November/December, 1976): 626–30.

Broute, Stephen. "The Most Powerful Men in Japan." *Euromoney,* June 1979, pp. 24–39.

Cook, Gary M., and Robert F. Williamson, Jr. "Improving U.S. Policy-Making in International Trade." *Columbia Journal of World Business* (Spring 1979): 15–24.

Destler, I. M. "Congress as Boss." *Foreign Policy* 42 (Spring 1981): 167–80.

Drew, Elizabeth. "Profiles: Equations (Robert Strauss)." *The New Yorker*, 7 May, 1979, pp. 50–129.

Drucker, Peter F. "Behind Japan's Success." *Harvard Business Review* (January–February 1981): 83–90.

_____. "What We Can Learn from Japanese Management." *Harvard Business Review* (March–April 1971): 110–22.

Evans, Rowland, Jr. "The Invisible Men Who Run Congress." *The Saturday Evening Post*, 8 June, 1963, pp. 13–17.

Givens, W. L. and W. L. Rapp. "What It Takes To Meet the Japanese Challenge." *Fortune*, 18 June, 1979, pp. 104–20.

Hata, Ikuhiko. "*Kanryoo No Kiniobiru Michi.*" [The Way Bureaucrats Survive]. *Shokun* (April 1977): pp. 8–9.

Higashi, Chikara. "*Nichibei Seisaku Keisei Katei No Chigai: Soko Kara Manaberu Mono, parts I, II and III.*" [Differences in Policy Formulation Processes Between the U.S. and Japan: What We Can Learn from Them]. *Finance* December 1978, Published by Ministry of Finance, vol. for part I, March 1979, vol. for part II, and May 1979, vol. for part III.

_____. "Alaskan Development and Japan: Interview with Senator Ted Stevens (R.-Alaska)." *Look Japan*, 10 July, 1981, pp. 10–11.

_____. "Are U.S.–Japan Relations Becoming Better? Interview with Robert Ingersoll, Former U.S. Ambassador to Japan (1972–1974) and Co-Chairman of the Wise Men's Group." *Look Japan*, 10 April, 1981, pp. 10–11.

_____. "Challenge and Response: Interview with Herman Kahn, Founder and Director of the Hudson Institute." *Look Japan*, 10 March, 1981, pp. 4–6.

_____. "Cultural Gap." *Look Japan*, 10 June, 1979, p. 5.

_____. "Declining Productivity in U.S." *Look Japan*, 10 September, 1979, p. 11.

_____. "Economic Structure and Crash." *Look Japan*, 10 November, 1979, p. 8.

_____. "How Open Is the Japanese Market?" *Look Japan*, 10 July, 1979, p. 15.

_____. "Japan's Role in the Global Context: Interview with Dale R. Tahtinen, Special Assistant to the President, American Enterprise Institute for Public Policy Research (AEI)." *Look Japan*, 10 June, 1981, pp. 11–12.

_____. "New Actions Are Needed to Overcome Tragic Undertones to Economic Relations." *The Japan Economic Journal,* 17 June, 1980, pp. 26–28.

_____. "Prospects for America, 1981: Interview with Paul W. McCracken, Edmund Ezra Day University Professor, Graduate School of Business Administration, The University of Michigan and Former Chairman of the Council of Economic Advisers under President Nixon." *Look Japan,* 10 February, 1981, pp. 10–12.

_____. "Reagan Daitoryo no Toojoo to Kongo no Beikoku Seiji Keizai Oyobi Nichi-Bei Kankei." (Reagan New President and Outlooks for the U.S. Politics and Economy and for U.S.–Japan Relations.) *Keizaijin* (Businessmen) (January 1981, published by Kansai Keidanren): 4–6.

_____. "Reagan's International Economic Policy and the Economic Summits: Interview with Henry Owen, Former Ambassador at Large and Special Representative of the President for International Economic Summits." *Look Japan,* 10 May, 1981, pp. 10–11.

_____. "Reagan Seiken-ka Nippon no Sentaku." (Japan's Choice Under the Reagan Administration), (co-authored with Eisuke Sakakibara). *Economist* (2 December, 1980, published by Mainichi Shinbun): 3–4.

_____. "The Automobile Issue and U.S.–Japan Relations. Interview with Congressman William Brodhead, U.S. House of Representatives (Democrat, Michigan)." (Parts 1 and 2) *Look Japan,* 10 July, 1980, pp. 8–9; 10 August, 1980, pp. 10–11.

_____. "The Automobile Issue: What is the Real Problem?" (Parts 1 and 2) *The Japan Economic Journal,* 28 October, 1980, p. 24; 4 November, 1980, p. 14.

_____. "Tokyo Summit, Energy and Cabinet Shake-up." *Look Japan,* 10 August, 1979, p. 7.

_____. "U.S. Economy, Politics and Relations with Japan: Interview with Senator Adlai Stevenson, III, U.S. Senate (Democrat, Illinois)." *Look Japan,* 10 June, 1980, pp. 8–9.

_____. "U.S. Foreign Economic Policies and Japan: Interview with Philip M. Klutznick, U.S. Secretary of Commerce." *Look Japan,* 10 October, 1980, pp. 8–9.

_____. "U.S. Foreign Policy and Auto Wars." *Look Japan,* 10 April, 1980, pp. 9–10.

_____. "U.S.–Japan Economic Relations." *Look Japan,* 10 October, 1979, p. 7.

_____. "U.S.–Japan Economic Relations and Industrial Policies: Interview with William V. Rapp, Vice-President of the Morgan Guaranty Trust Company and Visiting Professor, Columbia University." *Look Japan,* 10 September, 1980, pp. 8–10.

_____. "U.S.–Japan Relations and the Incoming Reagan Administration: Interview with Senator S. I. Hayakawa, U.S. Senate, (Republican, California)." *Look Japan* 10 January, 1981, pp. 10–11.

_____. "U.S.–Japan Relations and Iran." *Look Japan,* 10 January, 1980, p. 11.

_____. "U.S.–Japan Relations in Transition: Case of Japan's Defense Budget." (Parts 1 and 2). *The Japan Economic Journal* 3 February, 1981, p. 11; 10 February, 1981, p. 19.

_____. "U.S. Security Policy and Japan's Role: Interview with William Colby, former Director of the Central Intelligence Agency." *Look Japan,* 10 November, 1980, pp. 10–11.

_____. "U.S. Tighter Monetary Policy and Its Impact." *Finance* (December 1979, published by Ministry of Finance): 4–5.

_____. "Will Trade Frictions Recur?" *Look Japan,* 10 December, 1979, p. 11.

_____. "World Economic Outlook: Interview with Dr. Lawrence B. Krause, Senior Fellow in the Brookings Institution." *Look Japan,* 10 May, 1980, pp. 8–9.

"High-Technology Gateway." *Business Week,* 9 August, 1982, pp. 40–43.

Iida, Tsunehiko et al. "Hokaku Hakuchoo Jida: No Kanryoo" [Bureaucrats in the Era of Contending Conservatives and Liberals]. *Shokun* (April 1977): 8–9.

Imai, Kazuo. "Kanryo-Son Seitai to Uchimaku" [Bureaucracy—Its Organic Structure and Inside]. In Yoshimi Usui, ed. *Gendai Kanryo Zenshu,* vol. 21 (Modern Bureaucrats). Tokyo: Chikuma Shobo, 1960, pp. 21–26.

"It Takes Time and Strong Nerves." *Der Spiegel,* No. 1, 1983, pp. 80–86.

Japan External Trade Organization, "Tokyo Round: Bringing Home the Beef." *Focus Japan* 5 (March 1978): 4–6.

Japan. Ministry of Finance. *Zaisei Tokei Geppoo* (Monthly Financial Statistics) (June 1979).

Johnson, Richard Tanner, and William G. Ouichi. "Made in America (under Japanese Management)." *Harvard Business Review* (September–October 1974): 61–69.

Kaufman, Felix. "Decision Making—Eastern and Western Style." *Business Horizons* 13 (December, 1970): 81–86.

Kusayanagi, Daizo. "Yureru Kasumigaseki: Sengo Kanryoo No Bunkai Katei" [Rocked Kasumigaseki: Dissolving Process of Post-War Bureaucrats]. *Shokun* (April 1977): 20–27.

McConnell, Campbell R. "Why Is U.S. Productivity Slowing Down?" *Harvard Business Review* (March–April 1979): 36–60.

Nevin, John J. "Can U.S. Business Survive our Japanese Trade Policy?" *Harvard Business Review* (September–October 1978): 165–77.

Oka, Eitaro, et al. "Gyoosei Kaikaku: Gyosei Kaikaku wo Meguru Sho Mondai" [Administrative Reform: Issues in Reforming Administration]. *Jurist* (April 1978): 12–14.

Okita, Saburo. "Japan, China and the United States." *Foreign Affairs* (Summer 1979): 1090–110.

Passin, Herbert, et al. *"Toozai Hikaku Kanryoo Ron"* [Bureaucrats in the East and West]. *Shokun* (April 1977): 8–12.

Pauly, David, and Rich Thomas. "Battle of the Oranges." *Newsweek,* 18 September, 1978, p. 73.

"Pro and Con: Require U.S. Parts in Foreign Cars?" *U.S. News and World Report,* 7 February, 1983, p. 47.

Range, Peter Ross. "The Techonology War: Behind Japanese Lines." *Playboy,* February 1981, pp. 84–88, 190–96.

Rapp, William V. "Japan: Its Industrial Policies and Corporate Behavior." *Columbia Journal of World Business* (Spring 1977): 38–48.

"Reagan Misses 1981 Employment Targets." *National Journal,* 28 November, 1981, p. 2131.

Shapiro, Isaac. "The Risen Sun: Japanese Gaullism." *Foreign Policy* 42 (Winter 1980–1981): 62–81.

Shepherd, Stephen B., and Robert E. Farrell. "The Recovery May Just Be Better Than We Think (Interview with President Ronald Reagan)." *Business Week,* 14 February, 1983, pp. 119–22.

Shimaguchi, Mitsuaki, and Larry J. Rosenberg. "Demystifying Japanese Distribution." *Columbia Journal of World Business* (Spring 1979): 32–41.

"The Automobile Crisis and Public Policy: An Interview with Philip Caldwell." *Harvard Business Review* (January–February 1981): 73–82.

"The Course of U.S.–Japan Economic Relations." *Tradepia International* (1979): 4–9.

Thurow, Lester. "The Moral Equivalent of Defeat." *Foreign Policy* 42 (Spring 1981): 123–24.

Triffin, Robert. "The International Role of the Dollar." *Foreign Affairs* (Winter 1978/1979): 269–86.

Whitehall, Arthur M., and Shin-ichi, Takezawa. "Workplace Harmony: Another Japanese 'Miracle'?" *Columbia Journal of World Business* (Fall 1978): 25–39.

"World Trade: 'Steps in the Right Direction.' " (Interview with Robert S. Strauss, Special Representative for Trade Negotiations) *U.S. News and World Report*, 13 March, 1978, pp. 47–48.

"Wrapping Up the MTN Package." *Business America*, 23 April, 1979, pp. 3–8.

Young, Lewis H. "A Debate That Holds a Key to Japan's Future (Letter from Tokyo)." *Business Week*, 15 November, 1982, pp. 16–18.

Special Publications

Amaya, Naohiro. "On Japan's Trade and Industrial Policies." MITI Report JR-1 (73-2), Tokyo, February 1974.

Boston Consulting Group. *Trade Between Japan and the United States*. Prepared for the U.S. Department of the Treasury (April 1978).

Bureau of Public Affairs. "Agriculture in U.S. Foreign Economic Policy," Washington, D.C.: Department of State, January 1983.

Central Intelligence Agency. *Handbook of Economic Statistics 1979*. Washington, D.C.: Government Printing Office, 1980.

Central Intelligence Agency. *Handbook of Economic Statistics 1981*. Washington, D.C.: Government Printing Office, 1982.

Council of Economic Advisers. *1981 Economic Report of the President*. Washington, D.C.: U.S. Government Printing Office, 1981.

Crancall, Robert W. Senior Fellow, Brookings Institution. Statements before the U.S. Congress, House, Subcommittee on Commerce, Consumer and Monetary Affairs, Committee on Government Operations. 20 December, 1979 *mimeographed).

General Motors Stockholder Forum. Remarks by Thomas A. Murphy, Chairman, General Motors Corporation. Washington, D.C.: 8 April, 1980 (mimeographed).

Hodges, Luther H., Jr. Remarks to the Yomiuri International Economic Society. Tokyo, Japan, 15 October, 1979.

Hormats, Robert D. Deputy U.S. Trade Representative. Statement before the U.S. Congress, Senate, Subcommittee on Economic Stabilization, Committee on Banking, Housing and Urban Affairs. 3 April, 1980.

_____. Testimony presented to the U.S. Congress, House, Subcommittee on Asian and Pacific Affairs and Subcommittee on International Economic Policy and Trade, Committee on Foreign Affairs, 18 September, 1980.

Ingersoll, Robert S. Testimony presented to the U.S. Congress, House, Subcommittee on Asian and Pacific Affairs and Subcommittee on International Economic Policy, Committee on Foreign Affairs, 18 September, 1980.

International Labour Organization. *Yearbook of Labour Statistics 1979.* Geneva: ILO, 1980.

International Monetary Fund. *Direction of Trade Yearbook 1981.* Washington, D.C.: International Monetary Fund, 1981.

International Monetary Fund. *Direction of Trade Yearbook 1982.* Washington, D.C.: International Monetary Fund, 1982.

Japan Central Bank. *International Comparative Statistics 1980.*

Japan Central Bank. *International Comparative Statistics 1981.*

Japan Economic Institute. "Japan's National Diet," JEI Report No. 24, 26 June, 1981. Washington, D.C.: Japan Economic Institute, 1981.

_____. "Washington Applauds 'Wise Men's' Report on U.S.–Japan Economic Relations," Japan Insight No. 2, 16 January, 1981. Washington, D.C.: Japan Economic Institute, 1981.

_____. *Yearbook of U.S.–Japan Economic Relations in 1980.* Washington, D.C.: Japan Economic Institute, 1981.

_____. *Yearbook of U.S.–Japan Economic Relations in 1981.* Washington, D.C.: Japan Economic Institute, 1982.

Japan External Trade Organization. "A Study of American Leaders' Attitudes Toward U.S.–Japan Economic Relations." New York: Kane, Parsons, and Associates, 1980.

Japan. Ministry of Foreign Affairs. *Diplomatic Bluebook, 1980 Edition: Review of Recent Developments in Japan's Foreign Relations.*

Japan. Ministry of International Trade and Industry. *Tsuusho Hakushoo, Fiscal Year 1980* (Annual Report on International Trade for FY 1980).

Japan. Economic Planning Agency. *Annual Reports on the World Economy.* (1978 and 1979).

Japan. Economic Planning Agency. *Annual Reports on the Japanese Economy.* (1978 and 1979).

Japanese Government. *Eirikigo He No Shuushoku No Shoonin Nikansuru Nenji Hookoku Sho* [Annual Report on Admittance of Recruitment by Commercial Organizations]. Tokyo, Japan: Jinjiin [Personnel Agency], 1975.

Japanese Government. *Organization of the Government of Japan.* Tokyo, Japan: Administrative Management Agency, Prime Minister's Office, January 1978.

Japan. Ministry of International Trade and Industry. *Tsuushoo Hakusho* (Annual Report on International Trade). (1978 and 1979).

"Joint Communique Between Prime Minister Masayoshi Ohira and President Carter, May 2, 1979." In U.S.–Japan Trade Council, *Yearbook of U.S.–Japan Relations 1979*, Appendix A, pp. 78–80. Washington, D.C.: U.S.–Japan Trade Council, 1980.

Kaplan, Eugene J. "The United States and Japan: A New Economic Relationship." Washington, D.C.: U.S.–Japan Trade Council, 1975.

_____. "Japan's Trade Surplus with the United States: Its Causes and Cures, Tariff and Non-Tariff Barriers to Imports from the United States." A Paper Prepared for the Thirtieth Annual Meeting of the Association for Asian Studies. Chicago, Illinois, 1 April, 1978. Typewritten.

Mansfield, Ambassador Mike. "The Indispensible Relationship." An address delivered to the Southeast U.S.–Japan Association Conference in Nashville, Tennessee, on 17 September, 1982. Tokyo: United States Information Service, American Embassy, 1982.

Matsukawa, Michiya. "Japan–U.S. Economic Relationship." Address at the meeting of the Foreign Policy Association. New York City, 22 May, 1979.

Office of the United States Trade Representative. "Private Sector Advisory Committee System." Washington, D.C.: Office of the United States Trade Representative, 29 January, 1981. Typewritten.

Organization for Economic Cooperation and Development. *OECD Economic Outlook* July 1982. Paris Organization for Economic Cooperation and Development, 1982.

Organization for Economic Cooperation and Development. *OECD Bulletin Of Labour Statistics 1982–2.* Paris: Organization for Economic Cooperation and Development, 1982.

Organization for Economic Cooperation and Development (OECD), microfische tables. Washington, D.C.: Organization for Economic Cooperation and Development, 1982.

Report of the Japan–United States Economic Relations Group. By Nobuhiko Ushiba and Robert S. Ingersoll, Co-Chairmen. Washington, D.C. and Tokyo: The Japan–United States Economic Relations Group, 1981.

Schultze, Charles L. Chairman of Council of Economic Advisers, Testimony Before the U.S. Congress, Joint Economic Committee. 23 July, 1980.

Soejima, Minister Aritoshi. "Current Japanese Economic Issues." Speech before the International Economists Club. New York City, 15 November, 1979.

The Summary Report, Trade of Japan. Tokyo: Japan Tariff Association, 1979.

Toyota Executive Speaks Out Against Import Restrictions. News release from Toyota. Public Relations, Toyota Motor Sales, U.S.A. Inc. Torrance, Calif., 19 March, 1980.

Trezise, Philip H. "Japan: Cornerstone of Asian Policy." November 1979. (Unpublished paper).

Twenty-Fourth Annual Report of the President of the United States on The Trade Agreements Program 1979. Washington, D.C.: Government Printing Office, 1979.

U.S. Comptroller General. *Perspectives on Trade and International Payments Executive Summary.* Washington, D.C.: U.S. General Accounting Office, 1979.

U.S. Comptroller General. *United States–Japan Trade: Issues and Problems.* Washington, D.C.: General Accounting Office, 1979.

U.S. Congress. House. Committee on Foreign Affairs. *Export Administration Act Amendments of 1979.* House Report 96–200, 96th Cong., 1st sess., 1979.

U.S. Congress. House. Committee on Ways and Means. *Competitive Factors Influencing World Trade in Semiconductors. Hearings before a subcommittee of the House Committee on Ways and Means.* Serial 96-62. 96th Cong., 1st sess., 1979.

U.S. Congress. House. Committee on Ways and Means. *Task Force Report on United States–Japan Trade.* Committee Print 95-110. 95th Cong., 2nd sess., 1979. Washington, D.C.: Government Printing Office, 1979.

U.S. Congress. House. Committee on Ways and Means. *Report on Trade Mission to Far East.* Committee Print 97–27. 97th Cong., 1st sess., 1981. Washington, D.C.: Government Printing Office, 1981.

U.S. Congress. House. Committee on Ways and Means. *United States–Japan Trade Report.* Committee Print 96-68, 96th Cong., 2nd sess. Washington, D.C.: Government Printing Office, 1980.

U.S. Congress. House. Committee on Ways and Means. *U.S. Trade Policy.* Washington, D.C.: Government Printing Office, 1980.

U.S. Congress. Joint Economic Committee. *Economic Analysis and the Efficiency of Government. Hearings before a subcommittee of the Joint Economic Committee,* pt. 4., 91st Cong., 2nd sess., 1970.

U.S. Congress. Joint Economic Committee. *Export Policy: Role of Trade Reorganization.* Washington, D.C.: Government Printing Office, 1980.

U.S. Congress. Joint Economic Committee. "Bentsen Releases GAO Study on U.S.–Japan Trade; Protectionism Remains a Factor Though Diminishing." Press Release, 8 October 1979. Typewritten.

U.S. Congress. Joint Economic Committee. "Statement of Norman D. Lean, Senior Vice President, Toyota Motor Sales, U.S.A., Inc., on The Current and Future Health of the American Automobile Industry." Washington, D.C. March 19, 1980. (Mimeographed.)

U.S. Congress. Senate. Committee on Banking, Housing and Urban Affairs. *Preliminary Guide to Export Opportunities to Japan.* Washington, D.C.: Government Printing Office, 1978.

U.S. Congress. Senate. Committee on Banking, Housing and Urban Affairs. *The Effect of Expanding Japanese Automobile Imports on the Domestic Economy. Oversight hearings before a subcommittee of the Senate Committee on Banking, Housing and Urban Affairs,* 96th Cong., 2d sess., 1979.

U.S. Congress. Senate. Committee on Banking, Housing and Urban Affairs. *Multilateral Trade Negotiations. Hearings before a subcommittee of the Sen-*

ate Committee on Banking, Housing and Urban Affairs, 96th Cong., 1st sess., 1979.

U.S. Congress. Senate. Committee on Finance. *An Economic Analysis of the Effects of the Tokyo Round of Multilateral Trade Negotiations on the United States and the Other Major Industrialized Countries.* 96th Cong., 1st sess., 1979.

U.S. Congress. Senate. Committee on Finance. *Private Advisory Committee Reports on the Tokyo Round of Multilateral Trade Negotiations,* Committee Print 96–28, 96th Cong., 1st sess., 1979.

U.S. Congress. Senate. Committee on Finance. *United States/Japanese Trade Relations and the Status of the Multilateral Trade Negotiations,* 95th Congress, 2nd Session, 1979. Washington, D.C.: Government Printing Office, 1979.

U.S. Congress. Senate. Committee on Finance. *MTN Studies 2: Tokyo Geneva Round: Its Relations to U.S. Agriculture.* Washington, D.C.: Government Printing Office, 1979.

U.S. Congress. Senate. Committee on Governmental Affairs. Testimony of David R. MacDonald, 4 June, 1981.

U.S. Department of Agriculture. *U.S. Foreign Agricultural Trade Statistical Report, Calendar Year 1981: A Supplement to Foreign Agricultural Trade of the United States.* Washington, D.C.: International Economic Division, Economic Research Service, April 1982.

U.S. Department of Commerce. Bureau of the Census. *Statistical Abstract of the United States: 1979,* 100th ed. Washington, D.C.: Government Printing Office, 1980.

U.S. Department of Commerce. Bureau of the Census. *Statistical Abstract of the United States: 1980,* 101th ed. Washington, D.C.: Government Printing Office, 1980.

U.S. Department of Commerce. *U.S. Export Opportunities to Japan.* Washington, D.C.: Government Printing Office, 1978.

U.S. *Economic Report of the President* February 1982. Washington, D.C.: Government Printing Office, 1982.

U.S.–Japan Trade Council. "Are the Japanese Fair Competitors?" Washington, D.C.: U.S.–Japan Trade Council, 1977.

_____. *Inside Japan: A Symposium on U.S.–Japan Economic, Political, and Cultural Relations, 1975.* Washington, D.C.: U.S.–Japan Trade Council, 1975.

_____. *Yearbook of U.S.–Japan Economic Relations 1979.* Washington, D.C.: U.S.–Japan Trade Council, 1980.

_____. *Yearbook of U.S. Japan Economic Relations, 1978.* Washington, D.C.: U.S.–Japan Trade Council, 1979.

INDEX

Abe, Shintaro (MITI minister) 117

Adams, Fanueil, 125

Agency of Natural Resources and Energy. *See* Ministry of International Trade and Industry, bureaus, agencies; Ministry of International Trade and Industry, organization

Akigusa, Tokuji (president of NTT), 108; resignation due to government policy, 110

Amakadiri (one-way retirement), 67, 107

America-Oceania, Division of, (Japanese). *See* Ministry of International Trade and Industry, bureaus, divisions; Ministry of International Trade and Industry, organization.

automobile industry; Japan, 79; president of U.A.W. comments on "local content" legislation, 118-19; U.S. response to Japanese "voluntary" restraints, 117–18

balance of payments,15

balance of trade, 18; U.S.-Japan bilateral imbalance, 17–19, 25

Bank of Japan, exchange rate policies, 84

"Beef Caucus" (parliamentary League for the Promotion of the Livestock Industry), establishment of the Japanese Diet, 100

Begin, Menachim, 72

Bentsen, Lloyd, 93, 115; as chairman of Joint Economic Committee, 110, 122; speeches attacking "closed" nature of Japanese market, 122–23

Blaker, Michael K., 4–6, 8

Blumenthal, Michael: personal background, 88; talks with Finance Minister Murayama, 86–88, 126–27

Bonn summit conference, 90

Bretton Woods, 13; collapse of, 16

Brock, William (U.S. Special Trade Representative), 115; attends Trilateral Conference, 116; letter to MITI Minister Tanaka, 116–17; visit to Tokyo, 115, 118

Brodhead, William (former Congressman), 116

Brookings Institution, 91

Bureau of Basic Industries (Japanese), 37. *See also* Ministry of International Trade and Industry

Bureau of Consumer Goods (Japanese), 37. *See also* Ministry of International Trade and Industry

Bureau of Industrial Location and Environmental Protection (Japanese), 37. *See also* Ministry of International Trade and Industry

Bureau of Industrial Policy (Japanese), 37. *See also* Ministry of International Trade and Industry

Bureau of International Trade Administration (Japanese), 37. *See also* Ministry of International Trade and Industry

Bureau of International Trade Policy, 37; America-Oceania Division

ABOUT THE AUTHOR

Dr. Chikara Higashi received his Bachelor of Political Economics from the University of Tokyo in 1965, the Master of Economics university equivalent from the Japanese Ministry of Finance in 1968, and the Doctor of Business Administration (DBA) degree from The George Washington University in 1982.

Dr. Higashi entered the Ministry of Finance in 1965 and served in various positions, most recently as a Special Adviser to the Minister of Finance (1981–82). He was seconded from the Ministry of Finance to the World Bank in Washington D.C. from 1974 to 1978, and spent three years as a guest scholar at the Brookings Institution also in Washington D.C. from 1978 to 1981.

He is the founding President of the Research and Exploration Center for International Affairs in Tokyo and serves as an adviser to more than a dozen of the largest Japanese corporations. Dr. Higashi is the author of numerous articles on U.S.–Japanese trade relations, which have appeared, among others, in *Look Japan*, *The Japan Economic Journal*, *Japanese Finance* (Ministry of Finance), *Keizaijin* (Businessmen), published by Kansai Keidanren, the *Japanese Economist* (published by Mainichi Shinbun), and the *Japan Times*.